ONCE A
GRAND
DUCHESS

ALSO BY JOHN VAN DER KISTE

Published by Sutton Publishing unless stated otherwise

Frederick III: German Emperor 1888 (1981)
Queen Victoria's Family: A Select Bibliography (Clover, 1982)
Dearest Affie: Alfred, Duke of Edinburgh, Queen Victoria's Second
Son, 1844–1900 [with Bee Jordaan] (1984)
Queen Victoria's Children (1986; large print edition, ISIS, 1987)
Windsor and Habsburg: The British and Austrian Reigning Houses
1848–1922 (1987)
Edward VII's Children (1989)
Princess Victoria Melita, Grand Duchess Cyril of Russia,
1876–1936 (1991)
George V's Children (1991)
George III's Children (1992)
Crowns in a Changing World (1993)
King of the Hellenes: The Greek Kings 1863–1974 (1994)
Childhood at Court 1819–1914 (1995)
Northern Crowns: The Kings of Modern Scandinavia (1996)
King George II and Queen Caroline (1997)
The Romanovs 1818–1959: Alexander II of Russia
and his Family (1998)
Kaiser Wilhelm II: Germany's Last Emperor (1999)
The Georgian Princesses (2000)
Gilbert & Sullivan's Christmas (2000)
Dearest Vicky, Darling Fritz: Queen Victoria's Eldest Daughter and the
German Emperor (2001)
Royal Visits in Devon and Cornwall (Halsgrove, 2002)
William and Mary (2003)

Also by Coryne Hall
Little Mother of Russia: A Biography of the Empress Marie
Feodorovna (1847–1928). Shepheard-Walwyn, 1999

ONCE A GRAND DUCHESS

XENIA,
SISTER OF NICHOLAS II

JOHN VAN DER KISTE &
CORYNE HALL

SUTTON PUBLISHING

This book was first published in 2002

This new paperback edition first published in 2004 by
Sutton Publishing Limited · Phoenix Mill
Thrupp · Stroud · Gloucestershire · GL5 2BU

British Library Cataloguing in Publication Data
A catalogue record for this book is available from the British
Library

ISBN 0 7509 3521 9

*Coryne would like to dedicate this book to the memory of her
parents, Peggy & Ernie Bawcombe, and John to the memory of his
father, Wing-Commander Guy Van der Kiste.*

Typeset in 10/12pt Photina.
Typesetting and origination by
Sutton Publishing Limited.
Printed and bound in Great Britain by
J.H. Haynes & Co. Ltd, Sparkford.

Contents

Acknowledgements

We would like to acknowledge the gracious permission of Her Majesty The Queen to publish certain letters from the Royal Archives, Windsor, of which she owns the copyright; Her Majesty Queen Margrethe II of Denmark, for access to letters in the private royal archives, Copenhagen. Crown copyright material from the Public Record Office is reproduced by permission of Her Majesty's Stationery Office.

We are indebted to Her late Majesty Queen Elizabeth The Queen Mother, who graciously granted a private audience to give her recollections of Grand Duchess Xenia; and, for their invaluable reminiscences and general advice, to Prince Alexander Nikititch; Prince Andrew Andreievich; and Prince Michael Feodorovich, surviving grandsons of HIH Grand Duchess Xenia.

Prince Andrew Andreievich was kind enough to facilitate our access to Grand Duchess Xenia's papers in the Hoover Institution on War, Revolution & Peace, California. The Hoover Institution contains a vast archive on Russian affairs including thirteen boxes of material on Xenia. This was set up by gifts from the family in 1978 and consists of letters to Xenia and, most importantly, her diaries covering the period 1916–19. These relate to the Russian revolution, the abdication of Nicholas II, and the murders of both Rasputin and the Russian imperial family. Unfortunately, Xenia's handwriting, never easy to read, became increasingly worse under the stress of these events. This caused considerable difficulties for our researcher Dina Leytes and translator Natalia Stewart. Despite this, both did a first-class job deciphering the Grand Duchess's writing, which at times became impossible to read. Nevertheless, these diary entries remain a prime source for events up to Xenia's departure from Russia.

Only the discovery of a considerable quantity of further archive material has made it possible to complete the story. In the late summer of 2000, just as we embarked on research for this book, a remarkable collection of Grand Duchess Xenia's papers suddenly came to light. It comprised some four hundred documents and letters in English, Russian and French, plus some family photographs, dating from the time of her betrothal in 1894 until shortly before her death. Many of the documents are family letters from which, although information has been extracted and used, we have not quoted directly. Other letters come from nearly every royal family in Europe, to all of which she was closely related. The Grand Duchess preserved everything – poems, travel documents, Christmas cards, the invitation to the 1947 wedding of Princess Elizabeth, scores of telegrams of condolence sent on the death of her husband, even a 100 rouble banknote.

Although the letters are to Xenia, not from her, they have helped to fill out the wider picture to a remarkable degree. Without this wonderful archive, the Grand Duchess's life after the revolution would have been difficult to write, if not impossible. In making this previously unseen archive material available, and his unfailing generosity over a considerable period of time, Ian Shapiro of Argyll Etkin Ltd, London, who acquired these papers, has been a tower of strength. Without him the book would probably never have been written. Our thanks go to everyone at Argyll Etkin for stoically coping with the disruption in their offices caused by the sorting and photocopying of the documents for our research.

ADDITIONAL THANKS

Sue and Mike Woolmans, Karen Roth, Dina Leytes and Natalia Stewart have also been extremely helpful over a long spell with regard to general research, translation and deciphering of archive material, general advice and assistance beyond the call of duty. On a family level, Colin Hall and Kate Van der Kiste have been ever ready with support and general encouragement in the project.

We would also like to express our thanks to the following:

In Australia: Andrew and Elizabeth Briger.

In Britain: Ruth Abrahams; Arthur Addington; Theo Aronson; HRH Princess Margarita of Baden; Simon Bates; Mme Eunice Biedryski Bartell, President, Russian Ballet Society; Harold Brown; David Burdon-Davis; Lady Myra Butter; Pamela Clark and the staff of the Royal Archives, Windsor; David Cripps; Richard Davies, Brotherton Library, Leeds University; Frances Dimond, Curator, The Royal Photograph Collection; Robert Golden; Lady Natasha Gourlay;

ACKNOWLEDGEMENTS

Margaret Guyver; Jim Hanson, Argyll Etkin; Dale Headington; Joan Heath; Dr Edward Impey, Curator, Hampton Court Palace; Barbara Irvine, Russian Refugees Aid Society; Irina James and Sylvia Leone, Surrey University; Elizabeth, Baroness Maclean; Fr Dennis Mulliner, Chaplain, Chapel Royal, Hampton Court; Sarah Parker, HM Tower of London; Suzy Payne, Penhaligon's; Theresa Prout; Revd John Salter; John Thorneycroft, English Heritage; Dawn Tudor; Moya Vahey; Hugo Vickers; Katrina Warne; Mollie Whittaker-Axon; Marion Wynn; Charlotte Zeepvat; the staff of Kensington and Chelsea Public Libraries, Kingston Library; Portsmouth Library; and the Public Record Office, London.

In Canada: Paul C. Byington; Paul Gilbert, The Imperial Russian Historical Society.

In Denmark: Jørgen Bjerregård, Ballerup Egnsmuseum; Bjarne Steen Jensen; Anne Dyhr and Anne Orbæk Jensen, Det Kongelige Bibliotek; Paul Edward Kulikovsky; Mrs Ruth Kulikovsky; Anna Lerche-Lerchenborg and Marcus Mandal, Nordisk Film TV; Gerda Petri, Curator, Christian VIII's Palace, Amalienborg; Sigurd Rambusch and Marianne Reimer, Rigsarkiv.

In Eire: Anthony Summers.

In Finland: Ragnar Backström, Curator, Langinkoski Imperial Fishing Lodge Museum; Matti Bergström, Finnish Railway Museum.

In France: Marie-Agnes Domin; Jacques Ferrand; Laure de Margerie, Musée d'Orsay.

In Germany: Professor Dr E.G. Franz, Hessisches Statsarkiv, Darmstadt; Mignon Ubele, Secretary to Countess Bernadotte, Mainau.

In Russia: Pavel Bolwitschew; Dimitri Macedonsky; Larissa V. Kriatchkova and Dr Zinaida I. Peregudova, State Archives of the Russian Federation; Linda and Alexander Predovsky; Elena Yablochkina.

In Spain: Ricardo Mateos Sainz de Medrano.

In Switzerland: Prince Nicholas Romanoff; Mikhail Shishkin.

In the USA: Prince David Chavchavadze; Senta Driver; Marlene Eilers; Greg King; Carol Leadenham, The Hoover Institution on War, Revolution & Peace; Thomas Polk; Gary Zilaff.

Finally, our thanks to our editors at Sutton Publishing, Jaqueline Mitchell, Georgina Pates and Paul Ingrams, for all their hard work in seeing through this book from planning to completion.

Note on Dates,
Names and Currency

DATES

Russia used the Old Style Julian Calendar until 1 February 1918. This was twelve days behind the west in the nineteenth century and thirteen days behind in the twentieth century. Unless otherwise indicated, all dates before February 1918 are Old Style, and all dates after this are according to the New Style Calendar. At certain stages of the narrative we have indicated OS and NS where confusion might otherwise result.

NAMES

We have used the spelling of Russian names most familiar to English-speaking readers. The titles Emperor, Tsar, Empress, Tsarina are all correct and are used interchangeably. With quotations, however, we have deferred to the spelling in the original. 'Czar', for instance, was a popular alternative.

Russians have three names – their Christian name, patronymic (their father's name) and their surname. Xenia was therefore Xenia Alexandrovna, and her sister was Olga Alexandrovna. Nicholas II's daughter was Olga Nicolaievna. Since the revolution, members of the family use the spelling Romanoff, rather than Romanov, and this has been reflected in the text after 1919.

CURRENCY

In 1897 Russia joined the gold standard. From then until 1917 the exchange rate remained stable at 10 roubles to £1. After that inflation took hold and between 1917 and 1919 we have used the rate of 15 roubles to £1. (From 1919 onwards, the exchange rate between both currencies is no longer relevant for the purposes of the present work.)

TABLE 1 – THE DESCENDANTS OF GRAND DUCHESS XENIA

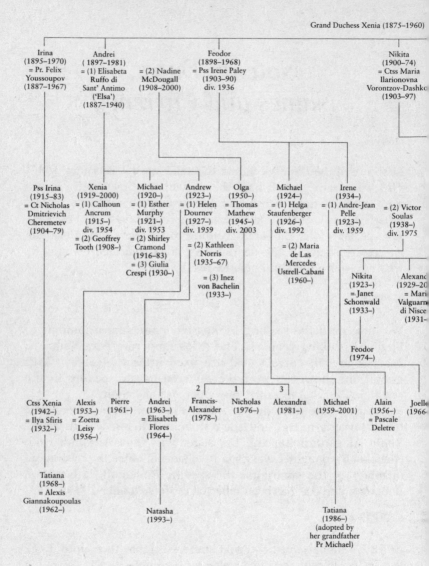

Grand Duchess Xenia (1875–1960)

Irina
(1895–1970)
= Pr. Felix
Youssoupov
(1887–1967)

Andrei
(1897–1981)
= (1) Elisabeta
Ruffo di
Sant' Antimo
('Elsa')
(1887–1940)

= (2) Nadine
McDougall
(1908–2000)

Feodor
(1898–1968)
= Pss Irene Paley
(1903–90)
div. 1936

Nikita
(1900–74)
= Ctss Maria
Ilarionovna
Vorontzov-Dashko
(1903–97)

Pss Irina
(1915–83)
= Ct Nicholas
Dmitrievich
Cheremetev
(1904–79)

Xenia
(1919–2000)
= (1) Calhoun
Ancrum
(1915–)
div. 1954
= (2) Geoffrey
Tooth (1908–)

Michael
(1920–)
= (1) Esther
Murphy
(1921–)
div. 1953
= (2) Shirley
Cramond
(1916–83)
= (3) Giulia
Crespi (1930–)

Andrew
(1923–)
= (1) Helen
Dournev
(1927–)
div. 1959

= (2) Kathleen
Norris
(1935–67)

= (3) Inez
von Bachelin
(1933–)

Olga
(1950–)
= Thomas
Mathew
(1945–)
div. 2003

Michael
(1924–)
= (1) Helga
Staufenberger
(1926–)
div. 1992

= (2) Maria
de Las
Mercedes
Ustrell-Cabani
(1960–)

Irene
(1934–)
= (1) Andre-Jean
Pelle
(1923–)
div. 1959

= (2) Victor
Soulas
(1938–)
div. 1975

Nikita
(1923–)
= Janet
Schonwald
(1933–)

Alexand
(1929–20
= Mari
Valguarn
di Nisce
(1931–

Feodor
(1974–)

Ctss Xenia
(1942–)
= Ilya Sfiris
(1932–)

Alexis
(1953–)
= Zoetta
Leisy
(1956–)

Pierre
(1961–)

Andrei
(1963–)
= Elisabeth
Flores
(1964–)

Francis-
Alexander
(1978–)

2

Nicholas
(1976–)

1

Alexandra
(1981–)

3

Michael
(1959–2001)

Alain
(1956–)
= Pascale
Deletre

Joelle
(1966–

Tatiana
(1968–)
= Alexis
Giannakoupoulas
(1962–)

Natasha
(1993–)

Tatiana
(1986–)
(adopted by
her grandfather
Pr Michael)

and Duke Alexander Michaelovich (1866–1933)

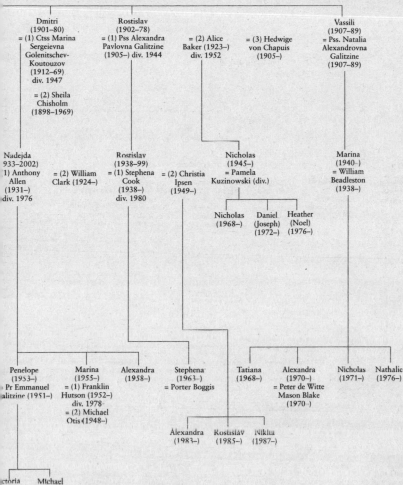

Dmitri
(1901–80)
= (1) Ctss Marina
Sergeievna
Golenitschev-
Koutouzov
(1912–69)
div. 1947

= (2) Sheila
Chisholm
(1898–1969)

Rostislav
(1902–78)
= (1) Pss Alexandra
Pavlovna Galitzine
(1905–) div. 1944

= (2) Alice
Baker (1923–)
div. 1952

= (3) Hedwige
von Chapuis
(1905–)

Vassili
(1907–89)
= Pss. Natalia
Alexandrovna
Galitzine
(1907–89)

Nadejda
(1933–2002)
= (1) Anthony
Allen
(1931–)
div. 1976

= (2) William
Clark (1924–)

Rostislav
(1938–99)
= (1) Stephena
Cook
(1938–)
div. 1980

= (2) Christia
Ipsen
(1949–)

Nicholas
(1945–)
= Pamela
Kuzinowski (div.)

Marina
(1940–)
= William
Beadleston
(1938–)

Nicholas
(1968–)

Daniel
(Joseph)
(1972–)

Heather
(Noel)
(1976–)

Penelope
(1953–)
= Pr Emmanuel
Galitzine (1951–)

Marina
(1955–)
= (1) Franklin
Hutson (1952–)
div. 1978
= (2) Michael
Otis (1948–)

Alexandra
(1958–)

Stephena
(1963–)
= Porter Boggis

Tatiana
(1968–)

Alexandra
(1970–)
= Peter de Witte
Mason Blake
(1970–)

Nicholas
(1971–)

Nathalie
(1976–)

Alexandra
(1983–)

Rostislav
(1985–)

Nikita
(1987–)

Victoria
(1985–)

Michael
(1993–)

TABLE 2 – THE RUSSIAN IMPERIAL FAMILY

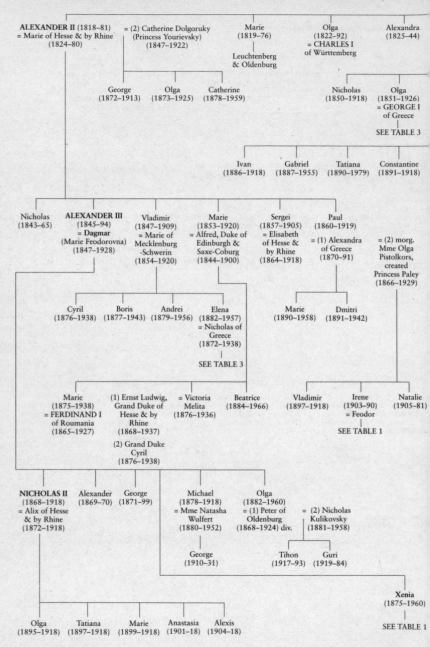

NICHOLAS I (1796–1855)

ALEXANDER II (1818–81) = (2) Catherine Dolgoruky (Princess Yourievsky) (1847–1922)
= Marie of Hesse & by Rhine (1824–80)

Marie (1819–76) — Leuchtenberg & Oldenburg

Olga (1822–92) = CHARLES I of Württemberg

Alexandra (1825–44)

George (1872–1913)   Olga (1873–1925)   Catherine (1878–1959)

Nicholas (1850–1918)   Olga (1851–1926) = GEORGE I of Greece — SEE TABLE 3

Ivan (1886–1918)   Gabriel (1887–1955)   Tatiana (1890–1979)   Constantine (1891–1918)

Nicholas (1843–65)

ALEXANDER III (1845–94) = Dagmar (Marie Feodorovna) (1847–1928)

Vladimir (1847–1909) = Marie of Mecklenburg-Schwerin (1854–1920)

Marie (1853–1920) = Alfred, Duke of Edinburgh & Saxe-Coburg (1844–1900)

Sergei (1857–1905) = Elisabeth of Hesse & by Rhine (1864–1918)

Paul (1860–1919) = (1) Alexandra of Greece (1870–91)

= (2) morg. Mme Olga Pistolkors, created Princess Paley (1866–1929)

Cyril (1876–1938)   Boris (1877–1943)   Andrei (1879–1956)   Elena (1882–1957) = Nicholas of Greece (1872–1938) — SEE TABLE 3

Marie (1890–1958)   Dmitri (1891–1942)

Marie (1875–1938) = FERDINAND I of Roumania (1865–1927)

(1) Ernst Ludwig, Grand Duke of Hesse & by Rhine (1868–1937)   = Victoria Melita (1876–1936)   Beatrice (1884–1966)

(2) Grand Duke Cyril (1876–1938)

Vladimir (1897–1918)   Irene (1903–90) = Feodor — SEE TABLE 1   Natalie (1905–81)

NICHOLAS II (1868–1918) = Alix of Hesse & by Rhine (1872–1918)

Alexander (1869–70)   George (1871–99)

Michael (1878–1918) = Mme Natasha Wulfert (1880–1952)

Olga (1882–1960) = (1) Peter of Oldenburg (1868–1924) div.   = (2) Nicholas Kulikovsky (1881–1958)

George (1910–31)

Tihon (1917–93)   Guri (1919–84)

Xenia (1875–1960) — SEE TABLE 1

Olga (1895–1918)   Tatiana (1897–1918)   Marie (1899–1918)   Anastasia (1901–18)   Alexis (1904–18)

Charlotte of Prussia (1798–1860)

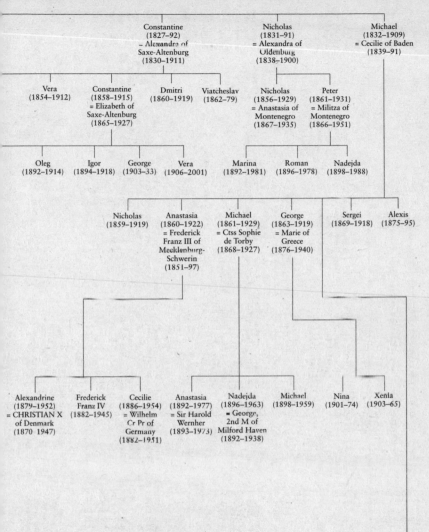

Constantine
(1827–92)
– Alexandra of
Saxe-Altenburg
(1830–1911)

Nicholas
(1831–91)
= Alexandra of
Oldenburg
(1838–1900)

Michael
(1832–1909)
= Cecilie of Baden
(1839–91)

Vera
(1854–1912)

Constantine
(1858–1915)
= Elizabeth of
Saxe-Altenburg
(1865–1927)

Dmitri
(1860–1919)

Viatcheslav
(1862–79)

Nicholas
(1856–1929)
= Anastasia of
Montenegro
(1867–1935)

Peter
(1861–1931)
= Militza of
Montenegro
(1866–1951)

Oleg
(1892–1914)

Igor
(1894–1918)

George
(1903–33)

Vera
(1906–2001)

Marina
(1892–1981)

Roman
(1896–1978)

Nadejda
(1898–1988)

Nicholas
(1859–1919)

Anastasia
(1860–1922)
= Frederick
Franz III of
Mecklenburg-
Schwerin
(1851–97)

Michael
(1861–1929)
= Ctss Sophie
de Torby
(1868–1927)

George
(1863–1919)
= Marie of
Greece
(1876–1940)

Sergei
(1869–1918)

Alexis
(1875–95)

Alexandrine
(1879–1952)
= CHRISTIAN X
of Denmark
(1870–1947)

Frederick
Franz IV
(1882–1945)

Cecilie
(1886–1954)
= Wilhelm
Cr Pr of
Germany
(1882–1951)

Anastasia
(1892–1977)
= Sir Harold
Wernher
(1893–1973)

Nadejda
(1896–1963)
= George,
2nd M of
Milford Haven
(1892–1938)

Michael
(1898–1959)

Nina
(1901–74)

Xenia
(1903–65)

= Alexander
('Sandro')
(1866–1933)

TABLE 3 – THE FAMILY OF CHRISTIAN IX OF DENMARK

CHRISTIAN IX of Denmark (1818–1906) = Louise of Hesse-Cassel (1817–98)

Children of Christian IX:

FREDERIK VIII (1843–1912) = Louise of Sweden (1851–1926)

Alexandra (1844–1925) = **EDWARD VII** (1841–1910)

GEORGE I of Greece (1845–1913) = Olga of Russia (1851–1926)

Dagmar (Marie Feodorovna) (1847–1928) = **ALEXANDER III** (1845–94)
SEE TABLE 2

Thyra (1853–1933) = Ernst August, Duke of Cumberland (1845–1923)

Waldemar (1858–1939) = Marie of Orléans (1865–1909)

Children of Frederik VIII:

CHRISTIAN X (1870–1947)

Carl (1872–1957) (HAAKON VII, King of Norway) = Maud (1869–1938)

Harald (1876–1949) = Helena of Glucksburg (1888–1962)

Ingeborg (1878–1958) = Carl of Sweden (1861–1951)

others

Children of George I of Greece:

CONSTANTINE I (1868–1923) = Sophie of Prussia (1870–1932)

George (1869–1957) = Marie Bonaparte (1882–1962)

Alexandra (1870–91) = Gr Duke Paul of Russia
SEE TABLE 2

Nicholas (1872–1938) = Elena of Russia (1882–1957)

Marie (1876–1940) = Gr Duke George of Russia
SEE TABLE 2

Andrew (1882–1944) = Alice of Battenberg (1885–1969)

Christopher (1888–1940) = (2) Françoise of Orléans (1902–53)

Children of Edward VII:

Albert Victor ('Eddy') (1864–92)

GEORGE V (1865–1936) = Victoria Mary 'May' of Teck (1867–1953)

Louise (1867–1931) = Alexander Duke of Fife (1849–1912)

Victoria (1868–1935)

Marie Louise (1879–1948) = Max of Baden (1867–1929)

Children of Constantine I:

George (1869–1957)

Olga (1903–97) = Paul of Yugoslavia (1893–1976)

Elizabeth (1904–55) = Charles-Theodore Count Toerring-Jettenbach (1900–67)

Marina (1906–68) = George, Duke of Kent (1902–42)

Children of Andrew:

Philip, Duke of Edinburgh (1921–)

Children of Dagmar / Alexander III line (SEE TABLE 2):

George (1880–1912)

Alexandra (1882–1963) = Frederick Franz IV of Mecklenburg-Schwerin (1882–1945)

Olga (1884–1958)

Christian (1885–1901)

Ernst August Duke of Brunswick-Lüneberg (1887–1953) = Victoria Louise, daughter of Kaiser Wilhelm II (1892–1980)

Axel (1888–1964) = Margaretha of Sweden (1899–1977)

Aage (1887–1940) = Mathilde Calvi di Bergolo (1885–1949)

Erik (1890–1950) = Lois Booth (1897–1941)

Viggo (1893–1970) = Eleanor Green (1895–1966)

Margarethe (1895–1992) = René of Bourbon-Parma (1894–1962)

Introduction

'Poor little Xenia, with such boys and her daughter married into that wicked family – and with such a false husband.' This dismissive verdict from the Empress Alexandra on her sister-in-law, written to the Tsar within less than a month of his abdication, now seems ironic. For 'poor little Xenia' was one of the survivors. The Empress might have been heading for the abyss, and in the view of many of the family she was more responsible for their tragic fate than anyone else, whereas Xenia, notwithstanding this apparently incorrigible family, remained to tell the tale. This was despite her precarious situation, for her daughter Irina was married to the man who, some six weeks before this letter was written, had turned conspirator and then murderer, leading a clandestine campaign to dispatch Rasputin in a vain effort to save the Russian Empire from collapse.

Born in 1875 during the reign of her grandfather Tsar Alexander II, Xenia had spent her early years in some security in the opulent courts of Russia. In her sixth year, his assassination presaged the constant campaign of bloodshed and eventually revolution which destroyed the world in which she had been brought up. Like her mother and sister she was fortunate to escape from Russia in 1919, and spent her remaining forty years in comfortable, though never wealthy, English exile, dying shortly after her eighty-fifth birthday in April 1960.

Her life, seen against the last years of Romanov grandeur, war, decline, and the first six decades of the turbulent twentieth century, was an extraordinary one by any standards. In recent years several biographers have chronicled the lives of most of her immediate family. Nicholas and Alexandra, her mother the Empress Marie Feodorovna, younger sister Olga and youngest brother Michael have all been immortalized in print, as has the notorious Rasputin. Her husband, Grand Duke Alexander ('Sandro') told his story (and occasionally hers) with more relish than historical accuracy in two volumes of memoirs, one published just before his death in 1933 and the other soon afterwards.

Yet Xenia's life has remained shrouded in some mystery. Thirteen boxes of material in the Hoover Institution, including diaries covering her dramatic departure from Russia, plus over four hundred documents that came to light in the summer of 2000, have revealed first-hand accounts of some momentous events. Using all this new material, it is possible for the first time to tell Xenia's story and see, often through her own eyes, what effect the Russian revolution had on her life.

Xenia's diary records her reaction to Rasputin's murder and the news that her son-in-law Prince Felix Youssoupov was implicated in the plot. Another entry shows her total disbelief and confusion as Russia spiralled into revolution, culminating in the abdication of her brother, the Tsar. More documents illuminate the relationship between Xenia and her husband: her feelings when he left her and, later, his emotional plea, which contradicts the version that was published in his own memoirs and was relied on by historians for nearly seventy years.

It has also been possible to cast new light on other members of the family. We see Xenia's sister Olga as a new mother, learn of her brother Michael's feelings on being suddenly nominated Tsar by their brother Nicholas II when he abdicated, and discover how Empress Alexandra Feodorovna felt about being exiled with her family to Tobolsk.

After the family's hurried departure from Russia, we find Xenia at the centre of a vast network of Russian emigrés and European royal relatives, more than one of whom expressed their feelings about Xenia's permanent exile from her motherland and the lack of help given the Romanovs at their time of greatest need by the British royal family. Thus, our book offers a fresh perspective on the problems faced in exile by the surviving members of the Russian imperial family.

1 (1864–90)

'A sense of happiness seemed to linger'

Nothing is more beautiful than this city of gold, on a horizon of silver, where the sky retains the paleness of dawn,'[1] wrote Théophile Gautier in 1858 when he caught his first sight of St Petersburg. This was the city of Grand Duchess Xenia's family and forebears since its inception by Peter the Great in 1703, on marshland seized from the Swedes, where the mouth of the River Neva meets the Gulf of Finland. By the nineteenth century it was one of the most beautiful capitals in Europe, elegantly classical with wide boulevards, enormous squares and majestic canals. For over six months in winter the city of St Petersburg froze in sub-zero temperatures under layers of ice and snow, with only four hours of daylight. In summer there were the 'white nights', twenty-two hours of daylight when the sun glistened on the golden domes of the churches and the city was bathed in the silvery-pearl haze so admired by Gautier. St Petersburg was very cosmopolitan. Along the 3-mile waterfront of the Neva, Italian architects had built splendid baroque palaces for the nobility, the largest and most lavish being the Winter Palace, the setting for the Imperial Court. This was the world that would form Xenia's earliest memories. Here she would come to realize that, as a child of Russia's ruling dynasty, she was a Grand Duchess, part of the most important and powerful imperial family in the world.

In the mid-nineteenth century the gorgeous Winter Palace was the residence of her grandparents, Tsar Alexander II and his wife Empress Marie Alexandrovna, formerly Princess Marie of Hesse. In the summer of 1864 Alexander II, seeking a wife for his heir, approached King Christian IX of Denmark with a proposal for his eldest unmarried daughter, Princess Dagmar, to marry the

1

Tsarevich, Grand Duke Nicholas Alexandrovich. At almost twenty-one, this sensitive youth had become a well-read adult with his father's liberal leanings, marked artistic interests, and little in common with his more boisterous brothers.

As a child Dagmar was less pretty than her elder sister Alexandra ('Alix'), who had married the Prince of Wales in 1863, but she had more personality, a sharper wit and wider interests, as well as the same sense of style and love of fine clothes. According to one of their playmates, Bernhard von Bülow, the future Chancellor of Imperial Germany, Dagmar was livelier and cleverer than her sister, 'but desperately hard-headed'.[2]

Accompanied by Count Stroganov and a large suite, the Tsarevich travelled to Copenhagen to meet the Danish royal family. A betrothal was virtually a foregone conclusion, but the two young people also fell deeply in love. Amid lavish family celebrations it was announced that they would marry in the spring of 1865. Yet it was not to be. On a visit to southern Europe Nicholas was confined to bed for several weeks while being treated for an abscess; he became too weak to return home and by Christmas he was evidently dying. Princess Dagmar and members of her family joined the sorrowing relations at his bedside at Nice as, on the evening of 24 April 1865 [NS], the thin, wasted young heir slipped away. After a suitable period of mourning a devastated Dagmar, knowing what was expected, dutifully transferred her affections to the new Tsarevich, the Tsar's second son Alexander.

Brought up as a soldier, noted one anonymous contemporary, 'without any political education, with a poor knowledge of languages for a man in his position, and with a disposition more given to self-indulgence than to work, the new heir-apparent found that time was above all things necessary to adapt himself to the altered state of things'.[3] Little attention had been paid to his education; as he was not heir to the throne, his tutors had made no effort to groom him as a future sovereign. They had thought him sluggish and ponderous beside his quick-witted elder brother. Uncomely, uncouth and bad-tempered, he was regarded as the ugly duckling of the family, clumsy, lacking in manners and too keen to use his fists. Court officials had always slighted or ignored him, and it must have given him satisfaction to consider that now he would be treated with more respect.

The two young people were not really in love. Dagmar was still coming to terms with the loss of Nicholas, while Alexander was in love with Princess Marie Mestchersky. Although he also knew that, as the eldest surviving son and heir, he could never marry her, Alexander needed considerable prompting as to where his dynastic duty lay. Princess Mestchersky was banished abroad and the new Tsarevich was sent to Copenhagen to propose to Princess Dagmar.

In the autumn of 1866 Dagmar arrived in St Petersburg to prepare for her new role as wife of the heir to the imperial throne. She was received into the Orthodox Church, and took the name Grand Duchess Marie Feodorovna. On 28 October they were married at the Winter Palace. In the family Dagmar was always 'Minny' while her husband was 'Sasha'. They made their home at the Anitchkov Palace on the Nevsky Prospekt, one of St Petersburg's main thoroughfares. Carlo Rossi's baroque building had lavishly decorated state rooms, a private chapel and a ballroom. Outside was a small garden with a pond. In 1874 Monighetti added a Winter Garden over the projecting front vestibule.

As their youngest daughter Olga would remark many years later, her parents had little in common, yet they complemented each other so well that their marriage could not have been happier.[4] Hating pomp, ostentation and court balls, Sasha was happiest at home. Dagmar enjoyed the high society life of St Petersburg and positively sparkled at court occasions. She loved riding and was a keen horsewoman, while he was not merely unsuited to mounting a horse with his great bulk, but also afraid of them.

During the next sixteen years they had six children. The eldest, Nicholas, destined to be the last Tsar of Russia, was born on 6 May 1868. Alexander was born on 26 May 1869 and died of meningitis on 20 April 1870, and a third son George followed on 27 April 1871. Three years elapsed before Dagmar was *enceinte* once more. She always suffered from nausea during her pregnancies, and her physician Dr Hirsch advised her to eat raw ham in bed each morning. As her confinement drew closer she told her mother, Queen Louise of Denmark, that this time she felt particularly fat and awkward as well.

The coming of spring, when the ice in the Neva broke, allowing the river to flow again, was always eagerly awaited by all St

Petersburg. To signal the start of 'navigation', cannons were fired from the SS Peter & Paul Fortress, from where the commander sailed forth in a decorated barge to present a crystal goblet of Neva water to the Tsar. It was around the time this event was being anticipated that at 4am on Tuesday 25 March 1875, at the Anitchkov, Dagmar gave birth to a daughter, who was named Xenia.[5]

'On the 25th day of the present month of March our well-beloved daughter-in-law H.I.H. the Czarevna, . . . wife of H.I.H. the Cesarevitch . . . brought into the world a daughter . . . who has received the name of Xenia,' ran the words of the manifesto issued by Alexander II. 'We welcome this increase of our Imperial Family as a new grace of Providence . . . and in announcing it to our faithful subjects we are convinced that they will raise with us fervent prayers to God for the happy growth and prosperity of the new-born Grand Duchess. We order that everywhere the title of Imperial Highness shall be given to our well-beloved grand-daughter the new-born Grand Duchess. . . .'[6] The parents were delighted that the latest addition to their family was a daughter.

In accordance with Orthodox tradition, the parents did not attend Xenia's christening, which took place on Thursday 17 April, the Tsar's birthday. At the service in the Winter Palace church, conducted by Their Majesties' confessor, the little Grand Duchess wore a christening gown made by her mother from cotton and lace. It had a detachable bib on which Dagmar embroidered a tiny double-headed eagle, the imperial crown and the year of Xenia's birth. The gown was worn by all Dagmar's children and a new bib was made for each baby. Xenia's godparents were her grandmother the Empress Marie Alexandrovna, her grandfather King Christian IX of Denmark, her father's brother Grand Duke Vladimir Alexandrovich and Princess Thyra of Denmark, her mother's younger sister. Xenia also received the customary gift, a gold crucifix.[7]

The nursery at the Anitchkov consisted of five sparsely furnished rooms. Anastasia Grigorievna ('Nastya', or 'Na') was engaged as Xenia's nanny. The baby may also have come under the care of Kitty Strutton, an Englishwoman who had nursed her father, as English ways had been fashionable at the Russian court for some years. Dagmar engaged a wet-nurse, as she had done for her sons.

From England, the Princess of Wales wrote full of concern for her sister's health:

> . . . thank God that it is all over and you got through it well, and that you have a little girl!!!! . . . My thoughts and prayers were with you in those moments, I think – since you did telegraph me that very morning. . . .
>   . . . did you suffer much? My poor little Minny – or did you have a little chloroform this time? You did promise that you would. . . .
>   *Xenia* or something like that the little child is called, yes that is a beautiful name, who has thought of it? I almost imagined that you yourself wanted to nurse her!!!!! I cannot help laughing when I think of my blessed father's daughter's breasts dripping!!!???? No, the thought of seeing you little Minny with the little one at your breast!!! is much too amusing to be true!! and think how I have always wanted it so much myself!! What do the boys say to little sister? [*English in the original*] Sasha could honestly really have written to me, I wanted it so much?????. . .[8]

In June, when Xenia was almost three months old, Sasha was sent abroad to represent the Tsar on official business. Dagmar took the children to Peterhof, the imperial summer estate on the Gulf of Finland. Around the Grand Palace, with its long canal and cascades of fountains stretching down to the sea, were numerous villas: Marly, Monplaisir, The Hermitage and the Farm, but the Tsarevich and his wife always used The Cottage, a pretty yellow and white neo-Gothic villa, a riot of small rooms with verandas, gables and balconies, which Xenia's brothers loved to explore. From there, Dagmar took the three children to visit their grandparents in Denmark, where they were later joined by Sasha.

The Princess of Wales took a special interest in Xenia as, according to the western NS calendar, she was born on the same date as Alix's son, who had died within twenty-four hours.* 'Your sweet little Xenia is surely a dear little thing,' Alix wrote on 26

---

* Prince Alexander John of Wales, born 6 April and died 7 April 1871.

October. 'I am really curious to see her. Please do have yourself photographed with her, so that I can see what she looks like!!!!'[9]

A few months later she enquired: 'How are your sweet children keeping? I fear that your sweet Nicky has forgotten me, which would make me sad as I love that angelic child. Little Georgie can of course not remember me, and I do not know baby Xenia yet, which is a pity!'[10]

The following spring, when Xenia was in the arms of her nurse at Livadia in the Crimea, they met a small boy who introduced himself as Grand Duke Alexander Michaelovich. This was Xenia's first meeting with her future husband.

Despite the presence of Nastya, Xenia was raised under her mother's direct supervision. As she had few official responsibilities, Dagmar was able to devote plenty of time to her family. 'All three children lay by the side of me on the bed', she told Queen Louise in 1877, 'and Nicky told a little story.'[11] Xenia had inherited her mother's lively intelligence and something of her charm of manner but had nothing of Dagmar's outgoing personality. She was very close to Nicholas and Georgie and when their French tutor, Monsieur Duperret, returned from a visit to Paris, he even brought a present for little Xenia – 'a small bird which looks almost alive', Nicky told their mother.[12]

On 21 November 1878 Xenia's brother Michael was born. Although Xenia became the favourite daughter, 'Misha' as the family called him was undoubtedly his parents' favourite son.

Dagmar had the last word with regard to the children's upbringing. They were raised in a Spartan manner, as their father had been, sleeping on camp beds, rising at 6am and taking a cold bath. Occasionally they were allowed a warm one in their mother's bathroom. For breakfast they had porridge and black bread, mutton cutlets or roast beef with peas and baked potatoes at lunch, and bread, butter and jam at tea, with cake kept as a treat for special occasions. They were not brought up in luxurious surroundings; while Nicholas and George had their own sitting room, dining room, playroom and bedroom, they were very simply furnished, the only finery being an icon surrounded with pearls and precious stones. Nevertheless Dagmar impressed on them throughout childhood that a happy family life was the most important thing, with the minimum of discipline for its own sake. When the children were a little older they dined with their parents, and friendly family arguments often escalated into battles in which they threw bread at each other. Alexander's aunt, Queen Olga of Württemberg, was grossly affronted at this lack of discipline.

Xenia became her mother's constant companion and received regular presents from Aunt Alix in England. 'I will give your little Xenie [sic] the little white dress with the ribbons pulled through,' the Princess of Wales told her sister in 1879. There seems to have been a mishap though, as Alix continued, 'the other two [dresses] were ordered by you. I am sorry, *they were certainly* so smart – but it wasn't poor Loue's fault. . . .'[13] It was customary for both parents to see the boys mid-morning to discuss their lessons and activities for the day. At bedtime, Dagmar saw her sons for a shorter period. Sometimes the children were allowed into her rooms while she dressed for dinner. She let them choose her gown and watch while Sophie, the Danish maid, went through the daily ritual of brushing and arranging her hair, before winding ropes of perfectly matched pearls around her neck.

All the children were brought up to believe in and respect the word of Tsar Alexander II, whose decision on any matter was final. Unfortunately, this smothered both their individuality and their independence of thought. Dagmar was well aware that, after her children, the next heir was her brother-in-law Vladimir and his ambitious German wife, the former Princess Marie of Mecklenburg-Schwerin, who, while taking the name Grand Duchess Marie Pavlovna ('Miechen'), still had not renounced her Lutheran faith. Dagmar and Sasha disliked her pro-German attitude and distrusted her friendship with Bismarck, for whom she was rumoured to be a secret agent. Relations between the two women would always be distant. There was no such rivalry between Sasha and his younger brothers – Alexis, who was to become the head of the Russian navy, Sergei, a future governor-general of Moscow, and the more scholarly Paul. The brothers had one sister, Marie, who had married Queen Victoria's second son Alfred, Duke of Edinburgh. She found the courts of England disappointingly provincial and lacking in splendour compared with the palaces of St Petersburg, and always relished her visits back to the land of her birth.

Sasha adored his young family, liking nothing more than a good romp. He insisted that they be brought up as normal healthy children. As they grew older he took pleasure in being with other children as well, and he soon became Uncle Sasha to a whole tribe of nephews and nieces, delightedly leading them into mischief.

Outside the Anitchkov nursery, events were taking place which would have a significant effect on Xenia's future. By this time Sasha's relations with his own father were becoming less cordial. The Tsar and Tsarina had drifted apart. Since the death of her eldest son she had become more ardently Orthodox, and her health, never good, deteriorated further. The distance between husband and wife left him open to the temptations of a mistress, and his affair with Catherine Dolgoruky, who was soon 'his wife in all but name' and bore him several children, created a gulf between father and son. Sasha and his brothers all deeply loved and revered their mother, and were outraged at their father's cavalier treatment of her. Moreover, owing to a complete difference in outlook between father and son, the Tsarevich had no involvement with affairs of state. Though he was permitted to attend ministerial meetings, he was easily influenced by his mother's confessor, Father Bashanov, and the ambitious, arch-conservative Constantine Pobedonostsev, who between them, impressed on him that reform was dangerous and the autocracy of Russia must be preserved at all costs. He was at odds with his father's policy and was soon associated with the reactionary opposition, and it was apparent that once he came to the throne all reforms would stop.

The terrorist movement known as the 'Nihilists' or 'People's Will', an organization devoted to the destruction of the old regime by violence, was now active again. In February 1880 its activists infiltrated the Winter Palace and an explosion occurred just as the imperial family should have been eating dinner. Their lives were saved because the meal was delayed that evening. Sasha moved his family to Yelagin Palace, on one of the islands of the Neva delta. It was far enough from the city centre to give them extra security, but close enough to allow the Tsarevich to make daily visits to his dying mother. For Xenia and her brothers there was the advantage of vast grounds running down to the river. 'The poor children . . . are happy to be out of the city and enjoy this dearest place immensely,' Dagmar told her mother.[14]

To the children's delight, their aunt Queen Olga of Greece soon arrived with her children Constantine, George, Alexandra, Nicholas and Marie. The park, with its giant oak trees, provided an ideal place for wild games. Xenia and her brothers always wore high leather boots outdoors and their Greek cousins pestered the Queen until she bought them identical pairs. A Russian Grand Duchess by birth, Queen Olga was married to King George of the Hellenes, the second brother of Dagmar.

The Empress died in her sleep on 22 May. After the funeral, Sasha and Dagmar moved to the Villa Brevern in Hapsal on the Baltic. Xenia played with her brothers on the beach and bathed in the sea, Sasha hunted wild duck with Finnish nobles and Dagmar went riding. In June, while the children remained at Hapsal in the care of Princess Julia Kurakin, their parents returned to St Petersburg for a service marking the fortieth day since the Empress's death. They were shocked at the indecent haste with which the Tsar had married Catherine Dolgoruky, who had now been created Princess Yourievsky. Two of Alexander's brothers and several ministers accepted the arrangement as perfectly natural, but the Tsarevich and his wife were furious. Nevertheless Sasha kept his own counsel. There had been several attempts on his father's life during the previous few years, and he suspected that he would be sovereign himself before long.

Early in 1881 the Tsarevich's children received an invitation to a party at the Winter Palace. Alexander II was anxious for them to meet Catherine's children, their young step-uncle and aunts, ten-year-old George, seven-year-old Olga and two year-old Catherine, all of whom had now been legitimized with the title of Prince or Princess Yourievsky. Other guests included people who would remain close to Xenia for life – the Tsar's brother Grand Duke Michael Nicholaievich and his children, including fourteen-year-old Alexander ('Sandro'); and the Vorontzov-Dashkovs, Vanya, Sandra, Sofka, Maya, Ira and Roman, whose parents were close friends of Sasha and Dagmar. They had been invited so that the Tsarevich's children would find some people they knew among the guests. The huge doors flew open and the Tsar entered with Princess Yourievsky and their family. One of the Vorontzovs later recalled racing round the state rooms and sliding down the wooden helter-skelter, led by Xenia's brother Nicky. Then there was a raffle at which everyone won a prize, including dolls or china figurines for Xenia and the other girls, before they went home.

It is doubtful whether five-year-old Xenia understood who the Yourievsky children were, although her brother Nicholas had certainly been informed. The Vorontzovs were told by their parents that the Tsar had married a widow, and these were her children from the previous marriage.

The following month there was an afternoon fancy dress party at the palace, with costumes provided by the Emperor. The Yourievsky children arrived already wearing specially made costumes, the other boys and girls were sent into rooms to change. They were then told to go and see Princess Yourievsky, whom they found in one of the bedrooms. An icon was propped up on the pillow, and a big basket on the floor contained a selection of masks, which caused much hilarity as the children made their choice. Suddenly Sasha appeared at the door and summoned Xenia, then the Vorontzov girls were called away. The children learnt afterwards that the princess had chosen to use the room in which the Empress had died, and the Tsarevich discovered them laughing when he went in to pray.

On 1 March 1881 a dramatic event put an end to the children's parties. As Tsar Alexander II was driving back to the Winter Palace, a bomb was thrown at his coach and several people were killed. Disregarding pleas to look to his own safety, he got out to see if he could help the wounded, and was immediately hit by another bomb. His legs were shattered and he was carried back to the palace semi-conscious, to die from his wounds later that day. A signed manifesto, paving the way for full franchise in the future, lay on his desk. Xenia's parents had come into their inheritance all too soon.

After his father's funeral, Tsar Alexander III had no hesitation in tearing up the signed manifesto. He would reign as an autocrat. No clemency would be shown to the assassins who had evidently planned his father's murder for several months, and within weeks they were brought to trial and executed in public.

Warned that his family's safety was at risk in the capital, Sasha moved them to Gatchina, a vast palace with towers, battlements and high walls 30 miles south-west of St Petersburg, which had formerly belonged to the Emperor Paul. Xenia and Misha both had colds and so could not go outside, and had to be left behind at the Anitchkov. Xenia pined for her parents and longed for the company of her elder brothers. The Empress found Gatchina 'cold, disgusting and full of workmen' and she tried to make it more habitable by transferring some Chinese and Japanese porcelain from Tsarskoe Selo to fill the empty corridors. 'This uninhabited, big, empty castle in the middle of winter cost me many tears,' she continued, 'hidden tears, for Sasha is happy to leave the city.'[15] Not until later could Xenia and Misha join the others. 'Little Xenia is so glad,' Dagmar reported.[16]

Alexander III shunned the luxurious state rooms in the central block, only using them for significant occasions. Instead they lived in the Arsenal Block, in a series of low, vaulted rooms which had formerly been occupied by Paul's court. From the upper state quarters a corridor led to a tiny staircase winding down to the mezzanine floor. The small, dark and stuffy apartments, barely seven-and-a-half feet high, were crammed with furniture, knick-knacks, photographs and china. The Empress noted that they lacked 'toilets and constraint' and reminded her of ships' cabins.[17] Their children pasted cartoons from Christmas numbers of the *Graphic* on the walls; on the stairwell were pictures of Victorian society beauties cut from magazines. There was a study for the Empress, a drawing room, billiard room and dining room. In the Tsar's modest, almost shabby working study, its desk covered with papers and family photographs, was a life-size wax figure of a man playing a hunting horn. Official reception rooms were on the first floor. Beyond the sitting rooms were bedrooms and nurseries – a visitor after the revolution noticed that toys were still lying around. Nicholas and Georgie's bedroom had 'two green Biedermayer sofas with hard backs that served as beds', with a china stove between. Nearby, sunk into the floor, was a bath.[18] It was traditional for Russian Grand Duchesses to sleep on a camp bed until their marriage, so Xenia had a hard bed like her brothers. A photograph of one of the ladies' bedrooms survives, showing a single bed, a dressing-table with a frilly valance and some comfortable chairs.

On the ground floor, through an outer hall full of stuffed bears and aurochs (known as 'the monagerie'), was the Arsenal Hall, where the principal part of family life took place. This was a large vaulted room with sofas, a dining table, billiard table and toys including a boat-shaped swing, an American mountain, a gymnasium, a railway, a dolls' house, a kitchen equipped for cooking and a fortress complete with soldiers. 'A sense of happiness seemed to linger', wrote a British visitor in the 1920s.[19] A staircase connected the Arsenal Hall directly to the Emperor's study. Security at the palace was tight, with cavalry patrolling the park boundaries and cossacks pacing up and down outside the imperial family's rooms every night. Visitors were carefully scrutinized and each security pass carried the bearer's photograph.

Although Nicky and Xenia both preferred St Petersburg, trips to the capital were at first kept to a minimum. Even playing in the park posed problems, and Dagmar told Queen Louise that the boys were never allowed out alone: 'They go out always with us, and we keep all that is sad and unpleasant away from them so that they do not feel the oppressive time we are experiencing.'[20]

Every morning Xenia and her brothers went to wish their father good morning before he began work in his study. Lunch, which always started with soup and usually comprised both French and Russian dishes, was served at 1pm. Afterwards, they waited for their father's command to get dressed. Xenia's maid Vera wrapped her in a pelisse or long cloak and high fur-lined boots. After a walk, with the snow crackling under their feet in the pale northern sunlight, the children returned to their lessons and the Tsar to his desk.

In the spring of 1882 they visited Peterhof, where on 1 June the Empress gave birth to her last child, Olga, the only one of the children 'born in the purple'. As Olga was delicate, they engaged an English nanny, Elizabeth Franklin, who established Olga's nursery in one of Gatchina's large tapestried salons, refusing to bring up 'her baby' in the gloomy entresol. 'Nana' ruled with a rod of iron, but the other children had the freedom of the nursery as long as they recognized her authority.

Sasha wanted all his children to receive an equally good education. At Gatchina they had several private tutors, with special emphasis on foreign languages. A favourite was Charles Heath (the 'old man' as the children called him), English tutor to Xenia's elder brothers, who lived at Gatchina with his wife and daughters, and taught the Emperor's children to fish, play games and never cheat. They all learnt English, French and German but, unlike Nicholas, Xenia never knew any Danish. Among the succession of French tutors (Monsieur Duperret was dismissed after an erotic scandal) was Ferdinand Thormeyer from Switzerland. Xenia's geography textbook is preserved, along with other books used by the imperial children at Gatchina.

The Emperor and Empress believed spare time should be usefully employed. The children therefore learnt cookery, joinery and how to make puppets for their theatre, including the clothes. As well as playing with her dolls (in which Misha enthusiastically joined), Xenia played battle games with her brothers' toy soldiers, watched pictures from a magic lantern and 'played billiards, tag, battledore & shuttlecock [and] cycled around the vast palace'.[21] Like other royal children of the day, she recorded each day's events in her diary.

From an early age Xenia showed artistic talent. In 1881 Dagmar told her mother that Xenia had grown a lot and was 'quite a big girl already. I believe she has a talent for drawing, she always has a pencil in her hand and draws small figures and faces perfectly accurately.'[22] She also learnt gymnastics, dancing (usually partnered by Misha) and played the piano. As the Tsar believed in an outdoor life, all the children were taught to ride in Gatchina's large riding school. They kept birds, rabbits and even a bear cub, which they had to look after themselves. When Xenia was nine, she and Misha were each given a donkey by their father. They were normal, healthy children who loved going to the circus and for family birthdays secretly made their own presents, usually pictures. Birthdays and Name Days were always marked by a church service, followed by lunch in the Arsenal Hall. As Sasha also believed in letting them indulge their high spirits, there was no rigid discipline. They attended celebrations on regimental holidays and accompanied their parents to military reviews.

Religion was also important, and in the spring of 1883 Xenia went to her first confession before accompanying her mother to communion. 'She was very serious the whole Friday [the day before] and one could see her thinking properly over it,'[23] Dagmar wrote. Xenia's participation was part of the preparation for her first appearance at a state occasion – her parents' coronation in May 1883.

There were genuine fears that an attempt would be made on the family's lives during the coronation. A few days before the ceremony, amid tight security, they moved to the Petrovsky Palace on the Tverskaya, the main road into Moscow. From here, in 1812, Napoleon had watched Moscow burn.

On 10 May the official state entry to Moscow took place, with a procession of Russian Grand Dukes and foreign princes escorting the Tsar to the Kremlin. He rode by himself in front, a squadron of horses forming the vanguard, announcing his approach to the troops and civilian population lining the streets of their march. A long file of golden carriages followed, the first containing the Tsarina and Xenia, the others the Russian Grand Duchesses, princesses of royal blood and elder ladies-in-waiting. Wearing a short version of the Russian court dress with the traditional half-moon-shaped *kokoshnik* on her head, Xenia sat beside her mother in the golden coach of Empress Elizabeth. As the long procession wound along the Tverskaya, Xenia copied the way the Empress bowed and waved to the people. Just outside Red Square the Tsar helped his wife and daughter from the coach and they went inside the Iverskaya Chapel for a few moments of silent prayer at one of the holiest shrines in Russia. The procession entered the Kremlin through the Spassky Gate to the strains of the national anthem. After prayers at the three great cathedrals, the Uspensky Sobor, the Archangel Michael, and the Annunciation, the imperial family mounted the Red Staircase to the Great Kremlin Palace. The day was very tiring, and when Dagmar was asked later what eight-year-old Xenia thought of it all, the answer was, 'she really didn't know – that she didn't speak, but looked at everything and bowed to all the people exactly as she did'.[24]

The coronation was on 15 May. The Emperor, wearing the dark green and gold uniform of the Preobrajensky Regiment, and the Empress in a silver brocade court dress slashed with the red ribbon of the Order of St Catherine, led the procession down the Red Staircase and along a raised walkway to the coronation cathedral, the Uspensky Sobor. Inside, Nicholas, George and Xenia took their places with other members of the imperial family alongside the dais.

After the long ceremony, during which the Tsar crowned himself, the imperial family paid homage to the sovereigns. First came the Emperor's brothers Vladimir and Alexis, who kissed the

Emperor and then kissed the Empress's hand. Then it was the turn of his sons Nicholas and George, in uniform with the blue ribbon of St Andrew, and Xenia in a short white dress and *kokoshnik* with her hair flowing loose. 'It was a pretty sight to see the children bowing and curtseying low to their parents,' recalled an observer.[25] After the Tsar had taken communion they stepped outside as the guns fired a salute and the bells of Moscow rang. The procession moved slowly round to the other great cathedrals, where prayers were said before they returned to the Kremlin. A whole round of banquets, balls, military reviews and other festivities followed, in which Xenia took little part, although she was at the consecration of the new Cathedral of Christ the Saviour on 25 May.

The imperial family were always glad to escape to their holidays in Denmark, visits which Sasha compared to being 'out of prison'. At Kronstadt Xenia, her parents, sister and brothers boarded the imperial yacht for Copenhagen, to stay with their Danish grandparents. In 1883 there was a particularly large gathering of the family of King Christian IX, 'the Father-in-law of Europe', and Queen Louise at Fredensborg, the King's summer palace set in a vast park north of Copenhagen.

Here Xenia was soon to find out that she was related to several of the other European crowned heads. Her mother's eldest brother Frederik was Crown Prince of Denmark, while the elder sister Alexandra was Princess of Wales. The second brother had been elected to the throne of Greece, where he reigned as King George I of the Hellenes with his wife Queen Olga. Dagmar's youngest sister Thyra, Xenia's godmother, married the Duke of Cumberland, whose family had ruled Hanover until dispossessed by Bismarck in 1866. Waldemar, the youngest brother, married Princess Marie of Orléans in 1885. As not everyone could come each year, they sometimes used the smaller Bernstorff palace, 10 miles from Copenhagen.

These family reunions were lively, noisy affairs, at which all political discussion was forbidden. Xenia's father seemed ten years younger as he indulged in boyish pranks, like turning a hose on the pompous King Oscar II of Sweden, who knew better than to come again next year. Another unpopular visitor was Kaiser Wilhelm, who came some years later for King Christian's eighty-fifth birthday, arriving 'because he said he wanted to', and went about slapping everybody on the back in his determinedly hearty manner, pretending how fond he was of everyone.[26] Like many of his other hosts before and after, they were all glad to see him go.

All the children loved these gatherings. Every morning after breakfast the Tsar, like the Pied Piper, led them on a walk around Fredensborg, taking them into muddy ponds to search for tadpoles or into the orchard to steal apples. Often he encouraged the Russian courtiers to lead them round and round the large galleried Cupola Hall on roller-skates. On wet days they played ball in this hall, throwing the ball up to the Tsar or King Christian as they passed by in the gallery above.

It was under the table in the Cupola Hall that Xenia first made the acquaintance of a cousin who was to become a life-long friend. Princess Marie of Greece ('Greek Minny'), a daughter of King George and Queen Olga, was almost a year younger. They had met before, but the meeting had obviously left no impression. Now the two girls quickly became best friends. Unlike Xenia, who showed signs of inheriting her mother's 'elfin beauty', Marie was rather plain. Another friendship formed in Denmark was with a slightly older cousin, Princess Victoria of Wales. 'Toria' was fifteen, the same age as Xenia's brother Nicky, who that summer had a teenage crush on her. While their parents left dignity behind and indulged in all sorts of practical jokes, the children walked in the woods, played hide-and-seek in the palace and generally enjoyed themselves. In later years there were tea parties at the Kejservilla, a modest house just outside the gates of Fredensborg purchased by Alexander III in 1885.

One of Xenia's earliest surviving letters, to Queen Louise, was written when she was ten years old: 'I very often think of the pleasant time we passed all together in Fredensborg. . . . I wish you a very Merry Christmas and happy New Year. We all look forward to Christmas. I wish we could be all together at that nice time. I hope another time when we will come to you that dear Aunt Thyra & the Greek cousins will be there & then it will be so very very nice.'[27] As on all her early letters, Xenia had drawn a flower in the top left-hand corner of the page.

Xenia must have been a well-known figure in Denmark at this time. In 1884, when she was nine years old, the Danish composer

Valdemar Vater wrote the 'Xenia Polka Mazurka' dedicated to the little Grand Duchess.[28]

From the early 1880s Xenia, Nicky and Georgie also had a particular group of Russian friends, the Vorontzov-Dashkov children, Vanya and his sisters Sandra, Sofka, Maya and Irina, their companions at Alexander II's parties at the Winter Palace. Their father Count Ilarion was Minister of the Court, his wife 'Lili' was the Empress's close friend and lady-in-waiting. With Dmitri and Paul Cheremetev, the Bariatinsky children and a few others, the Vorontzovs formed the nucleus of Xenia's childhood world. Every Sunday these friends took the 9.30 train to Gatchina for lunch. Afterwards they played games on the palace lawn, sometimes with Charles Heath, watched over by Xenia's nurse Nastya. They loved the miniature railway in the park with its tunnels, stations, bridges and its engines, replicas of real locomotives, which could reach speeds of 4 or 5mph. An even more exciting pastime was to walk into the Echo Grotto from its entrance by the Silver Lake, through an underground passage into the palace, and climb the towers.[29] Another playmate was a cousin, Grand Duke Alexis Michaelovich, who was the same age as Xenia and sometimes brought his brothers Sandro and Sergei. Often the Emperor would come and take the children for a walk, singling out one of them to talk to on the way. Tea was served back at the palace, or at the Huntsman's Lodge, with the Empress and her guests.

Like many youngsters they formed their own secret societies. The 'Potato Society' took its name from an incident on a paperchase when the pursuers were told the 'fox' had 'shot into the potatoes'. Every member had a golden charm shaped like a potato, made by Fabergé. There was also a 'Gatchina Society', whose golden badge, with the Tsarevich's monogram on one side, the inscription 'Anitchkov and Gatchina 1881–1885' and the owner's name on the other, was presented to friends by Nicholas after he came of age.

As they grew older, the Tsar's children attended theatrical performances in Gatchina's 'Bolshoi Theatre', or listened to operas and concerts relayed from St Petersburg by telephone. They gave parties, and staged amateur theatricals for friends Puppet shows, conjurers, gypsy ensembles and a 'mind reader' came to entertain. A group of balalaika players made a particularly good impression.[30]

Like other members of the family, Xenia was a keen angler. 'Mama and I went to the Admiralty where we were first feeding the ducks and then, taking a sailor and fishing rods with us, started in the *Moya* to the large bridge near the Menagerie, where we went ashore and began angling. It was very exciting! Mama was catching one perch after another while only roaches swallowed my bait and she caught so many that I got offended.'[31]

The Tsar took the children into the woods to teach them the secrets of nature. They cleared the gardens, making bonfires with twigs and baking potatoes over the hot cinders. There were picnics in the woods, the Tsar driving the children in a wagonette, and the Empress bringing her guests. When snow came they went sleighing, or tobogganing down the hill on a piece of board like the local children. 'We went out skiing in the afternoon,' Xenia wrote in 1884. 'It was marvellous. Hurrah! We were skiing all together and Mama too, she (and we all) laughed and shouted.'[32] Several days would usually be spent in making a giant snowman in front of the palace, and they regularly went skating. They loved watching the Emperor test the newly frozen ice on the pond; treading carefully until it gave way under his weight and he landed up to his knees in water.

As for most children, Christmas was a special time of year, and was always celebrated at Gatchina. Because etiquette forbade any member of the imperial family from entering a shop, the shopkeepers had to send their wares to the palaces on approval. Once a particular item had been purchased one year, the retailers assumed that it would be wanted every time, and so they sent the same things over and over again.

Moreover, as the children had never ventured out into the wide world, they had no idea about any novelties in the market, and the most important shops did not advertise in those days. Even if they had done so, the children would never have seen any advertisements, as newspapers were not allowed in the nursery. The Tsar's children had no pocket money, and everything they chose as personal gifts was paid for out of the privy purse. They had no idea of their relative financial value. Xenia was in the Tsarina's rooms when two ladies-in-waiting were unpacking cases of jewellery and bibelots sent by Cartier from Paris. She had not decided what she would give her mother until she saw a filigree scent bottle, its stopper studded with sapphires. To her innocent mind, the price did not matter; nothing else would do. Countess Stroganov, who was looking on, was entreated not to give the secret away. Xenia proudly presented it to her mother on Christmas Eve, and not wishing to spoil the occasion, the Tsarina accepted it with due enthusiasm, but afterwards she made it clear to her ladies that in future any boxes arriving from Cartier and other jewellers could be admired by the children – but no more. Neither she nor the Tsar gave their children any luxurious presents; they had toys, books and, when they were older, gardening implements.

Excitement was intense on Christmas Eve as the children, bursting with enthusiasm, tried to eat their dinner while waiting eagerly for the drawing-room doors to open. Finally the Emperor rang a small handbell, and the children stampeded into a large room filled with beautifully decorated Christmas trees and tables laden with gifts. In 1884 Xenia recorded that she 'received a lot of things' and 'fire-crackers were snapping on the Christmas Tree'.[33] After lunch on Christmas Day the imperial family attended the celebrations of the guards and the palace police in the riding school, at which the Empress personally distributed the presents.

Despite the imperial thrift, Christmas was an expensive time of year. All their relations, Russian and foreign, every member of the household, government officials, domestic servants, and soldiers and sailors attached to the household had to be given presents. The lists prepared in the Tsar's private chancery ran into many thousands, and every card attached to the gifts bore the imperial signature. So many presents could hardly have been chosen individually. These were mostly pieces of porcelain, glass and silver. Relations and intimate friends received jewellery.

They saw in the New Year with hot punch and apple pies, and at the beginning of January returned to St Petersburg so that the Emperor and Empress could preside over the 'season'. At the Anitchkov the lawn was flooded to form an ice rink and every afternoon the Vorontzovs joined the Tsar's children for skating and ice-hockey, or slides down the specially constructed ice-hill. Although Sasha joined in the ice-hockey, he never wore skates and stood on a patch of ice specially strewn with sand. One day the girls returned from the ice rink and changed into their dresses for tea, only to find their shoes had disappeared. Neither Nastya nor Vera knew where they were. Answering the Tsar's summons to Xenia's drawing room wearing hastily borrowed slippers, they found that Sasha had decorated the tea table with their freshly polished shoes arranged like a garland.

For Xenia and Nicky a favourite pastime was to stand and watch the passers-by through the high stone balustrade surrounding the palace and garden. There were daily meetings of the 'Potato Society' in Xenia's rooms and they also took part in a kind of 'fortune telling', which involved opening the Bible at random and picking out a passage with a finger and closed eyes.

Sometimes Xenia and the Vorontzov sisters had tea with Dagmar in her drawing-room overlooking the Nevsky Prospekt. In one corner was a table, just large enough for a samovar, the tea things and some biscuits. The Empress, dressed in a tea gown, made tea herself before she changed to go to the theatre.

After the end of the season, the family spent Lent quietly at Gatchina, preparing for Easter, the most important festival in the Orthodox calendar. Sometimes Sasha and Dagmar took their children to the Palm Market in St Petersburg, where toys, coloured paper flowers and brightly coloured eggs were sold. Shortly before Palm Sunday they rowed out to the islands for the ritual of planting willows.[34] On Good Friday the imperial family followed the religious procession of the carrying out of the Holy Shroud, as it wound its way along the corridors of Gatchina's kitchen block. For the Easter Service in the palace church, at which they all stood holding lighted candles, Xenia and the Empress donned high-necked white dresses. Afterwards the children rushed to greet everyone with the traditional three kisses of blessing, welcome and joy. Then there was the Easter feast, with all the delicious things forbidden during Lent, including *paskha*, a rich creamy pyramid-shaped dessert. On Easter Sunday, while the Emperor and Empress distributed porcelain eggs to the staff, eggs made of wood or straw and containing a little present were hidden in the downstairs rooms for the children to find. If they were away for Easter, greetings still had to be given to everyone on their return to Gatchina. The Emperor and Empress drove with their children to the park for this ceremony. 'At one o'clock I exchanged Easter kisses with lackeys, Cossacks, several little singers and coachmen,' Xenia recorded in her diary. 'For Easter Papa presented me with a brooch and Mama with a small inkpot,' she continued.[35]

Early summer was spent at The Cottage playing games, hunting for mushrooms or sailing. One day Nicky suggested a boat trip but Xenia hesitated, saying she would be given a 'boring chaperon' and it would be no fun. At tea that afternoon Nicholas persuaded his mother to allow Sandra Vorontzov, who was six years older, to take charge of his sister and the boat trip went ahead.[36]

In 1884 Grand Duke Ludwig IV of Hesse and his family arrived at Peterhof for the marriage of his second daughter Elisabeth ('Ella') to the Tsar's brother Grand Duke Sergei. Ludwig's wife Princess Alice, who had died in 1878, was the second daughter of Queen Victoria. Ella and her siblings were therefore the Queen's grandchildren and she had taken a large part in their upbringing. Among the party was Ella's twelve-year-old sister Alix ('Alicky'). Soon Xenia, Nicky, Misha, Alix and her brother Ernie were romping together happily, jumping on the net underneath the climbing mast which acted as a kind of trampoline, playing on the maypole and fooling around in the wigwam on Xenia's balcony. 'Everyone roared with laughter at the sight of Xenia running with her skirts hitched up,' Nicky wrote in his diary. 'We got covered in sand when we slid through hoops on to the ground. We returned home exhausted, filthy and soaked through with sweat.'[37] Before the family left, Nicholas gave Alix a small brooch. Shyly she accepted it, but then pressed it back into his hand during a children's party. A hurt Nicholas gave the brooch to Xenia who, not knowing what had happened, accepted it cheerfully. Ella soon became a regular visitor to Gatchina, where she appreciated the warm family life and became especially fond of Nicholas and Xenia.

All the family looked forward to the summer cruise in the Finnish Archipelago on board the yacht *Tsarevna*. They went ashore for picnics, played cards and generally relaxed, far from the tensions of St Petersburg. In later years the cruise included a stay at the Langinkoski Imperial fishing lodge, presented to the Tsar by the State and the people of Finland in 1889. Here they lived quite informally, the Tsar taking the children fishing for salmon in the River Kymi, while the Empress cooked salmon soup in the kitchen.

In the autumn, if there was no trip to Denmark, they went to their Crimean estate of Livadia on the Black Sea coast. The Crimea was the holiday resort of the Romanovs and many of the Grand Dukes had estates dotted along the coastline. Sasha had constructed the Maly (or Small) Palace, near his father's old palace, and went hunting while the children bathed in the sea and went on picnics or excursions into the mountains. Since 1857 Gatchina had been the main hunting preserve of the Tsars, but sometimes they visited the imperial hunting lodges of Bialoweiza and Spala in Poland. Although the Empress often organized her own shooting parties, neither Xenia nor Olga were ever taught to handle a gun. With the approach of winter they moved back to Gatchina, ready for the yearly round to begin again.

In the summer of 1886 Queen Olga of Greece brought her children Alexandra, Greek Minny and Andrew to Russia and Xenia invited Minny to stay with her at The Cottage. Minny and Xenia shared a bedroom, ate sweets to their hearts' content and lived like sisters. The Empress usually dressed Xenia and Olga in white dresses of lace, muslin or fine wool and she bought identical dresses for Minny. In the evening there were pillow fights when the Tsar came to say goodnight.

From Peterhof they went to the army camp at Krasnoe Selo for the manoeuvres. The Tsar's sister, the Duchess of Edinburgh, was also there with her elder daughters Marie ('Missy') and Victoria Melita ('Ducky'). The four girls were of a similar age but, unfortunately, Missy and Ducky took an instant dislike to Greek Minny, which she reciprocated. 'Xenia, who was always sweet-tempered, got on better with them,' Minny recalled.[38] For some reason Xenia's cousins gave her the nickname 'Jelly', and Greek Minny the name 'Grasshopper', which they used in letters even after they were all grown up.

Missy had fond memories of Alexander III joining in their games. 'In the garden stood a mast on which his sons learnt how to climb and handle ropes and sails. . . . To guard against bad falls a net had been suspended beneath the mast. . . . Uncle Sasha would pursue us over this net, and when he had cornered you he would jump up and down and his weight made you bounce like a ball . . . up and down, shrieking and laughing, a game for the gods.'[39]

Glimpses of Xenia from relatives outside the Romanov family circle are few and far between, but Missy, eventually Queen of

Roumania, found her 'a dear chum'. Missy was a year older, and the two met occasionally when family weddings and funerals brought them together. Yet in childhood they did not know each other well enough to form more than a fleeting impression, though Missy wrote of her 'immense admiration for Xenia', and her lack of comprehension for the good relationship she had with the sharp-tongued Marie of Greece.[40]

During the first few years of Tsar Alexander III's reign, the terrorists were kept largely dormant. Six years later there was a chilling reminder that the imperial family's worries were not yet over. Each year on 1 March they travelled by train to St Petersburg for a commemoration service for Tsar Alexander II. Each journey to and from the SS Peter & Paul Cathedral was heavily guarded by police. Nevertheless, in March 1887 they were about to take the train back to Gatchina when the Tsar was informed that several students had been arrested carrying bombs which they had intended to throw at the imperial family. One of the five students subsequently hanged was Alexander Ilyich Ulyanov, whose younger brother Vladimir, later to be known as Lenin, would exact full revenge on the family. Soon afterwards the Tsar received another letter from the Executive Committee of the People's Will, condemning him to death. He took his family to Novorossisk on the Black Sea, far away from the oppressive atmosphere in St Petersburg.

In October 1888 the imperial train was derailed when the family were travelling from the Caucasus. They were in the dining car when the train suddenly lurched violently twice and everything was thrown around; then there was a loud bang and several more jolts, as the rear carriages crashed into those in front, followed by silence. Xenia was the first of the children to appear from the wrecked carriage, emerging from behind a section of the roof hanging down to form a partition between her and Dagmar. Then Georgie, who had crawled up on to the roof, called down to say that Misha was safe, and last came Nicholas. The Tsar's leg was trapped and it took a while for him to be freed. All were severely shaken and most suffered injuries, apart from six-year-old Olga, who had been thrown clear and rolled down the embankment out of harm's way but was still terrified. Xenia and George had cuts on their hands from flying glass, while their parents sustained more severe wounds to arms and legs. For five hours, in relentless drizzle, the Emperor and Empress tended the wounded until a relief train arrived. At the next station the local priest said prayers, while the imperial family stood with tears streaming down their cheeks.

Although they all recovered from their injuries within a few weeks, the incident took its toll on their nerves. An official enquiry placed the blame on technical factors, but it was rumoured (and never ruled out) that a bomb had been smuggled aboard. Twenty-one people on the train were killed and many more injured, some for life. To Xenia as well as her brothers and sister, it was a horrifying reminder that their safety could never be taken for granted.

In the winter of 1888 Xenia caught typhoid. As she began to recover, Sandra Vorontzov came over to read aloud, or help cut out paper patterns. Xenia's beautiful hair was falling out, and the Emperor and Empress debated whether it should be cut short; they asked Sandra to decide. Photographs taken at Gmunden, the Austrian home of the Duke and Duchess of Cumberland at around that time, showing Xenia with a short boyish haircut, tell their own story.

In 1889 Princess Alix of Hesse, now a very attractive girl of seventeen, arrived to stay with her sister Ella. Nicky and Xenia met her frequently at the Anitchkov for skating, or at dances at the Vorontzovs' and balls at the Winter Palace. Everyone saw that twenty-year-old Nicholas was becoming increasingly attracted to Alix, but the Emperor and Empress did their best to discourage a romance. Xenia usually invited Alix to join the others for tea in her drawing room. The Empress, who had not been told, came in unexpectedly one day and there was an awkward moment. As soon as she had left Alix hastily departed, followed by the others. Xenia was summoned to her mother. 'I'm in for it now,' she muttered to Sandra Vorontzov. She was forbidden to invite the princess to tea again, leaving Xenia with the problem of what to do the following afternoon. She refused to cancel tea, so the Vorontzov girls decided on a ruse. After skating, all four sisters escorted Alix to the entrance, pretending they were also leaving. The princess's carriage arrived, she left – and they remained behind. Only on the eve of Alix's departure was Xenia allowed to issue an invitation.[41]

Xenia now began a sporadic correspondence with Alix, in which Xenia was 'chicken' and Alix 'the old hen'. That year the Greek royal family visited Russia for the marriage of Princess Alexandra ('Aline') to Xenia's uncle Grand Duke Paul. After the lavish ceremony at the Winter Palace, Sasha and Dagmar left for Peterhof taking Greek Minny with them. Missing her sister, she badly needed Xenia's company.

As she grew older Xenia was encouraged to take an interest in the many charitable organizations and educational establishments in Gatchina town, ranging from hospitals, almshouses and asylums to schools and a teachers' training college. She accompanied her mother to the children's asylum for the Christmas celebrations, for which the Empress had given a generous contribution towards decorations for the Christmas trees and presents for the children.[42] On 26 October 1893 Xenia was present at the consecration of a hospital for children with chronic diseases in St Petersburg. 'I and Mama examined the house which is very large and comfortable, and there is enough room!' Xenia recorded in her diary. 'Mama caressed the children and then we went away.'[43]

A real treat for Xenia was meeting girls from the outside world. In 1890 she was present when girls from the grammar schools and the Institutes (exclusive boarding schools) received their medals from the Empress. The girls, all about Xenia's age, watched her closely as she walked round Gatchina's Great Hall behind her mother, who was talking to teachers and pupils. 'She was dressed very simply in pink cotton with a broderie anglaise trim,' recalled one girl, 'her hair tied back with a white bow, and she returned our admiring looks with something of her mother's friendliness.'[44] After lunch, during which Xenia had to sit with the guests, the girls were amazed to be told to help themselves to the sweets and fruit as they went out into the garden.

That same year Xenia lost the company of one of her friends when Sandra Vorontzov announced her engagement – but the young Grand Duchess was soon to begin her own romance.

2 (1890–4)

'A seventh heaven of bliss'

By 1890 Xenia had matured from a tomboy into a pretty young girl. She had inherited Dagmar's wonderful large eyes, which earned her the nickname 'Owl' from her cousin Prince George of Wales. Unlike the Empress, Xenia was shy, and often blushed even in the company of her brothers. She loved skating, had a weakness for strawberries, liked to play four-hands on the piano with Misha, was becoming a keen photographer and had an 'irresistible inclination to laugh at the slightest provocation'. At a battleship launch, she and Nicky stood behind their parents with various dignitaries from the armed services. Nicholas was whispering to his sister, keeping up a running commentary on people and events, while Xenia was laughing until tears came into her eyes. Suddenly she laughed too loudly and the Tsar turned round. The two young people suddenly became alarmed. Having made them aware of his displeasure, their father turned back to the event while their mother shot them an amused glance.[1]

Xenia also suffered from a skin complaint which could have been of a nervous origin. In December 1889 she wrote to her grandmother, Queen Louise, that she had been unable to go out for six days:

Again, I am full of red spots on the face and arms, which is horrid! I am treated by a doctor who is famous for these sort of skin diseases but the *cure* I am going through is certainly an awful one!

. . . he forbids me to *wash* and to bathe for some time and this alone is already horrid. And then he puts some nasty ointment on my arms which burns and takes the skin off. It's most painful and I can't wear any tight fitting sleeves because they *rub* and that hurts dreadfully! I am obliged to wear a dressing gown, with enormous big sleeves![2]

The problem frequently recurred. 'All my nasty red spots are gone and the skin has nearly quite finished off peeling,' she told her grandmother in December 1891. 'My face is smooth and I am allowed to take my baths again, which is certainly the nicest thing in the world.'[3]

Among the imperial children's playmates were Grand Duke Michael Nicholaievich's six sons, the 'Wild Caucasians' – Nicholas ('Bimbo'), Michael ('Miche-Miche'), George, Alexander ('Sandro'), Sergei and Alexis. The boys and their sister Anastasia had been raised in the Caucasus, where their father was Viceroy for nineteen years. His wife Princess Cecilie of Baden, who took the name Grand Duchess Olga Feodorovna upon conversion to Orthodoxy, was a very intelligent woman who dominated her family. Against the background of boating, riding, tennis parties and visits to country estates, the children had known each other since Grand Duke Michael brought his family back to St Petersburg in 1880.

In 1886 twenty-year-old Sandro was serving in the navy and eleven-year old Xenia sent him a Christmas card when his ship was in Brazil: 'Best wishes and speedy return! Your sailor Xenia.' By the summer of 1889 he had noticed that she had grown up. 'She is fourteen. I think she likes me.'[4] That summer he and his brother Miche-Miche visited the International Exposition in Paris, from where he sent her a postcard: 'My lovely Xenia, I am writing to you from the top of the Eiffel Tower. . . . Goodbye, I am kissing [strongly] your dear little hand. Your Sandro.' She kept the card for the rest of her life.[5] At the small private balls the following season he danced only with her. In May 1890 he asked his brother George whether he thought Xenia preferred him or their brother Sergei and, more importantly, whether he considered the Tsar would allow either of them to marry his daughter.

That summer Sandro was invited to join the imperial family on their Finnish cruise. It was an idyllic time. During the day they went ashore to pick flowers and strawberries, or to hunt for mushrooms. They had merry picnics, at which the Emperor laid the table and everyone else helped prepare the food. Sandro cooked mushrooms, while Xenia cooked kebabs and lent her mother a hand with the potatoes. In the evenings they played 'a silly card game' called 'wolf'.[6] It was noticed that Xenia and Sandro spent a lot of time together on deck. Neither the Emperor nor the Empress liked Sandro much at this time, considering him too restless to settle down. Besides, Xenia was only fifteen and Dagmar certainly did not want her to marry young.

In September Sandro left on his yacht *Tamara* for India. Nicholas and Georgie also left for the Far East, on a nine-month-long journey to India and Japan, Georgie as a naval cadet, Nicky to complete his education. Xenia was left at home with only eleven-year-old Michael and eight-year-old Olga for company. Soon alarming reports arrived from Bombay about Georgie's health. Never strong, he now had acute bronchitis and was sent back to Athens to be treated by one of the imperial doctors. By March he was in Algiers. '[Georgie] likes Algier very much and finds it a lovely place,' Xenia wrote to Queen Louise. 'They go about in the mountains a great deal and then have picnics and all such things. I do wish we could go and *see him*, or *he* could come home again. I would give anything to see him home again.'[7]

Meanwhile, also in Bombay, Sandro learnt of his mother's death from a heart attack, brought on, it was said, by Miche-Miche's unsuitable marriage and subsequent banishment. Then came news that the Tsarevich had been attacked by a fanatic at Otsu in Japan, and was ordered home.

On 25 March 1891 it was Xenia's sixteenth birthday. This event in the life of a Tsar's daughter was usually marked by a gift of a pearl and diamond necklace from her parents. After attending the *Folle Journée*, the last big ball of the carnival season before Lent, the imperial family retired to Gatchina as usual, before spending some time in Moscow.

In June she went with her mother to meet Georgie's ship when he arrived in the Crimea. After the official reception and a private reunion in his cabin, they left for Livadia. Still unaware that he was suffering from tuberculosis, the family believed the doctors who said he could be completely cured if he spent the next two winters in Algiers. Xenia was delighted to have one of her brothers home. They all visited the caves at nearby Massandra and went on excursions along the cliffs, before joining the

Emperor and Michael on the *Tsarevna*. On 14 July they anchored at Kotka, where they enjoyed particularly fine weather at Langinkoski during their four-day stay. Although Georgie's health improved, the doctors recommended a change of air. When Cannes did not bring about the expected improvement he was sent to the dry mountain air of the Caucasus. He settled into a large, comfortable villa, but from then on he lived apart from the rest of the family. The following year work began on a palace for him at Abbas Touman.

In the summer Xenia accompanied her parents on an official visit to Finland. They arrived by train at Lappeenranta, which was 'magnificently decorated' for the visit, with a specially erected reception pavilion in front of the castle. The following day they attended military manoeuvres and visited the spectacular Imatra Falls, 'which, in the midst of their surroundings of dark, melancholy forests, belong to the rare sights of Finland'.[8] After a military parade the next day, which Xenia watched from the pavilion with her mother, they saw an exhibition of schoolchildren's handicrafts, the barracks and the church.

Alexander III's family had always been popular in Finland, but despite outward appearances this visit was not a success. 'The populace . . . kept entirely aloof from all contact with the Imperial family and they were met by only the official representatives,' *The Times* reported. 'The difference was so marked that both the Tsar and Tsarina were visibly affected . . . and made no secret of their disappointment.'[9]

After a visit to Denmark the imperial family returned to the Crimea in October with King Christian, Queen Louise, the Princess of Wales and her daughters Toria and Maud. Great celebrations were planned at Livadia for the Emperor and Empress's Silver Wedding anniversary, including a magnificent firework display. Georgie joined the party from Abbas Touman and, to Xenia's delight, he arrived with Sandro, who was serving with the Black Sea Fleet. The celebrations were overshadowed by mourning for Xenia's cousin Aline, who had died in childbirth, and by the unseasonably cold weather. Almost everyone was taken ill and then the Princess of Wales was summoned home by the news that her son George had typhoid. He recovered, but another family tragedy followed in January 1892 when the Prince of Wales's eldest son Albert Victor ('Eddy') died from influenza, leaving Prince George heir to the British throne. Mourning for Aline and Eddy also overshadowed the celebrations for King Christian and Queen Louise's Golden Wedding anniversary, which the imperial family attended in May.

By now Xenia and Sandro were in love, but her parents still did not approve. Sandro spoke to Georgie about his feelings when he visited him in the Caucasus. Xenia, meanwhile, was sulking about her father's disapproval. Georgie took his sister's side and refused to congratulate the Tsar on his birthday. When Dagmar took her children to Abbas Touman in April Sasha wrote: 'Kiss Georgy and Xenia for me, if they still remember me and love me!' He was particularly fond of his eldest daughter and saddened by her attitude. 'Xenia ignores me, I am an absolute stranger to her; she will not talk to me, she never asks questions, never asks for something and I would be so glad to please her in any possible way.' The relationship with Xenia, he told the Empress, would 'torture me throughout the winter'.[10]

In 1892 Sandro was safely out of sight serving with the Baltic Fleet, and the Emperor and Empress turned their attention to Nicholas, who was in love with Princess Alix of Hesse. When he told his father he intended to marry her, the Tsar was non-committal. With Georgie away, Nicholas's confidante was naturally his sister. They shared their secrets – his love for Alix, her growing feelings for Sandro. She now acted as a go-between, continuing her correspondence with Alix, exchanging photographs and sometimes enclosing a note from him. Nicky had confided his hopes to Ella and she began to work behind the scenes to bring them together, despite the opposition of the Emperor and Empress. But marriage to the Tsarevich would mean conversion to the Orthodox faith, and Alix refused to change her religion.

In the spring of 1893 Xenia reached the age of eighteen, and to mark the occasion she was painted by Serov. Sandro now saw no reason for them to wait any longer. After a discussion with Xenia he went to see the Emperor with two requests – a transfer to the *Dimitri Donskoi*, about to leave for America, which was granted, and Xenia's hand in marriage. The Tsar listened kindly but made it plain that, while he had no objection in principle, the Empress did not want her daughter to marry so young, and advised Sandro to raise the matter in a year's time. Disappointed, Xenia and Sandro resigned themselves to waiting and he left for America. At Fredensborg in October Xenia's grandfather King Christian decided to take a hand. To the Empress's chagrin, he tried to persuade her to agree to a betrothal. She was adamant: there would be no talk of marriage until Xenia was older.

She was also worried about Sasha's health. He had been suffering from bronchitis and it was hoped the trip to Denmark would do him good. He was too unwell to attend the banquet for his Name Day, more important to Russians than a birthday, and the church service had to be held on board the imperial yacht. As they left Copenhagen on 5 October the weather was wet and their spirits were low. None of them knew what tragedy the next twelve months would bring.

On 8 November 1893 Alix wrote to thank Xenia for her letter, begging her to continue their friendship and correspondence and not to let what she was about to say change anything. With a heavy heart, Alix had told Nicky that she loved him but still could not change her religion. All the same, she implored Xenia not to let them drift apart: 'that would be too hard'.[11]

Although Xenia was upset for Nicky, her own situation was about to improve.

When Sandro was back in St Petersburg his father urged him to try again. They knew that the problem was the Tsarina. Determined to resolve the issue, on 12 January Grand Duke Michael Nicholaievich lunched with the Emperor and Empress at the Anitchkov. Sandro knew his father adored Xenia and would do all he could to obtain her parents' consent, but he had no illusions regarding the Tsarina's antipathy to being contradicted or rushed, and feared she would say no 'in a manner precluding any further attempts on my part. I remember having broken a dozen pencils in father's study awaiting his return.'[12]

After lunch, Michael asked for Xenia's hand in marriage on behalf of his son. As anticipated, Dagmar was annoyed at being taken off guard. Grand Duke Michael's appearance was unwelcome, especially as she considered she had not been given a chance to discuss it with Sasha in private. According to Sandro, when his father returned from the talk, he said that she had abused him 'in a most disgraceful way', saying that Sandro was trying to break her happiness, had no right to steal her daughter, she would never speak to him again, and never expected a man of his age to act in such an appalling manner. She threatened to complain to the Tsar and ask him to punish their entire family. In fact, although the Empress was 'furious' that Michael had taken them by surprise, they both consented.

At 4.30 Sandro went to see Xenia. Her valet Beresin led him into her salon where only the day before they had held a merry tea party. 'Today everything seemed different,' recalled Sandro. Xenia came from the bedroom, her eyes riveted on the floor, wearing 'a simple white silk blouse, blue skirt, brown stockings and brown shoes'. They sat down and spoke in whispers. 'We used to kiss each other before but these were cousins' kisses. Now it was a kiss of possession.'[13] Later they went upstairs and were blessed in front of the icons by the Emperor, Empress and Grand Duke Michael.

The close blood-tie necessitated a special dispensation from the Holy Synod. When Sandro's sister Anastasia had married Frederick, Grand Duke of Mecklenburg-Schwerin, he had fumed inwardly against what he called the 'heartless law that forced the members of the Russian reigning house to marry foreigners of royal blood', and which 'continued its tyranny up to the year 1894, when I broke its validity' by his marriage to Xenia.[14] At first the Empress refused to set a date for the wedding, still insisting that her daughter was too young. As Grand Duchess Olga was later to point out, female members of the family had been married as early as sixteen. Dagmar simply dreaded losing control over Xenia, wanting her to stay on as a companion. Nevertheless Xenia and Sandro had known each other since childhood. 'In the end my father and my great-uncle, Michael, carried the day, and then, as usual, my mother made the best of it.'[15]

Messages of congratulation poured in – from the Empress's ladies-in-waiting 'Aprak' (Countess Apraxine) and the two Countesses Kutuzov; from Xenia's former German teacher and Sandra Vorontzov, now living in Moscow with her husband. 'I'm wishing you happiness forever from the bottom of my heart,' Sandra wrote. 'Please pass on my regards to their Royal

Highnesses [sic] and felicitations to your brothers. . . . I embrace you, wish you happiness and send you my best wishes.'[16]

Some of the letters expressed pleasure that the young couple would be making their home in Russia, a feeling echoed by Dagmar. She wrote of 'mixed feelings' on giving 'a loved child away. God send them his blessing and happiness,' she continued. 'Praise God, that we will at least have them here, that is my comfort.'[17] Sandro, she told King Christian, was becoming more like a son.

There was only one cloud on the horizon. The Tsar was still unwell and influenza now weakened him further. He suffered from frequent headaches and insomnia and complained that his shoes did not fit. Nobody noticed that his feet were swelling. The first court ball, which would mark Xenia's official debut into society, was postponed for a fortnight.

On 24 January, Xenia's Name Day, all the imperial family attended church. Although the Tsar was feeling better he was still not back at work. The season was in full swing and Xenia and Sandro, chaperoned by her mother and brother Nicholas, took their full part. They attended a performance of Delibes' ballet *Coppelia*, a costume ball at Count Cheremetev's at which Xenia appeared as a seventeenth-century 'boyarina' and Sandro as a guard commander, a ball at the Winter Palace and the *Folle Journée* at the Anitchkov ending at 1am.

Although Xenia's happiness was now complete, she was still concerned for Nicholas and broached the subject once more with Alix, but to no avail.

Concern over the Emperor's health made him look to the future. In April Alix's brother, Grand Duke Ernest Ludwig of Hesse ('Ernie'), was to marry Princess Victoria Melita of Edinburgh ('Ducky'). Nicholas was given permission to go to the wedding and speak to Alix. On the morning of his departure Xenia received a telegram from Alix saying that she would not convert to Orthodoxy. Distraught, Nicholas left for Coburg. When news of her brother's betrothal arrived, Xenia was one of the first to send congratulations: 'you cannot imagine my joy, I am terribly happy and you will understand why,' she wrote, enclosing an Easter present for Alix.[18]

Xenia and Sandro now found themselves pushed into the background. She admitted to Nicky that they were 'depressed' that nothing had yet been decided about their wedding; it was 'a terrible bore and *quite* impossible to bear'.[19] Sandro was equally upset; nobody, he said, seemed to be considering them any more, no plans were being made for their wedding, and no house had been bought for them. His protests at the delay brought forth the excuse that dressmakers and jewellers would need six months to prepare the trousseau.

Something may have been said, because the next day the Empress wrote to her brother King George of Greece that 'Xenia's wedding will probably be in July, but it is still not absolutely certain. That is not nice or pleasant for us. . . .'[20] With the wedding finally arranged for 25 July Xenia was in 'a seventh heaven of bliss', according to her mother.[21] At last they had a firm commitment. Yet Nicky was slightly shocked by their uninhibited behaviour, 'kissing, embracing and lying around on the furniture in the most improper manner'. Xenia in particular, he thought, had changed completely since becoming engaged.[22]

Early in May Xenia and Sandro accompanied the Tsarina to Abbas Touman, where Georgie was living as an invalid. Though he was delighted to see them, 'his pale, worn-out face bore witness to the progress of his fatal illness'.[23] During those four weeks together they drove into the mountains, organizing picnic parties, laughing, joking and dancing, doing their best to cheer up Georgie, who was growing weaker and had a premonition he would never see St Petersburg again. They feared that the sight of two healthy, happy people must have caused him additional pain, and were reluctant to talk of their plans in his presence, though to all outward appearances he remained the same kind, generous, faithful Georgie. He was equally affronted by their manners, complaining to Nicky at their indulgence in 'gymnastics, sucking, sniffing and similar activities', about the way they almost broke the ottoman and generally behaved in a most improper way, lying down on top of each other, 'even in my presence, in what you might call an attempt to play Papa and Mama. . . . It's a good thing there isn't long left until the wedding, otherwise it could all end badly! I tried to shame them, but to no avail.'[24]

In June they joined the Tsar aboard the imperial yacht *Tsarevna* for a cruise in Finnish waters and a short stay at Langinkoski. Like his son, he too was unwell, had lost considerable weight during their absence and was complaining of extreme fatigue. The doctors, the ever-optimistic court physicians, put it down to the consequences of long months of hard work, and prescribed plenty of rest and fresh air. As in previous summers, the betrothed couple visited their favourite places ashore, did a great deal of fishing, and entertained friends.

On 21 July they inspected the wedding presents and Xenia's trousseau, laid out in four large halls of Peterhof's Grand Palace. Xenia's dowry, including table silver and jewellery, had been commissioned from Fabergé, and some of the magnificent jewellery came from Bolin. Nicholas gave his sister a fan, on which he had painted 'a frightened hen which has laid several eggs out of which are hatching a whole army of paper cockerels',[25] probably a reference to the nicknames 'the old hen' and 'chicken' that Alix and Xenia used in their correspondence. Queen Victoria sent a table and a tea-set, and Xenia's Danish grandparents a vase.

Wedding presents had been sent from all over the world. Side by side with large collections of useless trinkets were beautiful things such as silver plate for about a hundred persons, a solid gold toilette set of one hundred and forty-four articles, dozens of gold-rimmed glasses, cups and dishes emblazoned with the imperial monograms, every kind of coat and wrap in ermine, chinchilla, mink, beaver and astrakhan, and vast tables loaded with linen, china and household articles. The jewellery comprised pearl necklaces, some with five strings, each holding more than a hundred pearls, and necklaces of diamonds, rubies, emeralds and sapphires, with matching tiaras and ear-rings.

According to custom, the Tsar's present to the groom was clothing, including 'four dozen of everything'. Also on display with the trousseau were the embroidered silver nightgowns, each weighing well over fifteen pounds, that by Romanov tradition an Imperial Grand Duke and Grand Duchess had to wear when entering the bridal chambers on their wedding night. 'This ridiculous rule', remarked the groom, was part of the same regulations which forbade him from seeing his bride the day before the wedding.[26]

The Grand Palace teemed with royal visitors from all corners of Europe. Though the Tsar was evidently very tired, and his family were shocked by his appearance, he made a special effort to enter into all the festivities for his daughter's wedding. As the Tsarina walked through the rooms where the trousseau and the wedding presents were displayed, she felt a mixture of happiness for her daughter and the sadness of a mother: 'What shall we do in a few weeks when she leaves us? I don't dare to think – even now I can *hardly ever* see her *alone* – he [Sandro] never leaves her for one minute.'[27] The Tsarina's ladies were convinced that she was bitterly jealous of Sandro for taking her beloved eldest daughter away from her in marriage.

His first cousin Grand Duke Constantine saw matters a little differently. In his view the Tsarina had never been well disposed towards her daughter's husband-to-be, and as the wedding drew closer she found him increasingly demanding and tactless. He had objected to the accommodation prepared for him and Xenia in Ropsha for the first two days after the wedding, in rooms where other members of the family had stayed with their wives, during manoeuvres, without complaint. On glancing at them he declared that they were not good enough, and demanded the apartments of the Tsar and Tsarina. He also found fault with the rooms in the Winter Palace which were being prepared for them to stay in during their first winter. The Tsar had offered his daughter the Michaelovsky Palace in the centre of St Petersburg, close to the Nevsky Prospekt, as a wedding present but Xenia thought it too large. Instead, he purchased Countess Vorontzov's house on the Moika embankment, which was due to be fully redecorated in a year's time.

Xenia found herself 'between two fires'; by acquiescing to Sandro's hopes and wishes, she was afraid of upsetting her parents, and vice versa. Constantine sympathized with his cousin to an extent, as Their Majesties had one very tiresome idiosyncrasy that was difficult to cope with; if a decision about anything was needed, one had to wait for a very long time, and everything was decided at the very last minute, so that their entourage was completely uninformed as to any plans and could make no preparations. It was unhelpful to make Sandro and Xenia wait for five months after their betrothal before giving them any idea as to the time and place of their wedding. If they asked any questions about plans for their future life, it was seen as a challenge to parental authority. However, such shortcomings on the part of the Emperor and Empress did not excuse Sandro's lack of discretion or his responsibility for a certain amount of unpleasantness and ill-feeling. 'I repeat: please God that this should all pass and turn out for the best.'[28]

After lunch on 25 July the Empress and her ladies dressed Xenia for her wedding. In the private apartments Xenia donned the heavy regalia worn by all Romanov brides. Over the silver brocade wedding dress with its long court train, made by Mme Olga Bulbenkova of St Petersburg, the Empress's ladies draped a long, ermine-lined crimson mantle with a short, ermine-lined cape on top. On her hair, carefully arranged in two long curls resting on her shoulders, was placed a diadem with a beautiful pink diamond in the centre and, behind this, the diamond Bride's Crown and the bridal veil. Then came more jewels – a diamond necklace, a triple-row diamond bracelet and diamond earrings so heavy that they were hung over Xenia's ears on hoops. When, after three hours, Xenia was finally ready she could hardly move for the weight of these robes. As the Emperor blessed her he appeared calm, but the Empress's eyes were red from crying.

Sandro, in naval uniform, was at last permitted to collect his bride and at 3pm the procession set off to the ornate cathedral of SS Peter & Paul in the Grand Palace. A 21-gun salute rang out as the Tsar and Tsarina led a long file consisting of members of the imperial family in strict order of precedence and the bride and bridegroom.[29] Between two and three thousand people had gathered to see the procession pass through the halls of the palace, the men in uniform, the ladies in court dress and sparkling jewels.

The bride's youngest brother and sister, Michael and Olga, were winking at Sandro, who had difficulty in preventing himself from laughing out loud. 'Dear little Xenia looked sweet as a bride, it was a dreadful day for her, fancy she had to have her crown & tiarra [sic] put on before us all,' Princess Maud of Wales wrote to the Duchess of York in her description of the day's events. 'I mean all the lady members of the family & 2 long curls she had to put on & a gorgeous velvet & ermine cloak on top of her silver dress. Every Gr Dss has to wear the Crown Jewels on their wedding day – the heat was too awful in Church as they have heaps of candles & heaps of people & very little room, you can imagine how pleasant it was – the service lasted nearly 2 hours.'[30] Eight bridesmen took turns in holding the heavy crowns over the couple's heads during the ceremony. These were, for Xenia, her brothers Nicholas and Michael and cousins Christian of Denmark and Nicholas of Greece; for Sandro, his brothers Nicholas, George, Sergei and Alexis.

On their return to the palace they walked in the same order as before, except that the newly married couple changed places with the Tsar and Tsarina. They all noticed how exhausted Sasha looked with the day's exertions but he was powerless to defy Romanov tradition. Therefore, after an hour's rest, there was a banquet, at which *The Times'* correspondent reported that the cost of the fish alone (fifty of the largest Sterlet) was £400. Then toasts were given, to a flourish of trumpets and artillery salutes.

All the guests were presented with a memento. For the men, the St Petersburg jewellers Hahn had made cuff-links, one with a miniature photograph of Xenia, the other with that of Sandro, surrounded by small diamonds and an enamel border. The ladies were given a similar gift in the form of two gold buttons.

It was after 11pm before Xenia and Sandro could change into more comfortable clothes and leave in a court carriage. Their destination was Ropsha, a pretty palace 12 miles south of Peterhof with terraced gardens running down to a lake and hundred-year-old trees in the park. Peter III was killed there in 1762 – so it was not, perhaps, the most auspicious place for a honeymoon.

The Palace of Ropsha and the adjoining village had been brilliantly illuminated for the occasion, and their nervous coachman, blinded by the lights, overlooked a small bridge and landed his three horses, carriage and two newly-weds flat in the brook. Xenia fell to the bottom of the carriage, and Sandro landed on top of her, while the coachman and the footman were thrown into the water. Nobody was hurt and they were promptly rescued by Xenia's servants in the second carriage. Her magnificent ostrich-feathered hat and ermine-trimmed coat were covered with mud, while Sandro's face and hands were absolutely black. They wondered what the reaction would be of General Wiazemsky, who was to meet them at the entrance to Ropsha Palace, but he said nothing. As far as he was concerned, remarked Sandro lightly, 'it may have been a new fashion among the newly-wed members of the imperial family to take a swim fully dressed'.[31]

At last Sandro and Xenia were on their own for the first time since their betrothal. Unable to believe their good fortune at the prospect of being allowed to eat their supper undisturbed, they glanced at the door suspiciously and then burst out laughing with relief. He took the box containing his mother's jewellery and presented it to his bride. Though she did not share her own mother's fascination with jewels, she admired a beautiful diamond diadem and a set of sapphires. At 1am they donned their 'wedding night uniforms'. Later in the day they would have to return to St Petersburg for the rest of the ceremony, consisting of a reception for members of the diplomatic corps in the Winter Palace, prayers at the tombs of their ancestors in the SS Peter & Paul Cathedral and at the miraculous icon of the Saviour. There would be telegrams to answer, including one from Queen Victoria at Osborne, a gala performance and a series of magnificent festivities at Peterhof. But for the moment, as he entered the bedroom looking like 'an operatic sultan in the grand finale',[32] Sandro and Xenia were completely alone.

3 (1894–1900)
'Of one thing she certainly is not shy'

Xenia and Sandro spent their honeymoon at his Crimean estate of Ai-Todor (St Theodore) on the Black Sea coast. The land had been purchased by Sandro's mother in 1869 when it was bare and barren; she had supervised the planting of every tree and flower, the estate had grown up with the children, and Sandro inherited the property on her death. Although the main entrance was on the Sevastopol High Road, the gardens and vineyards stretched right down to the sea. The young couple settled into the Old House, its outside walls covered with climbers and grapes. Everything remained as it was in Sandro's childhood, as he would not permit any alterations. When ivy began to poke through the bathroom floorboards, he simply let it flourish until it covered the walls. Xenia had a salon cluttered with ornaments, pictures and photographs; a boudoir with a comfortable chaise-longue and a dressing table with a large mirror; and a bedroom with icons above the bed. Her desk was covered with Fabergé photograph frames, and the Icon Salon lived up to its name – they covered the walls.

Their idyll was broken by disturbing news of the Tsar's health. He had insisted on going to hunt in Poland where, at his request, Georgie joined the party. Although at first Sasha was able to go out with the guns, his health soon deteriorated. The doctors diagnosed nephritis, a disease of the kidneys, for which there was no cure, but there was a chance that a warmer climate might help. They decided to go to the Crimea.

When the *Orel* docked at Yalta on 21 September Xenia and Sandro were waiting on the quay. Although blissfully happy, Xenia was having trouble adjusting to married life and could not wait for a reunion with her parents. As the Tsar came down the gangplank followed by his family and Prince Nicholas of Greece, the seriousness of his condition was evident. After greeting the waiting dignitaries, the sovereigns drove to the Maly Palace at Livadia. Though increasingly anxious about his father, the Tsarevich made time to visit his newly married sister and brother-in-law. After seeing them on one occasion, he wrote to Alicky afterwards how funny it was to see Xenia established with her own court, and how uninhibited she now seemed to be. In front of others, she still appeared shy – 'but of one thing she certainly is not shy – that is in kissing her husband – whenever she can she flies at him, her arms around his neck!'[1]

At first the Tsar seemed a little stronger. He and the Empress joined Xenia and Sandro on the beach at Oreanda, drove with them to the farm at Ereklik, near the wooden palace in the mountains west of Livadia built for Sasha's mother, and visited the palace of Massandra where they were offered strawberries, peaches and chestnuts by the steward. Xenia and Sandro frequently lunched and dined at Livadia, and one day the imperial family drove over to Ai-Todor for tea.

Nevertheless there was no putting off the inevitable. All they could do was wander down to the beach at Ai-Todor, watch the waves and worry about the future. Alicky was summoned from Darmstadt as the Tsar's condition worsened, and none of them now dared to stray far from the palace. Day by day he became weaker, as Xenia and Sandro joined the vigil with other members of the family. On 20 October the end was evidently near, and the family knelt in his room as the prayers for the dying were intoned. Outside that afternoon the late autumn fog grew thicker. As a clock in the distance struck 3pm and the sound died away, he sighed deeply and his head fell on to his wife's breast. Everyone else rose and silently kissed his forehead and hand.

Xenia described the scene in a letter to her grandmother in Denmark:

Oh! I cannot believe it yet, it seems impossible that our beloved Angel is gone, and has left his *poor, miserable, heart-broken*, family to weep and *mourn him*! But *he* is happy now; God did not want him to suffer *any longer*. . . . *Oh!* but it is *hard* to bear this trial, and I only pray to God that he might help poor

Motherdear! She is still so brave but I am so afraid for the future when the funeral and all is over, and when old life begins again! . . . It was such a peaceful, quiet end! He talked till the last moment nearly, and recognised us all. In fact it seemed as if he had gone to sleep, and when one looked at him sitting in the arm chair with his head bent down a little, one really could not think it possible that he was no more of this world. Motherdear was kneeling near him holding him in her arms till the last moment and would not leave him for a long time afterwards till at last we begged her to go in the other room to *rest*, while they undressed him and put him on the bed. Then when all was ready she came in again . . . till all at once she felt sick and *fainted*! I was so frightened but thank God it did not last long. . . . In the evening there were prayers like always.[2]

Xenia's brother was now Tsar Nicholas II. Everyone seemed in a daze until her uncle, the Prince of Wales, arrived and took over the funeral arrangements, while the Princess of Wales supported her grief-stricken sister.

Xenia's letter continued:

Papa had such a *heavenly* expression in the first two days, he had a lovely smile on his face and seemed so happy! But the third day it began to spoil and he swelled out dreadfully. (His stomach became enormous and the poor legs worse than ever . . .) and a smell began, which was quite unbearable. . . . So they quickly brought him downstairs in the big room, then they had to arrange everything. That smell haunted us everywhere and it remained in our noses! – Now of course he has changed completely, and it spoils the good impression of the beginning!

I am so pleased dear Aunt Alix is here now, she is such a comfort for poor Motherdear. . . .

Georgie was forbidden by the doctors to accompany the funeral cortège to the north, and was sent back to the Caucasus. 'It was too dreadful having to part with dear little Georgie again, just in this time of *sorrow*, and he looked so thin and miserable,' Xenia continued. '. . . Sandro's brother, George, went with him to Abas [sic] Touman, so as not to leave Georgie quite alone.'[3]

Alexander III's coffin was taken by warship to Sevastopol, where a funeral train was waiting. All along the 1,400-mile route soldiers lined the track and peasants knelt in the fields as they passed. Three days later they reached Moscow, where the coffin lay in state at the Archangel Cathedral in the Kremlin while funeral masses were said. Then the coffin was borne back to the station for the journey to St Petersburg, where the ladies entered black-draped carriages for the drive to the SS Peter & Paul Cathedral and yet more masses for the dead. 'Now we have them twice a day, . . . which is dreadfully tiring,' Xenia wrote. 'Mamma and I don't go in the evenings, it's too much.'[4]

Finally, wearing a long, black woollen dress with a Marie Stuart cap and a floor-length veil, Xenia took her place for the four-hour funeral service on 7 November. One week later, on the Dowager Empress's birthday, Nicholas and Alix were married in the Winter Palace church. The relations who had arrived for the funeral stayed for the wedding, and there was no honeymoon. Xenia had every sympathy for her new sister-in-law. 'Alicky is really *very nice* and such a help to poor Nicky! Poor boy, you can imagine what a state he is in!' she told her grandmother. 'She is such a dear to Motherdear, and she really feels deeply for us in this dreadful sorrow and then fancy what a sad position hers is?! Poor girl, it's really awful.'[5]

Xenia and Sandro were installed in the Winter Palace, where their rooms looked out towards the Admiralty. The apartments were reached from the Sobstveney (private) staircase of the Empress Marie Alexandrovna, through an anteroom opening on one side to the Cuirassier Hall 'We have got a lot of rooms, but only 4 are nicely arranged, by ourselves,' Xenia told Queen Louise. 'My little sitting room is a tiny little thing, and it's so cozy; the bedroom and dressing room are enormous, but very comfortable and pretty. Then comes his room, which is not *quite arranged* yet.'[6] Nicholas and Alix, now the Empress Alexandra Feodorovna, visited them four days after their wedding and formed a very favourable impression of these rooms, although Xenia had been sad to leave her two rooms at the Anitchkov, which she told her grandmother that she '*loved*'.

On Christmas Eve Xenia and Sandro joined the rest of the family in the Blue Drawing Room of the Anitchkov. 'Of course our

Xmas was not a gay and happy one,' she told Queen Louise, '. . . but still Mother dear wanted it to be like before, and so we each had a tree and a table, and got such *lovely* presents. It was dreadful for her but we all tried to cheer her up, and it was such a comfort to have darling Aunt Alix. . . .'[7]

As the New Year of 1895 dawned, Xenia was still trying to come to terms with her loss. Yet amid the grief was a ray of happiness: around the time of the Tsar's death Xenia had discovered she was pregnant. 'I am well, . . . though I get *sick* occasionally!' she wrote. 'I don't like that much but there is nothing to be done! I will take care of myself, besides Sandro takes too much *care* of me even!'[8] Unfortunately, as was only to be expected at a time of such great stress, the skin problems had returned. 'I feel quite well now,' she assured her grandmother at the end of December, 'though I still can't get rid of these horrid red spots, which come back perpetually, but today I look a little bit more decent!'[9] Nevertheless, she only went out in a carriage.

Nicholas sometimes came to lunch, especially if he had an official function at the Winter Palace, but because of court mourning there was no season and no merry skating parties. In March there was further sadness, when Sandro's youngest brother Alexis died of tuberculosis in San Remo.

In the spring Xenia and Sandro stayed with the Dowager Empress at Gatchina, where the late Emperor's rooms remained unchanged. In May, when Dagmar set off to visit Georgie in the Caucasus, they moved to Peterhof to await the birth of their baby. Peterhof occupied a special place in Xenia's heart because it had been the scene of her wedding. They stayed at The Farm, a yellow-painted Gothic house built in the 1830s and enlarged for Alexander II. Verandas ran along two sides, supported by metal columns painted to look like birch trees. Many of the upstairs rooms had balconies overlooking the garden, with striped canopies to keep out the sun. Inside was a large entrance hall, its yellow walls hung with engravings and its large bay windows draped with net curtains. A curved staircase with an iron balustrade led up to Alexander II's study, decorated in a vivid blue, and Marie Alexandrovna's sitting room with pale lilac and green flowered wallpaper. Since Alexander II's death The Farm had been used as a summer house for guests, for other members of the imperial family, or for receptions. Nearby was the St Alexander Nevsky chapel, consecrated on Xenia's wedding day.

On 3 July 1895 Xenia gave birth to a daughter, Irina. As the grand-daughter of a Tsar through the female line, she held the rank of Princess. The Dowager Empress, confident that she knew when to expect the baby despite the doctor's opinion, returned from Abbas Touman in good time but extremely agitated over her daughter's approaching confinement. Sandro had no sympathy for fathers who acted 'like helpless lunatics' when their children were born. Never squeamish, he was with her at the birth of all seven, and remained until the ordeal was over. In his memoirs he related how the court physician would administer a small dose of chloroform to ease the pains, 'causing her to laugh and say all sorts of funny things', while each time he would follow the ancient Russian customs of a father lighting the two candles held by him and his wife at their wedding, just as the first shrieks were heard in the room, and wrapping the new-born baby in the shirt worn by him the previous night. Though it might be 'a silly superstition', he admitted, 'it seemed to give Xenia more self-confidence'.[10]

A small bed and some baby clothes arrived from England. Xenia engaged an English nanny, an 'exceptional woman' who had already spent twelve years in Russia.[11] As the nanny got on well with the wet-nurse and the nurserymaid, domestic harmony reigned in the nursery.

In August, leaving Irina in the care of Nicky and Alix, Xenia and Sandro joined the Dowager Empress in Denmark. It was a depressing visit as Sandro was bored, Xenia sorely missed her father and baby Irina, and Georgie was confined to bed after coughing up blood again. To Xenia's dismay, all her female cousins were enthusiastically learning to ride bicycles. She noted with resignation that she would have to follow suit, 'although it seems to me I will never master how to do it'.[12]

In September they accompanied Georgie back to Abbas Touman before returning to St Petersburg in time for the birth of Alix's first baby, a daughter Olga, born on 3 November. The two baby cousins vied for the attention of the elder generation, and they would record in their diaries and letters during the first few months which weighed more, which was talking more, and which was able to walk first. For Xenia it was an exciting day when Irina could first be helped to stand on her feet and remain there for a few seconds unaided.

The two couples were still very close. When Nicholas and Alix moved to the Winter Palace, Xenia and Sandro spent the evenings with them in the library. Sandro even helped the Tsar to christen his new billiard room. Xenia was very fond of Alicky, and according to Olga the only members of the family who ever made an effort to understand her were both her sisters-in-law and their aunt Olga, Queen of Greece.[13] Otherwise the family were still relatively united at this stage, though Xenia and Olga, separated in age by seven years, were never really close.

In May 1896 Tsar Nicholas II was crowned. On the day of the ceremony Xenia, in a gown of pink and silver, walked in her mother's procession to the Uspensky Sobor, taking her place just below the dais to the right of the thrones. The service was reminiscent of the same occasion only thirteen years before, but this time Xenia could participate in all the festivities. As an adult, Xenia's resemblance to her mother was striking. At the Coronation ball she appeared dripping in emeralds, some an inch long; at yet another ball she borrowed a yellow and silver dress of her mother's, embroidered with coloured flowers. When she appeared wearing a diamond diadem and covered with jewels, the Dowager Empress thought she was looking at herself as a young girl again. To the boy who would eventually become her son-in-law, Felix Youssoupov, who had known Xenia from his childhood, 'her chief attraction lay not in her beauty but in the rare, delicate charm which she had inherited from her mother, the Empress'. As a youngster he always looked forward eagerly to her visits, and afterwards, when she had gone, he would wander around the rooms, 'rapturously sniffing a delicious odour of lilies of the valley which still lingered in the air'.[14]

At the festivities an incident occurred which began to drive Xenia and Olga apart, and certainly created divisions in the rest of the imperial family. One of the events held to celebrate the crowning of a new Tsar was the gathering at Khodynka Field, the military training area just outside the city, of thousands of his subjects to pay homage and receive the traditional gifts of sweets, drink and souvenirs decorated with the Romanov double-headed eagle. This time a rumour went around the crowd that there would not be enough for everyone. In the resulting stampede many people were injured and killed; the numbers were officially estimated at around 1,400 dead and 1,300 wounded but were probably much higher. Sandro and his brothers, referred to as the 'Mikhailovichi', told the Tsar that it would be politic to cancel the Coronation ball as a mark of respect, but he was dissuaded from doing so by his uncles, particularly Sergei, governor-general of Moscow. When the dancing started, Sandro and his brothers indignantly walked out. 'There go the four Imperial followers of Robespierre,'[15] muttered Grand Duke Alexis as they went.

Xenia thought Sergei's behaviour was beneath contempt; in her view, he had washed his hands of all responsibility, declared it was nothing to do with him, said Count Vorontzov was responsible for everything, and could not even take the trouble to visit the scene of the disaster.[16] Olga thought her cousins and, no doubt by implication, her elder sister, were being unjust to Sergei, and readily acknowledged his despair and his offer to resign the governor-generalship of Moscow, which the Tsar would not accept.

Ever since Xenia's marriage, the Dowager Empress had always hoped that she and Sandro would come and settle with her in Gatchina Palace. This led to an 'unpleasant conversation',[17] not helped by the fact that it took place while the Imperial family was still in shock after the horror of Khodynka. The former Vorontzov palace was already being redecorated for them and the Dowager Empress was forced to give in.

To ease the situation they spent the summer at Michaelovskoe, an Italian style house on the Gulf of Finland belonging to Sandro's father. Over tea with Nicholas and Alix at Peterhof, Xenia and Sandro tried to make them understand that the uncles supported Sergei in his decision to resign if Pahlen was appointed head of the Khodynka investigating commission. The Tsar said if they all resigned he would not try to keep them on. Grand Duke Alexis, head of the Russian navy, was already displeased with Sandro, who had written a pamphlet on the inadequacy of the Russian defence systems. After a quarrel, Sandro resigned from the navy.

Xenia and Sandro moved to Ai-Todor. Now pregnant again, Xenia had been unable to join the family reunion in Copenhagen. 'I am so sorry we could not come to Denmark,' she wrote to

Queen Louise, '. . . and especially that you did not see my sweet baby, who is getting sweeter every day and is such a . . . sharp little creature! She runs about all by herself now and chatters away!'[18] Xenia was looking forward to seeing Irina and Olga together at Gatchina in November. 'We both embrace you warmly,' she wrote to Nicky, 'although I cannot press your little daughter to my breast, as it would be difficult in my condition!'[19]

The baby was late. 'Please tell Xenia that . . . only *lady elephants* carry for 22 months,'[20] Nicholas wrote to their mother. Xenia's son Andrei was born in the Winter Palace on 12 January. Although his rank of Prince only entitled him to a 15-gun salute, every time Xenia gave birth to a son the Dowager Empress insisted on the salute of 21 guns reserved for a Grand Duke. 'Andrusha' was large, healthy and 'very ugly',[21] Nicholas told Georgie. Nicholas and Alexandra's second child, another daughter Tatiana, was born on 29 May. Xenia was soon losing so much weight that she became very thin and the Dowager Empress was concerned about her health. In May 1897 Emperor Franz Joseph of Austria, on a state visit to St Petersburg, paid a courtesy visit to Xenia in her apartments at the Winter Palace.

Later that year Xenia and Sandro moved to their new St Petersburg home at 106 Quai de la Moika, the only palace in the capital to have a large garden. The original interiors were by Monighetti, but the palace had been redecorated to Xenia's taste by Nicolai de Rochefort and Nicolai Sultanov. Its exterior layout was unusual. From the main gates, with their entwined monogram of 'KA', a path led to the main door on the right of the palace, and then continued through an arch into another courtyard, and then through a final arch to the back of the palace. Beyond the elaborate entrance doors was an elegant classical hallway, and a white marble staircase with frescoes on the walls. On every other stair Xenia placed an aspidistra. The interior was in classic Edwardian style. Xenia's drawing room was in blue and white, one of her favourite colour combinations. Flower-patterned chairs graced the salon, the mahogany shelves of Sandro's library housed his large collection of naval books, and his study was next door. Downstairs were the suites of guest rooms. The palace also had its own private chapel. Although Xenia's son Prince Nikita thought the house had a hundred rooms, her grandson Prince Alexander (who visited in the 1960s) considered fifty would be a better estimate.

Court regulations stipulated a minimum of ten staff for a Grand Duke, Sandro's thirteen included the Director of the Court (General Evreinoff), three personal servants, two ADCs (including Vladimir Chatelain, who in later years became Director of the Court), one ADC General, a physician, a chef and four kitchen hands. In addition, the large staff included cooks, pastrycooks and laundresses, a porter, valet, groom, coachman and Xenia's own personal staff. The Director of her Court was Counsellor of State Nicholas Petrovitch Vesselago. Anastasia Grigorievna had remained after Xenia's marriage, more in the capacity of a personal maid; and Xenia had a young lady-in-waiting, Sophia Dimietrievna Evreinoff, only four years her senior, plus the nanny and nursery maids for the children. It was a privileged existence. Whenever the Grand Duchess was ill, staff covered the road outside the palace with straw to deaden the noise of the traffic.

In April 1898 they attended the wedding of Sandro's niece Duchess Alexandrine of Mecklenburg-Schwerin (Adini), daughter of his only sister Anastasia, in Cannes. The bridegroom was Prince Christian of Denmark, eldest son of Xenia's uncle Crown Prince Frederik. From Cannes they went on to Monte Carlo, lured by the gambling tables, and Xenia admitted that their fortunes at the casinos were mixed. She was 'mad about the shops', and laughingly said she would soon be ruined as she could not stop buying, while Sandro was even worse – but that did not lessen his exasperation with her extravagance. Shopkeepers did their best 'to get you to buy everything, and it's hard to refuse'.[22] To Parisian traders, the sudden appearance of the Tsar's sister and her husband was obviously too good an opportunity to lose.

On the way home they visited King Christian and Queen Louise in Denmark, to give them an account of the wedding in Cannes, and one afternoon they all drove over to Sorgenfri, which was to be Christian and Adini's new home. The King's Lord Chamberlain, Rørdam, who had known Xenia since her childhood, described Sandro as 'a handsome, slim figure; good-looking, regular features; delightful eyes'.[23] It was probably Xenia's last meeting with Queen Louise, who died in September.

On 11 December Xenia's son Feodor was born in St Petersburg.

She made a quick recovery and was soon able to move on to her couch. The Dowager Empress still insisted that Xenia's sons be treated as Grand Dukes. This was emphasized when, in June, while cruising on Sandro's yacht *Tamara*, they were given the disappointing news that Alix had given birth to a third daughter. This still left Georgie as heir to the throne.

Only five years after the death of Sasha, Dowager Empress Marie had the grief of losing her second surviving son Georgie, who passed away in the summer of 1899. He had taken to riding about on a motorcycle, though the doctors had expressly forbidden it. In June he was found by a peasant woman by the road, having fallen off his vehicle, and evidently dying. Although three months pregnant, Xenia accompanied her mother, Misha and Uncle Alexis to Batum, to bring George's body back to St Petersburg for burial. In Moscow Nicholas joined them for the final stage of the journey.

The funeral on 14 July was an ordeal for everyone, particularly the Dowager Empress. After standing dry-eyed holding Xenia's hand for much of the funeral ceremony, she saw the coffin being lowered with the tombs of her husband and their baby son Alexander nearby. Suddenly she staggered, collapsed on to Xenia, insisting loudly that they must go home, as she could not stand any more, and then tried to tear herself away. The Tsar took hold of her other hand, and she tried to push past the open tomb to get out quickly. Xenia thought their mother was going to faint, and Sandro supported her. Without stopping to throw flowers on to the grave, she hurried out still clutching Georgie's hat.

George's death emphasized the problem of the succession. Misha was now heir and, after him, the crown would pass to Grand Duke Vladimir and his family. Nicholas's daughters could not succeed to the throne, nor could the crown pass through Xenia to her sons. Although their father was a Grand Duke, he was distant in the line of succession. It was becoming imperative that the Empress should give birth to a son.

In 1899 Sandro was reinstated in the navy, promoted to Captain of the *Rostislav* stationed in the Black Sea, and appointed to a post in the Ministry of Finance under Sergei Witte. He rose steadily in rank over the next few years, finally becoming Minister of Merchant Marine, the youngest member of the government.

When the Boer War broke out in South Africa that autumn, Russia was not involved, but Xenia shared in the general pro-Boer sympathy, telling Nicky that she thought there could be nobody except the English who was not on their side.[24] As the Empress was particularly pro-English and virtually regarded Queen Victoria as her mother, Xenia had to be discreet about her views.

After the autumn trip to Denmark, which this time included Irina and Andrei, Xenia and Sandro returned to St Petersburg. On 4 January she gave birth to her third son at the palace on the Moika. 'It was too stupid last night – the telephone muddled everything!' Olga wrote on a postcard she had painted herself. '. . . I congratulate you with dear baby Nikita. . . .'[25]

That summer she welcomed Greek Minny to Russia as the bride of Sandro's brother, Grand Duke George Michaelovich. Xenia's best friend was now also her sister-in-law and Minny was grateful for her support. 'Xenia has always been my guardian angel,'[26] she told her mother Queen Olga of Greece many years later. Xenia was living at The Farm and Minny often drove over from Michaelovskoe, just along the coast. In the autumn they all joined Sandro at Ai-Todor, where George had purchased some land from his brother on which to build a house.

When Minny left to visit her family in Greece, Xenia drove to Livadia, where she was surprised to find Nicholas Ill in bed. The doctors diagnosed influenza, but as his temperature rose over the next few days Xenia became increasingly alarmed. A second opinion was called for and her fears of typhoid were confirmed. Count Fredericks, the Minister of the Court, begged Xenia and Sandro to persuade the Empress to allow bulletins to be issued.

Xenia was also worried about Irina's illness. At one point her temperature was so high that her condition gave cause for concern; her recovery was slow and Xenia, who visited Livadia every morning, was torn between brother and child. To complicate matters Alix was in the early stages of pregnancy, and as the crisis approached there were urgent discussions over what to do if the Emperor were to die leaving a pregnant widow. Luckily Nicholas recovered, but his illness emphasized even more the need for a male heir.

4 (1901–5)

'Why are we being punished by God?'

By the summer of 1901 Xenia and Sandro had been married for seven years, and their fifth child, another son Dmitri, was born on 2 August. A few days earlier at Gatchina, Xenia's nineteen-year-old sister Olga married her distant cousin Prince Peter of Oldenburg, a surprise as Peter was said to have no interest in women. Also that season, in June, the Empress had given birth to her fourth child, Anastasia. Xenia, cruising on the *Tamara*, received the news by telegram, and shared in the general family disappointment that this baby was yet another girl.[1]

At the start of the year, on 22 January [NS] 1901, Queen Victoria had died, and Alicky lost the guiding influence which her mother-in-law was either unable or unwilling to provide. Though Xenia never knew the Grandmother of Europe personally, she shared in the general mood of sorrow, readily recognizing that the late sovereign had been 'everything that was best about England, she was so much loved, and exuded such enormous charm!'[2] Her sympathies were especially with her aunt Alix, now Queen Consort. Despite Tsar Alexander III's contempt for Queen Victoria, Xenia had clearly inherited none of his feelings on the subject.

Xenia and Alix were still close. On 7 November Alix wrote to her 'Darling Chicken' to say that her brother Ernie, the Grand Duke of Hesse, and his wife Ducky, at whose wedding in 1894 Nicholas and Alix had become betrothed, were to divorce. Their unhappy marriage had been an open secret throughout the European courts, and they had maintained a façade of togetherness largely in order not to upset Queen Victoria. Now she had passed away, they no longer felt it necessary to go on living a lie. The Empress begged her sister-in-law to do what she could as regards curtailing any gossip she might hear, for the sake of the whole family. All that anybody needed to know was that they went their separate ways 'as their characters could impossibly get on together'.[3]

The 'nasty gossip' concerned Ducky's relationship with another cousin, Grand Duke Cyril Vladimirovich. They had been in love for some years but, as first cousins, their marriage had been prohibited by the Orthodox Church and Ducky's marriage to Ernie had then been arranged. Now she had left her husband and daughter for Cyril. In 1903 he sought permission to marry Ducky secretly, but was refused by the Tsar. Xenia thought the whole thing was contrived so that Cyril could emerge unscathed from the episode. The only honourable thing, she was convinced, was to marry her and 'take the corresponding punishment', which he was evidently reluctant to do.[4] Unless Cyril was prepared to give up everything for a life in exile, he could only hope that the Tsar would relent. Meanwhile Xenia's widowed uncle Grand Duke Paul had married his mistress Mme Olga Pistolkors, a divorcee by whom he already had a son. Husband and wife, created Countess Hohenfelsen by the King of Bavaria, were promptly banished to Paris, leaving his two young children from his first marriage, Marie and Dmitri, in the guardianship of Sergei and Ella in Moscow.

Xenia spent the spring of 1902 at Ai-Todor, expecting another child. She spent much time fishing with the children, she still missed Sandro, who was with his ship, and freely admitted to her brother that she could never get used to these regular separations from her husband. Alix was also expecting a baby; desperate to give her husband a son, she had turned to the occult and fallen under the sway of Philippe Nizier-Vachot, a French faith healer, who convinced her that the child would be a boy. In August the whole country awaited the birth – but nothing happened. Finally, Xenia reported, there occurred 'a minor miscarriage – if it could be called a miscarriage at all! That is to say a tiny ovule came out!' The next day a bulletin was issued saying a miscarriage had ended the Empress's hopes, the doctors confirmed that there had been no pregnancy, and the symptoms were caused by anaemia. Xenia and the Dowager Empress both spoke to Nicholas about Philippe's influence, and her relief after the conversation was tempered by concern that they had 'failed to explain anything' as she told Dagmar's lady-in-waiting 'Aprak', and that they were no nearer finding out anything about the origins of the mysterious, if not bogus, Philippe.[5]

A week later Xenia returned to Ai-Todor, where her son Rostislav, named after Sandro's ship, was born in November. Though convinced that Alix's 'pregnancy' was auto-suggestion, she was worried that the association with Philippe would continue. She told Aprak that they refused to maintain their silence any longer. Diplomacy was required, but Nicky and Alix had clearly fallen completely under his malign influence. After some unwelcome publicity Nicholas was forced to send Philippe back to France, much to the relief of Xenia and Dagmar.

At around the dawn of the new century, Xenia and Sandro were among those who noticed that the Dowager Empress still had some influence over her son, before it gradually declined as Alicky gained in confidence. After this the Dowager Empress began to complain that Nicholas was doing his utmost to avoid all opportunities for a private meeting. Alarmed at what looked like at best a discomfiting lack of communication and at worst a widening breach between them, Xenia asked Nicholas to make every effort to discuss things with their mother more often. Dagmar seldom had a chance to see her son alone, even at Peterhof where the pace of life was more relaxed and informal.

Xenia and Sandro were always ready to take their place at glittering court functions. Sandro loved these social occasions, though for the shy Xenia it was more of a duty for which she had to steel herself. There was a particularly splendid dance at the Winter Palace in January 1903, which Sandro always remembered 'as it was to be the last spectacular ball in the history of the empire'. He recalled that a quarter of a century had elapsed since he and Nicky as young boys had watched Tsar Alexander II with Princess Yourievsky on his arm at a similar occasion. While some of the uniforms remained the same, the rest of the empire had undergone astonishing changes. He saw a new, hostile Russia which 'glared through the large windows of the palace', and smiled sadly to himself on reading the wording of the invitation which requested that all guests should come in seventeenth-century costumes. For at least one night, he saw, the Tsar wanted to be back in the glorious past of their family. Xenia was resplendent in the costume of a 'boyarina', richly embroidered and covered with glittering jewels; her halo-shaped headdress sparkled with emeralds and diamonds, and she carried an ostrich feather fan with a handle of pink enamel, rock crystal and diamonds made by Fabergé. Sandro himself was attired as a court falconer, in a white and gold long coat, with golden eagles embroidered on the front and back, a pink silk shirt, blue silk trousers and yellow leather boots.

The ball was considered a great success by all, he noted. 'This magnificent pageant of the seventeenth century must have made a strange impression on the foreign ambassadors; while we danced, the workers were striking and the clouds in the Far East were hanging dangerously low.'[6] Xenia and Sandro were probably more aware than the rest of the family that Russia was on the brink of momentous changes, though they could not have foreseen the 'abyss', culminating in the crash some fourteen years ahead.

Among her siblings Xenia was particularly devoted to the youngest brother Michael, or 'Misha', and shared his sadness when a prospective marriage to his first cousin 'Baby Bee', Princess Beatrice of Saxe-Coburg, was forbidden by the Church. The Tsar was sympathetic but firm; there could be no exceptions, and marriage between Michael and Baby Bee was therefore out of the question. As heir to the throne, Michael could not break Church law or marry without the Tsar's consent. After agonizing over it for weeks, in November 1903 he wrote to her with a heavy heart, breaking off their relationship. Afterwards Xenia reported with relief that he appeared in better spirits as a result.

A few days later, just before Christmas, Xenia received 'a terrible letter' from Baby Bee's elder sister Ducky, complaining bitterly about Michael, saying that 'he behaved in an ugly and dishonourable way towards her'.[7] Xenia thought this accusation unjustified as it came after one perfectly reasonable note in which Michael had written that, as they could not marry, it would be better if they stopped writing such letters to each other, but that he hoped they could remain on good terms. Beatrice, she understood, had become quite ill and was sent to Egypt, where she was getting thinner and spending much of her time weeping.

On 9 August 1903 Grand Duchess George (Greek Minny) gave

birth to her second daughter. The baby, Princess Xenia, was named after her aunt and godmother Grand Duchess Xenia. Shortly afterwards Sandro's father, whom Xenia always called 'Papa Michael', was found unconscious in his bedroom after suffering a stroke. For several weeks he was paralysed and hovered between life and death as the family gathered round. After a few weeks he recovered his powers of speech and some feeling in his body. He was taken to Cannes, where he lived in a small villa near his daughter Grand Duchess Anastasia of Mecklenburg-Schwerin. His journey by special train, which because of his condition could travel no faster than 24mph, threw the railway timetables of Europe into chaos.

By mid-January 1904 Xenia was in Cannes, where she had lunch one day with Ducky, Baby Bee and their mother, the Dowager Duchess of Coburg. She was shocked to see that Baby Bee, once so pretty and bright-eyed, was now an object of pity, extremely thin and unwell, and according to her anxious sister, in danger of losing her reason. Afterwards the Dowager Duchess raised the question of marriage again, but Xenia could only say that the Tsar had made it clear that they could not marry, and that Michael himself had reluctantly accepted the matter. Not for another year did the recriminations die down, but by then Michael had met someone else.

'War has been declared!! May the Lord help us!!'[8] With these dramatic words Xenia began her diary entry for 25 January 1904. Angered by Russia's penetration of Korea and Manchuria, Japan had launched a surprise attack on the Russian naval base at Port Arthur without any declaration of war. Only three weeks earlier, at the New Year reception at the Winter Palace, Xenia, glittering in white and gold, had watched avidly as the Tsar spoke to the Japanese Ambassador. In December, as tension mounted, she had insisted to the War Minister Kuropatkin that there would be no war, that the Tsar did not want any armed conflict, 'that there was no need to fight Japan and that Russia did not need Korea'.[9] Kuropatkin had replied that the decision might be taken out of Russia's hands.

Xenia and Sandro immediately returned from Cannes to St Petersburg. The war proved a disaster for Russia, with humiliating defeats on land and at sea. In what Xenia called the worst day since the declaration of war,[10] the *Petropavlovsk* was sunk by a mine. Of the 711 men and officers on board, only eighty survived, including Grand Duke Cyril. The whole imperial family, stunned by the loss of over six hundred lives, attended the Te Deum.

Outwardly life carried on as normal. Xenia and the children spent the early summer at Gatchina with her mother, enjoying picnics at the Finnish log cabin in the park with Michael and Olga, feeding the deer, going fishing and strolling in the woods. Sometimes they went on motor excursions, and one day Sandro drove Nicholas and Alix over to Gatchina in his new car. The Dowager Empress had put pressure on Nicholas to ensure that Sandro would not have to go to the front, and he remained in St Petersburg at the Ministry of Merchant Marine. Xenia, appointed Chief of the 15th Regiment of the Ukrainsky Hussars on her wedding day, had always attended regimental events and now supported her Hussars in any way she could during time of war. Gatchina was a garrison town, home of the Blue Cuirassiers, of which the Dowager Empress was Colonel-in-Chief. On a visit to the hospital Xenia planted a tree in the grounds.

By late July they were all at Peterhof, where Alix gave birth to the longed-for son, Tsarevich Alexis, the first heir born to a reigning monarch since the seventeenth century. The imperial family were jubilant, especially Michael who said he could now retire as heir. The lavish christening was noteworthy for the first appearance at a ceremony of Xenia's daughter Irina and her cousins Olga and Tatiana, who all wore short blue and silver satin court dresses with silver braid and buttons, silver shoes and blue velvet *kokoshniks* embroidered with pearls.

The Tsar and Tsarina's joy soon turned to uneasiness. In September Alexis haemorrhaged from his navel, and though the bleeding stopped suspicion remained. A few months later their fears were confirmed; he had haemophilia, a disease passed on by the mother that prevents the blood from clotting. Any knock or bump could be fatal, and Alexis could die at any time. Fearing for the future of the dynasty if the news became public, the secret was known to only a few trusted people.

After the Tsarevich's birth, Alicky's ascendancy was complete and there were no rivals for influence over her mild husband. All the same, as mother of the Tsar, Dagmar's status as matriarch of the family was unassailable. In Olga's opinion, Sandro was often the only male member of the family from whom the Tsar could seek advice. Sandro always liked his cousin and his advice was generally valued, but as Sandro and Xenia began to drift apart, Nicky felt increasingly isolated[11] and subsequently fell more under the sway of his determined wife.

In the autumn of 1904 Xenia and Sandro were back at Ai-Todor. Two of the villas in the park near the sea had been converted into convalescent hospitals, one for officers and one for privates, and Xenia paid frequent visits. In the Crimean sunshine they called at neighbouring estates of relations and friends, the Youssoupovs at Koreiz, the Vorontzovs at Alupka, and Grand Duke Peter at Djulber. Excavations for the building of Grand Duke George's house at Harax had begun and they went to see the progress. One day they organized a hunt.

By December they had returned to St Petersburg, and Xenia's gloom was evident from her letter to 'Apapa', King Christian IX, thanking him for his Christmas present.

We spent Xmas Eve as usual altogether at Gatchina, but it was a sad one, this year, as you can imagine. We are going through such a *hard* time, *every thing* is sad & seems to be against us & one feels quite *depressed* & miserable.

We are here since a month (came straight from the Crimea) and will remain here as long as Mamma does – and probably later on, we shall all go over to town.

We often go to Petersburg as there is always a lot to see there and Sandro has got his work and lots to do – Mamma looks well, thank God, but is in despair *about everything* & this war drives her mad, simply.[12]

In an increasingly oppressive Russia, there was unrest over the conduct of the war. Several defeats had shattered army morale and the people, who did not know what they were fighting for anyway, began to demand their own voice in the government of the country. All court functions had been cancelled but on 6 January the traditional ceremony of Blessing of the Waters took place on the frozen River Neva outside the Winter Palace.

After a service in the palace church, the imperial ladies made their way to one of the state rooms overlooking the Neva. From here they watched as the clergy, singing anthems and carrying lighted tapers, led the Emperor and the Grand Dukes out on to the ice. After prayers, the Metropolitan dipped his cross three times through a hole in the ice as a salute was fired from the SS Peter & Paul Fortress. Suddenly one of the palace windows near the imperial ladies shattered under the impact of a live shell. For a moment there was confusion, as ministers and court officials were thrown into a panic, while police and soldiers rushed around everywhere. The Tsar, who was unharmed, thought terrorists had planted a live shell in one of the guns.

Three days later came the ill-fated protest which was to go down in Russian history as 'Bloody Sunday'. Father Gapon, leader of an authorized labour union, placed himself at the head of a peaceful demonstration of workers who planned to go to the Winter Palace and personally present Tsar Nicholas II with a petition asking for a minimum wage and an eight-hour day. Though the Tsar was forewarned the night before, he was advised not to stay in the capital to receive it. The St Petersburg police called in the army to help maintain control, and as the crowd – estimated to number 200,000 – approached the palace, troops opened fire and over 2,000 were killed or wounded.

Xenia and Sandro had received a New Year's greeting card from Sergei and Ella at the beginning of 1905. In February Sergei met the same fate as his father, being blown to pieces by a terrorist bomb as his carriage left the Kremlin. While she and Sandro could shed few tears for the dead man, their hearts ached for Ella, widowed in such horrific circumstances. Full of sympathy, Xenia longed to go straight to the side of the bereaved widow, all alone, and comfort her, but Moscow was too dangerous to visit during this terrible time. The imperial family were advised not even to attend the funeral as the police could not guarantee their safety.

Worse was to come. In May Xenia and Sandro were at Gatchina, where they attended a military parade and Xenia relaxed in the park with her children, the dog Bachka and the horse Flight. During a picnic, a messenger arrived with news of a disastrous encounter between the Russian and Japanese fleets in the Straits of Tsushima, with the Russian fleet annihilated in less than an hour. All of the family were stunned.

Everywhere Xenia looked, there seemed to be nothing but bad news. The ignominious war was in its final stages when they learnt of mutiny on the battleship *Potemkin*, with a commander and several officers killed. 'How terrible, what a nightmare!' she wrote in her diary. 'Why, why are we being punished by God?! I am walking as if in a dream, unable to understand anything!'[13] Defeat was unavoidable and peace was declared in August 1905, but Xenia was angry that they had hardly been consulted when peace terms were drawn up, maintaining that the war had started without reason, continued thus 'and ended even more stupidly!'[14]

Later in the summer they moved to Ai-Todor, where the estate was enlarged as Sandro's family grew. More land was bought from the Tartars, and he laid out a little path between Ai-Todor and Livadia. 'The Tsar's Path' was used by Nicholas and Alix for their frequent visits. As Sandro still refused to have any alterations made to the Old House, new buildings were added. A passage connected it to a small house where Feodor and Nikita eventually lived. Opposite the Old House the architect Nicolai Krasnov constructed the New House, where the younger boys had their bedrooms, sitting rooms and bathrooms. A little further down the slope was the Suites House, used by the ladies and gentlemen of the household.

Sandro planted new trees and supervised the production and marketing of his wine, fruit and flowers. The vineyards were extensive, occupying land on both sides of the lower road. Proud of his wine, he made a point of always being present when it was bottled. Among varieties for sale were Bordeaux at 70 kopeks a bottle, or 40 kopeks for a half bottle; Madeira (1 rouble 50, or 80 kopeks); Claret (60 or 35 kopeks); and Reisling (75 or 40 kopeks).[15]

Like the other Crimean properties Ai-Todor remained completely unspoilt. When it was proposed to extend the railway line Xenia was determined to prevent it going through their estate.[16] Even with all the alterations, there was little spare room. When Grand Duke and Grand Duchess George arrived with their daughters they were given the three-roomed flat over the wine cellar in Sandro's vineyard. Later Misha, Olga and Prince Peter of Oldenburg joined the party, and they all met in the Old House for meals. Xenia and Olga wrote to their mother, who was in

Denmark, to say how much they were enjoying themselves. After supper they formed an amateur orchestra of balalaikas.

This was more an effort to cheer themselves up than anything else, as alarming news was beginning to filter through. All over the empire there were strikes and disturbances. By October the whole of European Russia was gripped by a paralysing general strike as disillusioned soldiers drifted back to their homes, telephone communications were cut, and there was no postal service. The Black Sea Fleet mutinied, there were skirmishes at nearby Yalta and a priest was murdered during a service. A company of soldiers arrived at Ai-Todor for protection. Mutinous ships were expected to arrive at Yalta at any moment and at Ai-Todor the guards were doubled. The children were forbidden to go outside without armed guards. It seemed as if a general strike was fast turning into revolution.

Xenia tried to send telegrams to St Petersburg to reassure Nicholas that they were safe, but the messages did not arrive. In Denmark a few telegrams reached the Dowager Empress, who was desperate for news of her family, but even these soon stopped. Once the situation calmed down a little, Misha, Olga and Peter left for the capital. They were advised not to have any lights on in their train, as the previous one had been attacked by the mob.

In October, when the Tsar put his signature to a manifesto approving the establishment of the Duma, or 'the end of Russian autocracy' as some of the family saw it, Xenia's mood darkened. Throughout Russia, she felt, there seemed to be nothing but the 'sorrow and disgrace' of disturbances, strikes, and meetings.[17] She could only hope for better times ahead, while remaining fearful for the future and anxious as to what the new year held in store for them. Sandro resigned his post at the Ministry of Merchant Marine. They were forced to remain at Ai-Todor for Christmas, together with George and Minny. Normally they would have attended the service at the village church, but this year the priest was summoned to the house. Having been warned that he might be killed, the poor man was driven to Ai-Todor and back 'in a closed landau under escort of a cavalry posse'.[18] All wounded officers from the hospital were invited to join the royal couple round the Christmas tree.

On 29 January 1906 [NS] Christian IX died in Copenhagen. As the situation in the Crimea had eased, Xenia and her family returned at once to St Petersburg. From there she travelled to Copenhagen with Misha, Olga, Peter and Greek Minny. Nicholas was unable to leave Russia.

After the funeral Xenia returned to St Petersburg, where the first signs of coolness between her and Alix occurred. The fault was that of the Empress, who 'needled' Xenia about the preparations she and Sandro had made to flee abroad on the yacht if necessary. When Xenia mentioned 'all the horrors we have lived through', Alix said: 'Only those who were there, really know what it was. . . .'[19] Xenia maintained a diplomatic silence.

On 27 April all the imperial family assembled in the white and gold St George's Hall in the Winter Palace for the state opening of the Duma. Xenia was unimpressed by the Duma members, with their 'repulsive faces and insolent disdainful expressions!', especially as they just stood looking around without either crossing themselves or bowing throughout the Te Deum.[20] As Nicholas read the speech from the throne, only his shaking hands betrayed his emotion. 'It was a great historic moment, unforgettable for those who witnessed it,' Xenia wrote. When the choir sang 'God Save the Tsar' she found herself caught up in the emotions of the moment, and even Nicholas could not hold back his tears. Even so, her impressions of the momentous day were that the Duma was 'filth' and 'such a nest of revolutionaries, that it's disgusting and shaming for the rest of Russia in front of the whole world'.[21]

5 (1906–13)

'A great woman and a wonderful mother'

After the disastrous Russo-Japanese war of 1904–5 Sandro was appointed to the command of the new torpedo boat HIMS *Almaz*. Xenia was spending the summer of 1906 with her mother at Gatchina, from where she visited Sandro once a week.

Soon she found herself involved in another of her youngest brother's ill-fated romances, the lady in question this time being 'Dina', Alexandra Kossikovskaya, a lady-in-waiting to their sister Olga. The rest of the family assumed it would be a temporary infatuation, until in 1906 Michael asked the Tsar for permission to marry. This was refused, and the Dowager Empress dismissed Dina from her post, advising her to go abroad and stay there. Less than a year later Dina returned to St Petersburg, and it emerged that Michael had found a priest who was prepared to marry them secretly in the country for a generous fee. Xenia was convinced that Dina and her father were doing their utmost to ensnare him at any cost.[1]

As they could not wed in Russia, they planned a runaway marriage in Italy. Michael knew Dina had been forbidden to follow him abroad, or even to leave the capital, and he told Xenia, whom he still trusted, how upset he was by such a measure. He and Dina still intended to defy the order, but the *Okhrana* (secret police) arrested her at Odessa as she planned to leave for Naples, and returned her to St Petersburg. After spending some time with his mother in Denmark, Michael decided to go to Ai-Todor with Xenia rather than return directly to St Petersburg, where a distressed Dina was waiting. At length he accepted with equanimity, as well as Xenia's understanding and sympathy, that the odds against their marriage were too great.

Meanwhile Xenia's eight-year-old son Feodor was taken dangerously ill with scarlet fever. Sandro was immediately summoned home. 'The first days of poor little Feodor's illness are difficult to imagine,' the Dowager Empress told Nicholas. 'Poor Xenia was in despair.'[2] Then Irina caught the illness; the sick children were completely separated from the rest of the household, and once Irina was on the road to recovery, their rooms and all possessions were disinfected. Feodor and Irina were particular favourites of the Dowager Empress, and she complained that she had not seen her granddaughter for nearly three weeks. Xenia was afraid to write to Nicholas at all for fear of infection. Sandro then heard that the crew of the *Almaz* had mutinied, and intended to take him hostage on his return. The Tsar advised him that he had no choice but to resign from the navy, as the government could not take the chance of delivering a member of the imperial family into the hands of the revolutionaries.[3]

Sandro was determined to leave Russia, for which he now confessed his hatred. The children's illness provided him and Xenia with a perfect excuse, and he told Nicky that the doctors recommended a change of climate. Wise enough not to give his brother-in-law an inkling of his understanding of the real reasons for the family's flight, the Tsar readily assented. When Feodor and Irina were out of quarantine, Sandro took them all for the first of many visits to Biarritz, situated on the border between France and Spain. Made fashionable by Napoleon III and Empress Eugenie, Biarritz had grown from a small Basque fishing village to a place renowned as the first name in holiday resorts for European royalty, with its superb weather and beaches. A sizeable Russian colony established itself there every year between August and November, headed by Xenia's uncle Grand Duke Alexis, who was seldom without female company, and Alexander II's widow Princess Yourievsky, who lived at the Villa Sofia. The Hotel du Palais, Hotel des Ambassadors, and the Continental were patronized by the Oldenburgs, Orlovs and other aristocrats who gambled at the casino and considered Biarritz an ideal place to spend their money.

As everyone in St Petersburg spoke French, there was no language barrier. When they arrived at the Villa Espoir, their party, said Sandro, 'resembled a migration of nomads', with himself, Xenia, six children, three nurses, English and French teachers, Irina's governess, Xenia's lady-in-waiting, his aide-de-camp, five maids and four butlers. Olga had arrived just before them and was installed at the Hotel du Palais. The morning after their arrival, a little the worse for September heat, 'with our faces swollen from an all-night battle with the mosquitoes, we ran to the Grande Plage and buried our bodies in the sand. Our hearts sang: we had escaped from Russia. I thought we would never go back. . . . I thanked the Lord for giving me such a convenient opportunity for getting out of the inferno.'[4]

Away from Russia they regained their previous high spirits. One of the favourite amusements of Xenia and Olga was throwing cushions at the heads of other guests in the lounge of the Hotel du Palais. But etiquette prevailed, at least on this first visit and the ladies had to be presented to Xenia. The Grand Duchess had lost none of her shyness with strangers, and as the ladies approached to make their curtsey they were somewhat disconcerted to note that the Grand Duke, standing behind his wife, was whispering something in her ear which made her laugh. In fact, every time a lady approached, he murmured, 'Come on, give her your little paw', causing Xenia to giggle behind a fan and extend her hand.[5]

At the Villa Espoir they gave numerous receptions, and towards the end of the evening Xenia discreetly indicated to their special friends that supper would be served. These privileged few, who included Xenia's close friend Mme Leglise, known to her intimates as 'la Mouche', pretended to leave with the others, then returned up the back stairs to rooms where the evening finished with a lively meal.

Sandro enjoyed mixing with 'the smart set', and threw himself with zest into golf on the links opposite their villa. As the Tsar of Russia's brother-in-law, it was inevitable that he would become the centre of attention. Though he remarked later that throughout twelve years of marriage he had never yet looked at another woman, amid the heady whirl of social contacts, invitations to dinner parties and the like, forbidden fruits began to appeal.

Their original plan had been to stay at Biarritz for three months, but when December came Sandro had no desire to return home, and he persuaded Xenia to stay a little longer. For the first time they spent Christmas abroad, and for him at least it was their happiest and most carefree in twelve years. There were no dreary court receptions to attend, no exchanges of visits with equally bored relatives or pompous ministers and councillors, just 'a real human holiday spent with our children and friends'. They waited for the hunting season, with its programme of luncheons in the country and dinners in Biarritz 'in an atmosphere of intimacy, happy fatigue and pleasant excitement'.[6]

For Sandro, there was more than 'pleasant excitement' in this temporary home from home. Gradually he became infatuated with a woman who regularly visited their villa. At first he found her 'clever in a charming, unaggressive way, free from the fireworks of cocktail-bred brilliance. Her Spanish-Italian ancestry accounted for her solid culture and had taught her that real refinement is an arch-foe of self-consciousness.' They spent an increasing amount of time in one another's company, and friendship soon turned into deeper mutual attraction. Sandro was playing with fire, 'prepared to taste bitter poison at the bottom of that cup' as he began to compare his feelings towards his wife and his new amour. 'I did not know which one of the two I needed more. One stood for all that was best in my character, another promised a possibility of tearing away from the strain and terror of the past.' He admitted that the very thought of making a choice between them 'horrified' him, as a husband and father of six children, with a seventh expected shortly.[7]

In March Xenia's uncle King Edward VII arrived with his mistress, Mrs Keppel. Xenia and Sandro often met him for dinner, bridge or walking on the golf course. Hardly had the King departed when the Dowager Empress's 'White Train' pulled into the Gare de Negresse, complete with Cossack bodyguards and personnel in exotic uniforms. She was met by Xenia, Sandro, their children and a large reception committee before driving to the Hotel du Palais. The local police sent for reinforcements from Paris.

The children, Irina, Andrei, Feodor, Nikita, Dmitri and Rostislav, became an endless source of delight to their grandmother. As there was always such a distance between her and Alicky, she found the pleasure in her daughter's family that she could not find in Nicky's. By day they all toured the countryside in Sandro's Delauney-Belleville, and in the evenings there were regular parties. Xenia and Sandro were delighted that Dagmar mixed with their friends and would readily join in with anything.

A few weeks after celebrating Xenia's thirty-second birthday, they had to return home for the birth of her baby. They all left Biarritz in the Dowager Empress's train, one carriage of which was completely filled with flowers.

Perhaps remembering the scent bottle she had given her mother as a child, Xenia had begun to patronize Cartier. On their way home they stopped in Paris, where Xenia took her mother to Cartier's establishment on the rue de la Paix. The previous year, when Xenia purchased a few small items, her necklace of matchless black pearls had caused quite a stir in Cartier's showroom. The Dowager Empress was impressed with the jewellery Cartier brought out, and both ladies expressed a wish to be able to buy his range in St Petersburg. They were delighted to learn that a Christmas exhibition was being planned in the Hotel d'Europe. Xenia remained a loyal client of Cartier and this patronage reached its culmination with the wedding of her daughter.

She also patronized the House of Faberge, whose exquisite bibelots and objets d'art included the famous easter eggs presented to both Empresses every year. She had several Fabergé picture frames and parasol handles, one in gold nephrite, diamonds, rubies and enamel. Her Christmas and Name Day presents to Nicholas and Sandro were usually Fabergé jewelled tie-pins, cigarette cases or cuff-links.

In March 1902 Xenia attended the Fabergé exhibition at the von Dervis Mansion in St Petersburg. Many of the imperial family had lent items for the occasion and they viewed the exhibition before retiring to a champagne buffet in aid of charity. Xenia and Sandro had lent a 'silver service in the form of Empire vases' and a collection of animals carved from semi-precious stones.[8]

Xenia and Sandro returned to Gatchina in time for the birth of their last child, Vassili, on 24 June 1907. He was a sickly infant and at first there was some doubt as to whether he would survive. A priest was summoned to baptize him in the nursery, thereby saving all of them 'the ordeal of military parades and shouting crowds'.[9]

Xenia was soon to experience her own heartbreak. Although they stayed in Russia until early autumn, Sandro's thoughts were elsewhere. At last they could travel abroad again, stopping at Baden-Baden to visit his father before going with him to Cannes,

Here they met up with Sandro's sister Anastasia and brother Miche-Miche, accompanied by his wife Sophie, Countess de Torby, and their daughters Nadejda (Nada) and Anastasia (Zia). Between Miche-Miche's endless tea parties and his sister's gambling in Monte Carlo, Sandro was eagerly anticipating a meeting with his lady friend in Rome and they booked into the Grand Hotel. Prince Dmitri later recalled a visit to the Vatican with his parents, where they were received by Pope Pius X.

Sandro's lady friend arrived and they went briefly to Venice, leaving Xenia and the children behind in Rome. Soon after he returned, with their trunks packed and bills settled, their son Dmitri complained of a headache. Scarlet fever was diagnosed, and all their plans were changed. Xenia and the other six children left for Biarritz, but Sandro stayed with Dmitri. The complications so often accompanying scarlet fever had set in, and the doctors warned that a major operation might be necessary. For four weeks he sat by his son's side, grieving and brooding.

After Dmitri's recovery they joined the rest of the family at Biarritz. This time Xenia and Sandro occupied the Villa les Vagues, rue Louison Bobet, a late nineteenth-century stone villa built for the Doux family, and rented out to tenants in their absence. Nothing had changed since the previous year; there was the same social round, the whirl of endless parties, functions and flirtations. Sandro now knew he had to choose between the two women in his life, but his companion turned down his pleas for 'an open and permanent association', and would accept nothing short of marriage, with a church wedding. He pleaded, argued and talked to Xenia. Though she had long suspected something of the sort, she was saddened at this open revelation that her husband no longer loved her, and wept, partly out of misery and partly with relief. Though the truth might be unpalatable, they agreed it was better than living a lie. Sandro claimed that he never stopped loving Xenia, though in an entirely different way from his feelings towards his companion at Biarritz. His wife, the mother of his children, 'radiated security and personified the established order of things', and 'stood for those traits of my character which were developed by years of military grind, by lectures on duties and responsibilities, by ceremonies of the Court, by Te Deums and Masses in cathedrals'.[10]

By the end of June they were back at Gatchina, where Xenia was upset by gossip that she and Sandro were on the point of divorce, and on asking around she was told that 'there had been rumours from abroad'.[11] In view of the marital problems of other members of the Tsar's family, such a solution appeared less shocking than it might have two or three decades earlier. Nevertheless they decided to stay together for the sake of their children. They remained friends, in Sandro's words, 'even closer friends than before because our friendship withstood the shock of calamity. All glory lay on her side, all blame on mine. She showed herself a great woman and a wonderful mother.'[12] Matters were complicated by the fact that Xenia was at the same time having her own affair with a man long believed to be the husband of Sandro's companion, whom she identified in her private diaries only as 'F', while Sandro's lover was 'M.I.', Maria Ivanova. One summer day Xenia and 'F' drove to Fontainebleau, had tea together in a little restaurant in the forest, and such an intimate heart-to-heart talk that she was overcome with sympathy for him: 'he loves me so much, it will be so painful for him to part from me.'[13]

'F' was in fact an Englishman called Fane whose christian name is currently unknown, although there are several possible contenders.[14] It was also long rumoured that the man in question was Prince Sergei Dolgoruky, a member of the Dowager Empress' household. This cannot be substantiated by hard facts or written evidence. Sergei Dolgoruky was an ADC to the Emperor, an officer in the Horse Guards and the Dowager Empress's equerry. Photographs from the 1890s show a handsome, dark-haired, slim man with a moustache, much taller than the diminutive Xenia, who was three years younger, though later pictures show him balding and stouter. In 1919 Robert Ingham, who knew him in Malta, described him as a big, stout man, very businesslike, who spoke broken English, a renowned collector who had furnished his St Petersburg home with many rare prints and photographs.

One source states that Sandro was having an affair with the wife of 'F',[15] but this was not substantiated. It also appears that Xenia may have been involved with Sergei Dolgoruky at a later date. His marriage in 1914 to a first cousin once removed, Princess Irina Vassilievna Vorontzov-Dashkov, née Naryshkine, a close friend of Xenia, was to have repercussions later.

By the standards of others in the family, Xenia and Sandro's behaviour was hardly scandalous – incompatible with their marriage vows, perhaps, but at least conducted with discretion. Other members of the family were not so discreet. After surviving the sinking of the *Petropavlovsk*, Cyril had the temerity to marry Ducky against the Tsar's express command. He was deprived of his army rank, titles, privileges and income and banished from Russia. It was several months before Nicholas restored Cyril's title, but the couple remained in exile. In 1903 Grand Duchess Olga had fallen in love with Nicholas Kulikovsky, a young officer in her brother Michael's regiment. Refused a divorce by her husband, Olga and Nicholas were seen openly together around Gatchina and lived in a kind of *ménage à trois* with Prince Peter. Grand Duke Paul brought his morganatic wife, for whom he was demanding a fitting title, to Biarritz every year, where they stayed with their three children in the Villa Coquette.

All these Grand Dukes, Sandro commented rather grandly, were displaying 'a complete disrespect for the wishes of the Emperor' as well as showing a bad example to Russian society. Yet he acknowledged that he was in no position to cast the first stone against those who had led Russia to what he called 'the threshold of moral decadence. Myself more than anyone else.'[16]

Sandro had founded the first Military Aviation School in Russia, near Sevastopol. Still hopelessly in love with his friend whom he met from time to time in Biarritz and Paris, Sandro envisaged a future together for them, and in the spring of 1910 he asked her to leave Europe and accompany him to Australia. He was ready to relinquish his title and buy a farm near Sydney. Fortunately for his reputation as well as hers, she firmly reminded him of his duty, telling him for good measure that she would never see him again unless he persevered in his aviation work in Russia and stayed where he belonged.

It was ironic that Xenia became the mother of six healthy sons, while her sister-in-law Alicky was only able to produce four daughters and a sickly haemophiliac son. The Tsar's daughters lived a very sheltered life, and the only people with whom they came into contact regularly apart from their parents and the suite were Xenia's children, who were often invited for afternoon tea and games of tennis. All the latter enjoyed a happy childhood. They had the same English nanny, who stayed for over twenty years and taught them to read English from a book called *Reading Without Tears*. On Sundays they had children's parties at their St Petersburg palace or went to see friends, but the Empress always discouraged them from playing with the frail Alexis.

The boys were considered 'rather wild'.[17] Grand Duke Peter's son, Prince Roman, recalled playing at Peterhof with Xenia's children, who turned somersaults down a grass slope with 'such zeal and wildness that our governess became terrified'. Once, to the children's delight, Xenia joined in, throwing herself down the slope despite disapproving looks from the governess.[18] As the children became older, various tutors were engaged: a Swiss tutor for French; a physics master, a fencing master, and a governess for Irina. Miss Coster became governess to Dmitri, Rostislav and Vassili, while their English tutor, Herbert Galloway Stewart, stayed with them until the revolution. 'Popular and respected', he was remembered with affection by his pupils, especially Nikita. Being typical children they quarrelled and fought, and at the Maryinsky Theatre they were always seated in the lower imperial box with their parents, as Xenia and Sandro feared brawls if they were left in the upper loge without supervision.

They loved the freedom of Ai-Todor where they swam in the sea, collected pebbles from the beach and dipped them in candlewax until they shone, and rode through the countryside on their ponies, accompanied by Tartar grooms. Sometimes they helped Xenia cut the roses, which she loved to arrange in Ai-Todor's rooms, snipping off deadheads as they went round the garden. Belaoussoff, the old lady in charge of overseeing the palace laundry, often played card games with the children.

In 1907 they arrived in the Crimea by car for the first time. This did not endear them to the Tartar population, who complained that Sandro's automobile upset their horses. At Ai-Todor they often had visitors. Xenia's young cousin, Grand Duchess Marie Pavlovna and her brother Grand Duke Dmitri, both staying at the nearby Youssoupov estate of Koreiz with their aunt Grand Duchess Ella, were shown around. Xenia 'was very nice and I believe glad to see us,' Marie told her fiancé, Prince William of Sweden.[19]

Grand Duke and Duchess George had finally moved into Harax. Greek Minny took Marie and Dmitri riding and they often stopped off at Ai-Todor. Marie soon revised her initial impression of her cousin. 'Xenia, I must say, I don't like so much,' she told her fiancé. 'She is rather strange in her manner in general and she does not seem to me clever. But Aunt Minny and she are the best friends, so there must be something in her which is hidden from my sharp eye. . . .'[20]

In the autumn of 1908 Xenia, Sandro and their children visited Denmark with the Dowager Empress on the *Polar Star*, where Queen Alexandra was awaiting them. The Queen and the Empress had bought a white Italianate-style villa, Hvidøre, situated on the coast road north of Copenhagen, two years previously. Although the villa had been altered and refurnished to both sisters' tastes, it was too small to hold Xenia's large entourage. She, Sandro and the children therefore lived on board the yacht, going ashore to the villa every day.

In November Grand Duke Alexis died in Paris, where he had lived since resigning from the navy after the disaster of Tsushima. Three months later Xenia's godfather Grand Duke Vladimir died suddenly in his palace in St Petersburg. Shortly before his death, perhaps with her eye on her sons' future, Vladimir's wife, the haughty Miechen, had finally converted to Orthodoxy.

A third loss was even nearer to home. In December Papa Michael died in his villa at Cannes, with only his son Nicholas present.* After an impressive funeral service at the Russian Church, with a black-draped, horse-drawn catafalque decorated with ostrich feathers, his body was brought back to Sevastopol on a warship sent by the Tsar. Sandro, Xenia and other members of the family, including the Tsar and Tsarina, met the coffin and were taken by special train to St Petersburg. The funeral in the SS Peter & Paul Cathedral was noteworthy for the attendance of Miche-Miche, allowed out of banishment for the occasion. Countess Torby had refused to set foot in Russia but Sandro and the other men followed the coffin on foot, bareheaded in a snowstorm, while Xenia and the ladies drove in carriages.

Like the other imperial ladies, Xenia was heavily involved in charity work. She was a member of the Women's Patriotic

---

* Papa Michael lived to the age of seventy-seven, a record for male members of the imperial family.

Association; from 1903 patron of the Crêche Society, which looked after children of poor working-class families in St Petersburg while their parents were working; and was active on the commissions for the organization of tubercular hospitals in Yalta and boarding houses attached to the Yalta Alexandrovsky Gymnasium. Shortly after her betrothal she became patron of the Maritime Naval Welfare Association which provided help to the widows and children of seamen. At a fund-raising bazaar in March 1894 her mother donated three prizes for the raffle.

At the end of 1911 the Grand Duchess founded the Xenia Association for the Welfare of Children of Workers and Airmen. Among those on the board of this society were Vladimir Chatelain, Director of Sandro's Court, and Xenia's friend and lady-in-waiting Sophie Evreinoff. Xenia started the society with the gift of two significant donations of money from charities which had started during the Russo-Japanese war but were no longer operational. Irina also played her part, organizing a charity bazaar in December 1912 and a musical evening the following February, with proceeds from both going to the Xenia Association.

Xenia frequently received appeals for help. A typical example was a request from her aunt, Queen Olga of Greece:

You have probably received Doctor Baron Kosinsky's petition . . . to find a Government-supported place for his daughter at the Kiev Institute – if at all possible, I would like to entreat you to fulfil his request, as he is a very nice man who carries out his duties not just conscientiously, but with complete dedication. . . .

The worst thing of all was the fact that 4 or 5 years ago his wife left him and their three children and married somebody else. . . . He had to join up for the sake of his children and it is a very difficult and even daunting task to raise a girl without a mother and he sent her to a grammar school in Sevastopol but he is afraid that all the children who go there, whose parents come from various classes and professions, may have a bad influence on her upbringing.

He is afraid that the girl might succumb to such influences and her education will suffer. So, I am writing to you and implore you to help this worthy man.[21]

In 1894 Alexander III had founded the 'Xenia Institute', a boarding school for 350 middle-class students named in honour of his daughter. The school was housed from 1895 in the former palace of Grand Duke Nicholas Nicolaievich senior in Annunciation Square near St Petersburg's English Quay, which had been sold to the Ministry of the Court after the Grand Duke's death to cancel his massive debts, and the building was altered to give the girls spacious bedrooms, bathrooms, a sitting room and a large dining room. The Institute was placed under Xenia's patronage. She made informal visits two or three times a year and often found herself 'mobbed' by the girls as she descended the marble staircase to leave. One of the pupils recalled that the Grand Duchess was warm and gracious, made everyone feel that they mattered, and had her mother's knack of remembering names and faces.

Among the teachers was the father of the writer Edith Almedingen, who gave up his work at the university to teach chemistry at the Institute. Edith was admitted free as a 'Grand Ducal pupil', as it was 'H.I.H.'s personal wish' that she attend 'the school which owed so much to [her] father'. Xenia always made a short speech at the graduation ceremony. 'She spoke very little. She said so much,' recalled Miss Almedingen of Xenia's 1916 speech. 'She made 30 girls feel that faith in God and love for one's fellow man could overcome the knottiest difficulties in life.'[22] From 1906 to 1914 the Principal was Princess Eugenie Alexandrovna Galitzine, but Xenia remained the patron until the building was taken over by the Trades Union Council in 1917.

Xenia and Sandro were together and apparently united in Biarritz in the spring of 1910, where her uncle Bertie, King Edward VII, was staying. The social round of parties and balls continued, and at one costume ball Xenia wore the authentic coronation gown of Empress Josephine. Though the weather was bad and the King was in poor health, he seemed reluctant to leave and prolonged his stay for as long as possible. Nevertheless, Xenia was shocked to hear of her uncle's sudden death soon after his return home.

'Georgie – you poor dear – I do so feel for you, I can't tell you!' she wrote to the cousin who had just succeeded as King George V. 'It's too cruel, all so sudden & you must feel crushed! God help you to bear it all. And to think that we saw him, yr dear Father, only the other day – looking so well & pleased & full of life. *Everything* here does remind one so of him, the place is simply haunted by him! For years running we used to meet here & he was always so kind & nice to us.'[23]

Shortly afterwards Xenia paid her first visit to London, where she had a chance to meet Georgie's wife. 'May', Princess Victoria Mary of Teck, had originally been engaged to Georgie's brother Eddy. On his death in 1892, in an echo of Dagmar and Sasha, May had dutifully transferred her affections to Georgie and they were married in the summer of 1893. 'I was so glad to have seen you this summer,' George wrote to Xenia that Christmas, adding that 'now that you have at last been to England, I hope you will soon come again'.[24] Little did he know how poignant his words would seem one day.

Xenia was still torn between her husband and 'F'. Six happy if rather guilt-ridden months came to an end in November 1911, when they had one petty argument too many and 'F' told her it was time for him to go. He said he was 'sick of the whole set up and everything'.[25] She was depressed by his imminent departure and his refusal to leave Ai-Todor with the rest of the family; the gossiping had started, she knew, and the fault was theirs, but she resented not being able to choose her confidantes without constant criticism. Two weeks later he had packed and left, and Xenia was bitterly upset at not knowing when she would see him again.

All this travelling disguised Xenia and Sandro's growing concern over the situation in Russia and their increasingly cool relations with the Empress. Xenia's sympathies were all with her brother, who she felt was being misled on many aspects of government business because he was upset and preoccupied by his wife's health. Alix appeared to be suffering from heart trouble, but more than one observer felt that her illness was psychosomatic, brought on by the stress of Alexis's haemophilia. Court life had ceased, as Alexandra shut Nicky and the children into their own cloistered little world at Tsarskoe Selo, seeing few people.

For Xenia and Sandro the yearly round continued – Biarritz, Paris and Ai-Todor, spaced between visits to the Dowager Empress at Peterhof or Gatchina and occasional trips to Denmark. By now it was common knowledge in society that they were leading separate lives. Sandro was understood to have moved to a separate bedroom and Xenia reportedly looked 'ill and sad' in consequence.[26] Olga noticed that they were having 'serious disagreements'.[27]

Yet their marital disharmony was nothing to the family discord which followed the appearance of Grigory Rasputin, the lecherous, drunken Siberian peasant and self-proclaimed 'Holy Man' who was introduced to the Tsar and Tsarina in 1905. When Alexis suffered a haemorrhage, Rasputin prayed at his bedside and the flow of blood ceased. It was clear that his presence had a calming effect on Alicky.

Like nearly every other member of the family, Xenia was thoroughly sceptical about 'that sinister Grigory',[28] aware of the most appalling rumours about him, and tried to reason with Alicky but the latter would not listen. Maybe Xenia feared the close association between Rasputin and her sister-in-law and its effect on public opinion in Russia more than anything else. Her sister Olga came to his defence, telling her that she found it difficult not to believe in him when the Tsarevich felt better the moment Rasputin was near, or prayed for him, yet she too was appalled by the stories that came to her ears.

By 1911 Rasputin moved confidently in society and his influence could open almost any door. To the dismay of Xenia and other members of the family, he had begun to control Church appointments and the Empress was now asking him to evaluate potential ministers. Over dinner with the Youssoupovs, or at the Anitchkov with her mother, he was the only topic of conversation. In February 1912 the Dowager Empress decided to go to Tsarskoe Selo and talk to Nicholas, but her words had no effect. Ella, too, tackled Nicholas about Rasputin's influence. After her husband's assassination she had founded the Convent of Martha & Mary in Moscow, becoming its Abbess and devoting her life to the poor and needy. She had also heard the rumours about Rasputin, and after speaking to Nicholas, wrote a strongly worded letter to Xenia:

Ever so hearty thanks for your letter and news partly good and partly the old sad, sad words I have heard so often. To *him* I only spoke (of course, he tells her everything), as she being so far from well he did not like me doing so, but all of no good. . . .
. . . and now does not one feel a devilish atmosphere of spite

and filth and intrigue which like a black wave is now being over all washed by the different passions the false prophet 'a wolf in sheep's skin' has awakened. May God help and hear our prayers. . . . Now they are bitter and unjust and poor things that *nasty* little circle of flatterers who stick to them and keep up their unbelief in all who are true to them, is working hard to 'break our necks'. . . .

. . . kiss darling Mama and Sandro – I don't write to her as N. once tipped me 'please *never* speak with Mama about this. . . .[29]

Rumour was rife in St Petersburg about the nature of Rasputin's hold over the Empress, which most people assumed was sexual. Only in the spring of 1912 did Xenia learn from her sister that Alix had finally admitted Alexis had haemophilia, that the strain had made her ill and that she would never fully recover.

Easter 1912 was particularly lively in the Crimea, with dances at Livadia, Djulber and Harax. At Ai-Todor guests danced to the music of an accordion. The area around Ai-Todor had once been the site of a Roman fortress and Sandro had started a series of archaeological digs. Grand Duke Dmitri Pavlovich and the Tsar were among the most enthusiastic excavators, though Nicholas always complained that the most exciting things were discovered when he was not present. The most interesting finds – coins, vases, statues, even a third-century brick – were placed in a special museum.

Xenia remained close to Nicky. He still visited regularly, often walking over from Livadia with Olga and Tatiana. Alix was a less frequent guest and there was now a perceptible coolness between her and Xenia. Despite this, Xenia usually had a stall at the Empress's charity bazaar in Yalta, where other participants included Grand Duchess Militza, Greek Minny, Princess Youssoupov and Princess Barlatinsky. All money raised was donated to the numerous Crimean sanatoria.

Xenia left for her now usual summer visit to London with Irina, before moving on to join her mother in Denmark. While she was in Copenhagen, they learned that Alexis had suffered his most serious haemophiliac crisis ever, and was on the brink of death. As every bulletin brought worse news, Xenia could only comfort her mother and pray for a miracle. The miracle came in the form of a reassuring telegram to Alix from Rasputin. She immediately stopped worrying. Next day the bleeding ceased and Alexis began to recover.

Shortly afterwards both Xenia and the Dowager Empress were stunned to learn that Michael had married his twice-divorced mistress, Natasha Wulfert, by whom he already had a two-year-old son. Forbidden to marry by the Tsar, but fearing that if Alexis died Michael would be forced to make a more suitable marriage, they had slipped away and were married in the Serbian Orthodox Church in Vienna. Nicholas faced his brother with a stark choice – renounce his rights to the throne or divorce Natasha. When Michael flatly refused to do either, he and his wife were banished abroad.

Sandro's brother George now proposed that, as Alexis was ill and Michael had been banished, Xenia's children should inherit the rights of succession, effectively by-passing the children of Grand Duke Vladimir. It was also rumoured that, to mark the tercentenary of the Romanov dynasty in 1913, Nicholas was planning to raise the eldest son of each Grand Duke from Prince to Grand Duke, a move that would have affected Xenia's son Andrusha, but nothing came of either idea. As the hollow celebrations proceeded, Xenia was disturbed to note that Rasputin's presence once again seemed all-pervasive, much to the anger of the clergy.[30]

An anonymous observer has left a description of Xenia in those last years of peace. The Grand Duchess was 'very shy with strangers, which makes her at times appear stiff. She feels completely at ease only in her own intimate set. She has inherited her mother's lovely eyes and beautiful skin, but her manner lacks the latter's assurance. She dresses well and is very elegant in all her appointments. When she comes into a ballroom or a theatre, she tries to slip in without attracting too much attention.'[31] Rørdam, former Chamberlain to Christian IX, recalled that she was about the same height and figure as her mother, with the same eyes and a similar engaging smile.[32]

Lacking Dagmar's assurance in society, Xenia preferred informal dinners and dances at her palace on the Moika. She found the long celebrations for the tercentenary a strain, finishing the season exhausted in mind and body.

Under the circumstances Xenia played a major role in efforts to heal the family's wounds and forgive Michael. While the unforgiving Olga would not speak to him, let alone speak to or see Natasha, Xenia wanted to let bygones be bygones and bring about a reconciliation. Difficult marital experiences had made her more understanding of Michael's weaknesses than the rest of their siblings. Their cousin Grand Duke Andrei, who had a long-standing relationship with the dancer Mathilde Kschessinska, readily sympathized with Michael's predicament and cordially received him and Natasha in Cannes early in 1913. From there the couple went to Paris, staying at the Hotel Mirabeau. In March Michael telegraphed to Xenia in St Petersburg inviting her to come and see him in Paris next week. Though unable to travel that quickly she arranged to join him two weeks later. Before leaving she went to see the Tsar, and they talked a great deal about Michael's problems. Nicholas made it clear that he could return home whenever he wanted to, but Natasha was strictly forbidden from entering Russia.

Xenia met her brother in Paris on 19 March and they talked together for two hours. With tears in her eyes, she told him about the many crosses borne by their mother, who suffered from the severe winter, her health undermined by distress about the family about Michael himself, about 'Nicky' and the effect that Alexis's illness was having on them all. At this point, she noticed, he became particularly attentive, occasionally making a comment or asking a question. He defended his past behaviour by saying he could not have acted otherwise, suffered greatly 'for Mama' and deeply regretted having to break his word to Nicky. There were many more subjects that she would have liked to discuss, but they did not have enough time.[33]

Xenia stayed in Paris for a further three days, seeing Michael again just before she left to go to England. The parting tugged at her heartstrings, especially as she did not know when they would meet again. She found her brother's behaviour particularly touching, and was moved by his persistent gratitude for her coming to see him. It was 'hurtful and sad that he has slipped away from us again'.[34]

Upset by her son's complaints that nobody ever wrote or made an effort to keep in touch, the Dowager Empress made efforts to see him. In June Sandro's eldest brother Nicholas had arrived at

Xenia's Paris hotel with a confidential letter from Michael complaining bitterly about them all, that they did not write to him, and no longer cared about him or did anything he asked. A furious Xenia was 'completely destroyed for the whole day, the whole thing is untrue!'[35] A week later she received another long letter from her brother, still full of complaints. She also remarked that the Dowager Empress, then in London, had telegraphed, hoping he might come to England if it could be arranged. More in hope than expectation, Xenia wrote to him personally to try to fix a meeting. A week later she was in England with her mother, and spent a tearful session with her talking about Michael. She was desperate to see him, Xenia noted, and Sandro sent him a telegram saying he had to come.[36]

On 11 July Xenia travelled with the Dowager Empress from Sandringham to London, to be met at Liverpool Street Station by 'Prince F', ('Prince Finiken', the nickname of Prince Schervashidze, her mother's Grand Master of the Court) who said that he had seen Michael – with Natasha – 'and that he looked rather embarrassed for her!' Michael and Natasha were staying at the Ritz Hotel in Piccadilly and the Dowager Empress was at Marlborough House, where her widowed sister Dowager Queen Alexandra was living. It was within walking distance of the Ritz and Michael went there on foot for the first meeting, leaving Natasha behind. Their mother had been 'very agitated at the prospect of seeing him' and was so excited and upset at the prospect that she could not sleep. Despite her apprehension, their reunion passed off without any ill-feeling.

That evening Michael came back again, this time with Natasha, and he and his mother had another reasonable conversation, after which it was Natasha's turn to face the Dowager Empress Marie Feodorovna, and let her speak her mind. Natasha was a proud-spirited woman, but it was not the occasion for answering back, and all the nervous young woman could do was to ride out the storm. The Dowager Empress told her a few home truths in front of Michael, which she repeated to Xenia in his presence. Xenia was distressed at the breach between their mother and her brother, regretting the unpleasantness on all sides. Nevertheless another, more pressing piece of family business was about to occupy her mind.

At eighteen Xenia's daughter Irina was a beauty, and Grand Duke Dmitri considered himself a suitor for her hand. Like her mother, Irina was painfully shy. Invited to participate in a tennis tournament at Znamenka, Grand Duke Peter's estate near Peterhof, Irina was too shy to go on to the court when it came to her turn to play. In 1913 she announced her intention of marrying 26-year-old Prince Felix Youssoupov, much to the consternation of some of the elder generation. Xenia discussed the situation with her mother, who was unconvinced of Felix's suitability.

The son of Princess Zenaide Youssoupov, Felix was heir to the largest private fortune in Russia, the family having over forty estates scattered throughout the Russian Empire. He had a notorious past, including a sojourn of study at Oxford, experimenting with drugs, going out in public dressed in women's clothes (once, in Paris, so convincingly that even the wandering eye of King Edward VII was dazzled) and affairs with other men and women. Gossips in St Petersburg suggested that he and Grand Duke Dmitri had been lovers at one stage. Now, under pressure from his family to marry and produce an heir, Felix decided he had found his ideal woman in Princess Irina. With Irina's engagement hanging in the balance, Xenia left with the children for the Grand Hotel at Treport, near Dieppe, where 'F.' was staying. Sandro had gone to America, and Xenia was 'bothered and upset' to receive a letter saying he was really happy to be with his lady friend 'M.I.'. Sandro intended to return in a couple of weeks and take the children to St Petersburg, but he wanted to know whether Xenia preferred to go to Ai-Todor and return to Paris in November when M.I. would be there. The situation, she admitted, was very vague, but 'F.' was a great comfort at such moments of melancholy.[37]

They were reunited at Ai-Todor in the autumn. By now, Irina and Felix's engagement seemed to be an open secret, but doubts still remained. Xenia was alarmed at giving her blessing to a marriage between her daughter and a man with such a history, while Sandro heard gossip in Paris and wrote to her admitting he was 'very upset' by rumours about Felix's reputation. Nevertheless they were prepared to give him the benefit of the doubt. As there was no hurry, they felt obliged to put him to the test; if his behaviour proved satisfactory, then the wedding could proceed. If they heard anything unfavourable about him again, they were prepared to cancel the festivities.

Irina had led a very sheltered life. She and her mother were ordering the trousseau and Felix was to meet them in Paris. Xenia was more prepared to be sceptical about the gossip, while the more worldly Sandro, suspecting there was no smoke without fire, sent Count Mordvinoff to ask Felix what truth there was in these stories. Felix assured him that his wild days were all in the past, and, as Sandro was on the verge of cancelling the wedding, he went straight to the hotel where they were staying and persuaded them to change their minds. Meanwhile, also perturbed by the rumours, the Dowager Empress summoned Felix to Denmark, determined to decide the matter. Xenia and Irina had already arrived at the royal palace, Amalienborg, in Copenhagen. After lunch, during which the Dowager Empress observed Felix keenly, she took him into an adjoining room. Aware that Irina was her favourite granddaughter, Felix used all his considerable personal charm. When the verdict came, it was favourable. 'Do not worry, I will do all that I can for your happiness,'[38] she said.

The formal betrothal took place on 22 December with a Te Deum attended by both families and members of the Grand Ducal household. Fifteen-year-old Feodor was particularly hostile to Felix, and Xenia was afraid he would not attend. He duly arrived with a very sour expression on his face that made Xenia want to burst into tears.

Sandro had given the young couple a piece of land on the Ai-Todor estate, where they chose a spot to build a house. In St Petersburg they would occupy a ground-floor wing of the Youssoupov Palace on the Moika Embankment. Felix also gave his fiancée a small house near the Youssoupov estate of Kokoz in the Crimea, consisting of one large room and a small bedroom. The two mothers were quite overcome by this touching gift, but Irina was too shy to thank Felix properly, until Xenia persuaded her to kiss her husband-to-be.

A few days before the wedding Irina received her presents, most of them purchased by Xenia from Cartier: a sapphire necklace; Xenia's emerald brooch with diamonds and rubies; three pearl sprays and a diamond chain with a large pearl at the end; a diamond and pearl brooch from the Dowager Empress; and some loose emeralds for the diadem Felix had ordered for his bride. Before the marriage, Irina had to renounce her rights to the throne, as Felix was not of royal blood.

The wedding took place on 9 February. As Irina was not a Grand Duchess she did not have to wear all the heavy imperial regalia. Instead she was attired in a white satin gown embroidered with silver, with a long train, and a tiara of rock crystal and diamonds made by Cartier, which held Xenia's wedding veil in place. Xenia and Sandro blessed Irina in their bedroom before she set out for the Anitchkov Palace in a state coach drawn by four white horses.

The bride was given away by the Tsar and preceded by Prince Vassili, who acted as Icon Boy. 'Whenever we came to a place where I didn't know the way to go, the Emperor would prod me with his knee in the right direction,' he recalled years later.[39] Xenia walked behind with Sandro and her mother. In the small chapel, which the Danish Ambassador's wife thought not much larger than an ordinary sitting room, Grand Duke Dmitri was among six bridesmen holding the golden crowns. In the middle of the ceremony, the nervous bride dropped her handkerchief and Anastasia darted forward to pick it up.

Afterwards there was a champagne reception in the Winter Garden and a wedding breakfast of *blinis* (Russian pancakes), consommé, roe cutlets and a baked apple dessert, all served on solid gold plates. Male guests were given a pale blue satin bag embroidered with the bridal pair's initials, containing almonds; ladies, a blue and white fan inscribed 'Anitchkov, 1914'. Throughout the day Xenia tried hard to contain her emotions, but it required a considerable effort of will, and she was relieved when it was all over.

At 6pm Xenia and Sandro returned home, where they welcomed the newly-weds with the traditional offering of bread and salt. Then they had tea for the last time together, before accompanying Felix and Irina to the station. Xenia felt the departure of her daughter keenly, bemoaning how empty the house seemed after the excitement and bustle of the previous few days, and how painful it was to realize she would never be coming back as their unmarried child.

6 (1914–17)
'. . . if dear Papa were
still alive?'

After Irina and Felix had gone on honeymoon, Xenia and Sandro returned to Ai-Todor, a feeling of sadness in their hearts that the colours of spring for once failed to dispel. Prince Feodor did his best to lift their spirits as he recorded the season's guests with his camera – the Tsar with his elder daughters and his sister Olga; Grand Duke and Duchess George; Prince Schervashidze, Grand Master of the Court of the Dowager Empress; and the younger Grand Duchess Marie Pavlovna, who had returned from Sweden after the break-up of her marriage. Little did any of them realize that it was to be their last stay at Ai-Todor in peacetime.

By June Xenia and Sandro were staying at the Piccadilly Hotel in London, where the season was in full swing. Xenia's mother was staying with her sister Queen Alexandra at Marlborough House; Felix and Irina arrived on the latest stage of their wedding tour, and took up residence in his Knightsbridge flat; Grand Duchess George was staying at Claridges with her daughters Nina and Xenia, on their way to Harrogate to take the cure.

On 28 June (NS) the heir to the Austro-Hungarian Empire, Archduke Franz Ferdinand, and his morganatic wife Sophie, paid an official visit to the Bosnian capital, Sarajevo. For Gavrilo Princip, one of the young Serbian anarchists motivated by a burning hatred of the Habsburgs, it was a providential moment, and the bullets from his revolver which claimed the lives of the heir and his wife would prove to be the most fateful assassination of the era. Although all heads of state and governments throughout Europe were shocked by the crime, very few realized it would lead to war. Sandro later claimed with hindsight in his memoirs that he had long been aware of what he called 'the suicide of a continent',[1] and that 'the common sense of the nations "happened" to be on leave'.[2] While he was probably less well informed at the time than his memoirs made out, he tried – and failed – to impress Xenia and her mother with the seriousness of the situation. With despair in his heart he left for Constanza, where he had arranged to be met by a cruiser from the Black Sea Fleet. Xenia went to France, while the Empress remained in London with her sister. Irina and Felix left to meet his parents in Kissingen.

Fane had returned from Bordeaux where his sister was very ill and Xenia arranged to meet him at Vittel, where she was taking the waters. He was ostensibly to act as her gentleman-in-waiting. After the gossip in 1911 he refused to go to Ai-Todor again, to Xenia's disappointment.

Increasingly urgent telegrams passed from one European head of state to another, but it was clear that the Russian, German and Austrian Emperors no longer trusted one anothers' governments, and matters had passed the bounds of monarchical diplomacy. On 1 August (NS) Tsar Nicholas II mobilized his army. Increasingly urgent messages from Russia and the Russian Ambassador, Count Alexander Benkendorff, persuaded the Dowager Empress that she must go home without delay. Next day Austria, France and Germany mobilized and Germany declared war on Russia. The Tsar dispatched a telegram to King George V, entreating him to support France and Russia in fighting to maintain the balance of power in Europe. It never reached its destination, but it proved unnecessary, as by then Britain had declared war on Germany.

Xenia had to leave Fane at Vittel. During the war he served with the British army in France. Xenia hoped he could be sent to Russia on some kind of mission and to this end she corresponded with the British Royal family, without success. The affair appears not to have been rekindled after the war.

After arranging to meet Xenia at Calais, Dagmar bade an emotional farewell to her sister. Grand Duchess George decided to stay in London with her daughters. In France Xenia was delayed as her attendants had lost all their luggage. When the Dowager Empress arrived for the rendezvous at Calais, where her private train was waiting, to her dismay there was no sign of her daughter. She pressed on towards the Belgian border, to cries of 'Vive la Russie!' all along the route, where she finally met up with

Xenia. Though both ladies had been confident that the Kaiser would let them pass through Germany, when they reached Berlin they found the line to Russia already closed.

Determined not to appeal to the Kaiser for help, the Empress and Xenia sat in the train in stifling heat surrounded by armed guards. As word of their arrival spread, the Russian imperial insignia on the train became a popular target for insult, and through closed curtains they could hear the ribald songs and jibes of crowds on the platform. They were unaware that only the Kaiser's fear of international repercussions had prevented their internment. Hearing that the Youssoupovs had reached Berlin and were in danger of imminent arrest, the Empress tried to send a message to them to join the train. Crowds were smashing the windows and tearing down the curtains, and when one of the retainers tried to go out for food the sentries thrust him roughly back. Seeing a group of stranded Russians huddled together on the platform, Dagmar ordered her staff to bring them on board immediately. At length Count Mirbach of the Ministry of Foreign Affairs appeared, told Dagmar that Russia had declared war on Germany (which, she informed him, was a lie), and gave her a choice of going back via England, Holland or Switzerland, or proceeding directly to Denmark. She chose the latter, and they left after a two-hour delay without being able to wait for the Youssoupovs. The journey was a nightmare, their carriages packed with the large imperial retinue and stranded Russians whom the Empress refused to leave behind. Soldiers with fixed bayonets guarded the locked doors, and their slow progress was frequently halted to let troop trains pass. In this overcharged atmosphere it was a relief to reach the Danish frontier.

At Klampenborg station the Russian Minister, Baron Buxhoeveden, was waiting on the platform with King Christian X and Queen Alexandrine. Though glad to be back at Hvidøre Dagmar had no intention of staying; with reports of unrest in Finland, they had to get home. While making preparations, Xenia heard that the Youssoupovs had arrived at the Hotel d'Angleterre after an eleventh-hour escape with the departing Russian Ambassador. Xenia and her mother, both 'extremely agitated' by the recent happenings, immediately drove over to see them. Irina was unwell and expecting her first child, but the Dowager Empress decided they must return to Russia immediately.

By the first few days of August (NS), every major European power had taken one side or other. Germany declared war on France and marched into Belgium; Austria declared war on Russia; and England entered the conflict alongside Russia and France. In neutral Denmark arrangements were made to take the Dowager Empress and Xenia home via Finland. Crossing by ferry to Sweden, they travelled by train to Stockholm and then transferred to cars for the journey to Torneo, close to the Arctic Circle, where the old Finnish imperial train, not used since the days of Alexander III, was waiting. Just before their arrival, the triumphal arch erected at the Finnish customs house collapsed in a thunderstorm, an accident which many saw as a bad omen.

They sat at the station as one delay followed another. While Xenia and her mother were having tea, a train arrived from Russia and they were surprised to see familiar faces approaching – Princess Victoria of Battenberg and her daughter Louise, who had been visiting the Tsarina. There was just time for a few words through the open window before the Battenbergs hurried across the footbridge into Sweden. Finally the train moved off on what was to become a triumphal progress through Finland. The Dowager Empress was still extremely popular with the Finns, and Xenia could bask in her mother's reflected glory. On 27 July (OS) they reached Peterhof after a nine-day journey across Europe.

Sandro's journey had been almost as eventful. Travelling through Austria, the Orient Express had been stopped at Vienna where the passengers were forced to wait for several hours while negotiations took place, and at length consent was given for the train to proceed to the Roumanian border. Sandro then had to walk several miles to meet the special train provided for him by the Roumanian government. In Constanza he found his old ship the *Almaz* waiting to transport him to Yalta.

Reunited with Sandro in the capital, Xenia and her family moved to the Yelagin Palace with the Dowager Empress. She had lost no time in telling Nicholas that in time of war his brother's place was at home. Michael had already asked permission to come back with his family, and after travelling across Norway, Sweden and Finland he was reunited with his mother and sister on 11 August. Reconciled with the Tsar, he was given command of a division in Galicia and later awarded the Order of St George for bravery. Although they were pleased to see Misha, his wife was not so welcome. Grand Duke Paul had also returned, demanding a better title for his morganatic wife. Alicky feared Michael would do the same, and Natasha was never officially received by the imperial family.

Xenia and Sandro shared Dagmar's distress at the family's being on opposite sides in the conflict. In England Aunt Alix was an ally, but Aunt Thyra was not, as her only surviving son Ernst August, who succeeded to his father's Duchy of Brunswick, was married to the Kaiser's daughter Victoria Louise. In Greece Xenia's cousin King Constantine was neutral, but his Queen consort was the Kaiser's sister Sophie. Though there had never been any love lost between Sophie and her eldest brother in Berlin, he spared no effort in trying to enlist their support for Germany. Alicky's brother Ernie, Grand Duke of Hesse and the Rhine, and her sister Irene, wife of the Kaiser's only surviving brother Henry, were in Germany; her eldest sister Victoria was married to Prince Louis of Battenberg, First Sea Lord in England.

Sandro had one brother in England. Miche-Miche and his wife Sophie had rented Ken Wood, on Hampstead Heath, where he entertained a succession of royal relatives and became president of several local associations. On the outbreak of war he offered his services to the Tsar, 'burning', he said, to return to Russia at this 'sacred hour'. The offer, which was unlikely to have been accepted, was soon rescinded for health reasons.[3] His sister Anastasia, widowed Grand Duchess of Mecklenburg-Schwerin, who managed to reach neutral Switzerland, was the mother of Queen Alexandrine of Denmark and of Cecilie, German Crown Princess. Barely a dynasty had any siblings whose loyalties were not bitterly divided in similar manner.

The old world of international family gatherings, last seen in all its glory at the wedding of Ernst August and Victoria Louise at Berlin in May 1913, was now a mere memory of a golden age swept away. For the next few years, the only way royal cousins, brothers and sisters could receive news of their relatives in the opposing camp would be through the neutral courts of Scandinavia, largely through Crown Princess Margaret of Sweden and Dagmar's nephew Prince Aage, who passed on family news from Denmark and reports on her beloved Hvidøre.

Russia was in no state to shoulder the burden of a prolonged conflict. The distances involved and her incomplete railways were barriers to effective mobilization, while reserves of rifles and ammunition were severely limited with field guns, heavy artillery and shells in pitifully short supply. A British military observer arriving in the empire was horrified to notice 1,800 raw infantry replacements arriving at the front during one attack, none with his own rifle. They had been sent to reserve trenches to wait until casualties in the firing line would make rifles available. Only in manpower was the empire supreme, with more than 1,400,000 men mobilized and another 1,300,000 reserves. The Germans knew their hopes of victory rested on crushing France before the 'Russian steamroller' could turn on them, and within a month they were only 30 miles north of Paris. A wave of anti-German hysteria swept over St Petersburg: German-owned shops were looted and the embassy was sacked. In August the Tsar changed the German name of St Petersburg to the Slavic Petrograd.

Sandro left for the front, assigned by the Commander-in-Chief Grand Duke Nicholas Nicolaievich ['Nicholasha'] to be 'stationed in the headquarters of the fourth army as a collaborator of its commander Baron Saltza', a former ADC of Sandro's father.[1] Soon afterwards, Irina caught measles, the family went into quarantine and it was mid-December before Xenia could move from Yelagin. She and the Dowager Empress spent a lonely Christmas Eve together, without the company of Nicholas, who was ill. The war was going badly for Russia. Losses were astronomical and, despite the initial burst of patriotism, morale was sinking.

Like other imperial ladies, Xenia turned her attention to war work. She supervised a large hospital for wounded and convalescent soldiers and equipped her own hospital train, which in July 1915 alone carried 77 wounded officers and 1,677 lower ranks. The Grand Duchess also made regular visits to her regiment, the 15th Ukrainsky Hussars, where she was photographed in 1915, and to the Youssoupov hospital, established in Princess Zenaide's large house on the Liteiny Prospekt. In addition she chaired the 'Xenia Committee', administered by G.G. Witte from the Ministry of Internal Affairs, which issued artificial limbs to disabled ex-servicemen and trained them in a trade or craft which would enable them to earn a living. She also supervised a storeroom for medical supplies. Olga became a nurse and Alicky enrolled on a nursing course with her elder daughters, doing even the most menial jobs in the hospital at Tsarskoe Selo.

On 8 March 1915 Irina gave birth to a daughter. She was named Irina after her mother, but always called Bébé. Despite the assistance of Mme Glinst, the midwife, poor Irina suffered terribly but bravely tried to lessen her own mother's anxiety. Nicky and Alix were amused, the latter noting, 'It would have seemed more natural, had I heard that Xenia herself had borne a Baby. . . .'[5] In an undated letter to a friend many years later, Xenia said she 'was proud to be a grandmother at 39'.[6] At Bébé's christening in the Youssoupov Chapel on 28 March the priest performed the ceremony very badly; Bébé swallowed a lot of water and Xenia's first grandchild nearly drowned in the baptismal font.

In April Xenia visited newly conquered Lvov, the capital of Galicia, where Olga was nursing at the hospital. On the 10th, both sisters were waiting behind the guard of honour when Nicholas arrived to address the troops from the riding school balcony. After having dinner with his sisters, Nicholas left. One member of the family they did not see was Misha, who had fallen out with Olga over his marriage. Though his headquarters were not far from Lvov, which he had visited several times, he was not invited, and only learnt of Nicholas's visit from the newspapers.

Back in Petrograd, Xenia frequently visited Alix during Nicky's absence at the front, or had lunch with Irina at the Youssoupovs' Moika Palace. She attended committee meetings with her brother-in-law Grand Duke George and Alexis Polivanov, head of the General Staff, and paid frequent visits to her mother, who was in a terrible state over the war and often could not stop crying. On 22 July there was a tea party in honour of the Dowager Empress's Name Day. Xenia, Sandro and Nicky came with all their children. Only Alix was absent.

By now Nicholas, urged on by Alix and Rasputin, had decided he would take personal command of the army. In Nicholas's absence the government would be in the hands of the Tsarina and her 'evil genius'. The family were horrified, and at Yelagin the Dowager Empress pleaded with him not to take this drastic step, but to no avail.

On 18 August Xenia accompanied her mother to Tsarskoe Selo,

'to try my luck,' as the Dowager Empress wrote in her diary.[7] Nicholas was at Kronstadt and did not return until 7pm. Meanwhile, they had tea with Alix, who spoke about everything except what was uppermost in their minds. To their frustration, when Nicholas returned, the conversation again had no result, and the family put this down to the influence of Alix and Rasputin. In May Princess Zenaide Youssoupov had visited Yelagin and implored the family to protest about Rasputin's malign influence over the Empress.

Xenia returned to live at Yelagin with her mother, Feodor, Nikita and Rostislav. Feodor was thin and unwell, while Andrei and Dmitri were in the Crimea with Irina, who was also in poor health. Xenia was reported to be 'fidgety' because her children were separated. Alix was now concerned at opposition coming from Yelagin, particularly from Prince Schervashidze, who she believed was turning her mother-in-law and Xenia against her, 'instead of keeping them up bravely and squashing gossip'.[8]

After a brief stay at Ai-Todor, Xenia went to Kiev to visit Olga, whose hospital had moved there after the reverses earlier in the year, and to see Sandro, now stationed there as head of Military Aviation. She was still there when Nicholas visited on 14 December, and they spent a happy couple of hours having tea in his train.

Xenia returned to Petrograd for Christmas but by the New Year she was unwell. Dr Brunner diagnosed influenza. To her delight Sandro visited, but found his wife very weak and even ten days later she was only able to get up for part of the day. Then the Dowager Empress was taken ill, so Xenia was deprived of her mother's company for several days. When Nicky's daughters came to tea on 14 January they found their aunt still looking unwell.

When Sandro returned to Petrograd in February Xenia was able to walk for a little while in the garden. A month later she was feverish again and unable to go out, but received daily visits from her mother. Alix told Nicky that 'she and Motherdear ought to go to Kiev for 2 weeks to get a change and have their rooms, which are full of microbes, thoroughly aired'.[9] By March Xenia had been in bed again for a week with a cold but she was unable to leave Petrograd, as Nikita had undergone an operation on his ear. Concerned, Alix visited Xenia's palace for the first time in two years.

As Xenia prepared to go south to Ai-Todor, she heard from her sister in Kiev, where their mother was also now living. Her patience exhausted by the interference of Alix and Rasputin in government affairs and the conduct of the war, the Dowager Empress had established herself in Rastrelli's Baroque-style Maryinsky Palace on the right bank of the River Dnieper, where she found the atmosphere more to her liking. Inside, among the twenty-six richly decorated suites and rooms on the first floor, were many grand reception rooms with glazed tiled stoves and parquet floors, including the Green Room, the Baroque Hall and the White Ballroom, which formed the central hall of the palace.

'Your Mama is here. We met her at the station . . . then we went to St Sophia's Cathedral, . . .' Olga told Xenia on 5 May. 'Our rooms are not nice – awful furniture, stuffy air in the bedroom because there are curtains round the bed and soft awful dark blue chinz. 6th May. Couldn't write a line. I shall never be able to any more! Of course I *might* write there [the Maryinsky Palace] but as you also know Mama would want at once to read it – so I won't. We have more work and are occupied till 1 [pm] and at 2 I already start [for the hospital] to get there at 3 (I walk for exercise as we don't have the garden). . . . Sandro will tell you bits so I needn't write. . . .

'I kiss you and Nikita awfully much. . . . Have the time of your life there in your dear Crimea. Sorry you were pestered with people coming and living with you! One is my fault perhaps!'[10]

Xenia was able to see the situation for herself when she spent two weeks with the Dowager Empress in July, also visiting Sandro and Olga. Earlier in the year she had discussed with Olga her sister's wish to ask for an annulment of her marriage, so she could marry Nicholas Kulikovsky. They both now agreed that it would be better to proceed while everyone's minds were on the war. Olga began petitioning the Tsar and, when her wish was finally granted, Xenia received a full report of the November wedding from her mother.

In the autumn of 1916 Xenia, described as looking 'sad and poorly',[11] arrived at Ai-Todor where the children were unwell. Irina was staying nearby at Koreiz, with Felix's parents. The Grand Duchess remained in the Crimea throughout the autumn, as the situation in Petrograd deteriorated.

Xenia was becoming increasingly distressed at the direction of Russia under her brother's rule. 'What would have happened if dear Papa were still alive?' she wrote to the Dowager Empress on 28 October. 'Would there have been war – disorder, intellectual ferment, dissents – in a word, everything that is happening, or not – I think not – at least *much of it* would not be taking place, and that we can say with certainty.'[12]

On the insistence of the Dowager Empress and her daughters, Grand Duke Nicholas Michaelovich wrote to the Tsar warning him about Alix's influence in government affairs. The Tsar gave the unopened letter to his wife, who responded with a hysterical outburst accusing the Grand Duke of 'crawling behind your mother and sisters'.[13]

Little information reached Xenia at Ai-Todor. The newspapers contained almost no political news and all letters, even those from the Dowager Empress, were tampered with by the Secret Police. She had planned to visit her mother, who was about to celebrate the fiftieth anniversary of her arrival in Russia as a bride, but when the moment came she was unable to travel as Irina, who had moved to Ai-Todor, was ill in bed. By Irina's own admission, the illness was probably neurasthenia, but in an almost hysterical letter to Felix she said she could not leave the Crimea. Luckily, Bébé had remained at Koreiz with Princess Zenaide.

At least Xenia had all her children under one roof, an increasingly rare occurrence these days. Andrusha had joined the army and been promoted to an officer in the prestigious Chevalier Guards during 1916; Feodor and Nikita had enrolled in the Corps des Pages and were photographed in the distinctive black tunic with gold collar and cuffs, black trousers with a thin red line and the obligatory white gloves.

By now the imperial family were united in the belief that Rasputin must be sent away and Alexandra's interference in government affairs must cease. Some of them decided to take matters into their own hands. One evening in mid-December 1916 Rasputin was lured to a room in the Youssoupovs' Moika Palace in Petrograd on the pretext of meeting Irina. It was part of a conspiracy organized by Prince Felix Youssoupov, the Tsar's cousin Grand Duke Dmitri Pavlovich, and the right-wing Duma deputy Vladimir Purishkevich. Felix plied him with poisoned cakes and wine, and when this failed to work the desperate Youssoupov shot him in the back. A few further bullets were necessary to dispatch him, and his body was wrapped in a curtain, secured with rope and pushed through a hole in the ice on the River Neva. He was found three days later.

As the mother-in-law of one of those responsible, Xenia was thoroughly embarrassed by the episode. Perhaps the most disturbing aspect was the fact that, on the night of the murder, Felix was staying at her Petrograd palace while his new apartments were being finished. Her three eldest sons had also returned there. According to Felix's own account, when he returned to his mother-in-law's palace at 5 o'clock the next morning, he was met and questioned by Feodor. It was even rumoured that both Feodor and Nikita had been present in the Moika Palace on the night of the murder, though they certainly never admitted it. The Danish Ambassador's wife also heard that four women were present. It was at Xenia's palace that the police interviewed Felix the morning after the murder and, after trying to leave by train with his brothers-in-law to join Irina in the Crimea, it was to Xenia's palace that he was returned and kept under guard.

Xenia was staying with her mother in Kiev when she heard the news, as she wrote in her diary on 18 December (OS):

> Slept little. There is a rumour that Rasputin is murdered! Already yesterday evening and today towards the evening there is talk that the murderer was Felix! . . . God knows what is happening and do not know what to believe . . . there was not any extra news all day. . . .
>
> Feodor and Nikita were going to the Crimea yesterday with Felix. . . .
>
> Later went to Mama. Olga came. . . . She is already f.w.!! [Olga was pregnant.] She is feeling a bit sick – so soon! . . . I will be an Aunt!
>
> . . . There is a different mood about Rasputin's murder by Felix. There is talk only about that.[14]

Although Andrusha and Feodor remained with Felix, it was decided that Nikita should go to Ai-Todor with his tutor Mr Stewart. Felix moved to the palace of his fellow conspirator Grand

Duke Dmitri. Rumours that Rasputin was killed in the Youssoupovs' Moika Palace had already reached Xenia.

> Schervashidze came in the morning. Now . . . [it has] become clear that Felix himself and only himself in person killed him. . . .
>
> Everybody here is rejoicing and everywhere is celebration that he was killed! This is terrible! I do not know what to think, they say everybody was questioned!
>
> It looks like the murder had taken place in Youssoupov's house. The body was thrown from Petrovski Bridge opposite Krestovski! Everything is so terribly twisted. . . .[15]

While Sandro could not be expected to shed any tears for Rasputin, he was one of the first to recognize that an event which looked at first like deliverance would create more problems than it solved. The Dowager Empress was mortified that her granddaughter's husband and her nephew should have stooped to murder, and as a Christian she was firmly opposed to the shedding of blood.

The family were united in asking Sandro to go and plead the case of the murderers before Nicky. He had already intended to do so, although with misgivings. Secretly 'nauseated' by 'their ravings and cruelty', he thought that they were behaving as if they expected their sovereign to decorate them for having committed murder.[16] Nevertheless he asked the Tsar not to treat them as common murderers, but rather as misguided patriots inspired by a desire to help their country. Matters were made even worse when Princess Youssoupov sent an ill-considered letter to Xenia, stating that although as Felix's mother she felt her son's position deeply, she congratulated the Grand Duchess on her husband's conduct in the affair, implying that he had saved the whole situation as his request for immunity for all concerned would have to be granted. Her only regret was that the principals had been unable to bring their enterprise to the desired end, and that there still remained the task of confining 'Her', namely the Tsarina. This message was intercepted by the Minister of the Interior, who took it to the Tsar.[17]

The imperial family then presented a joint letter to Nicholas, asking for leniency for the conspirators, especially Dmitri who was in indifferent health. The Tsar replied that nobody had the right to kill, yet the punishments he administered were relatively light. Dmitri was sent to the Persian front, a banishment from Russia which ironically was to save his life, while Felix was exiled to his country estate near Kursk.

It fell to those still left behind to watch the final dismembering of the Russian Empire and the fall of the dynasty.

7 (1917)

'Poor little Xenia'

Xenia had returned to Ai-Todor, and was still there early in January 1917 when she received what she considered a strange letter from Felix, asking her not to regard the murderer of Rasputin as a criminal but 'an instrument of Providence'.[1] She asked Irina to return with her to Petrograd, but she replied from Kursk that Felix forbade it, as he felt it was too dangerous. The investigators into Rasputin's murder had recently interviewed Felix and she gave Xenia an account of their visit.

Sharing the rest of the family's exasperation at the Tsarina's meddling, Xenia fervently wished her mother could be more assertive and do what she could to help save the empire, even if it was only a word in the ear of a son who might just listen to her when he would take advice from nobody else but his misguided wife. 'If you speak you must and shall be listened to', she wrote in despair; 'if things don't change it will be the end of everything. People seem to have put their last hope in you and if that fails – it may only be fatal.'[2]

The Tsarina's attitude towards her sister-in-law was one of condescension and pity. 'Poor little Xenia with such boys and her daughter married into that wicked family – and with such a false husband.'[3]

Almost at the end of her tether, Dagmar told Xenia that she could see no future other than being flung into the abyss. She had no intention of returning to live in Petrograd, preferring to remain in Kiev, shielded from intrigues and hoping against hope that Nicholas, from whom she now received letters very rarely, would stop following his wife's disastrous counsel. Sandro and Felix hoped that once the Tsar went back to the front, they and the Dowager Empress could go to Petrograd, call for the arrest of Protopopov and Shcheglovaty, Chairman of the State Council, and demand that Alicky and her confidante Anna Vyrubova be sent to the Crimea. Only thus, Felix felt, could disaster be avoided.

When Princess Julia Cantacuzene lunched with Xenia she passed on all the latest news from Petrograd. Shortly afterwards Grand Duke Dmitri Constantinovich came over from his nearby estate of Kishkine, where he and his niece Princess Tatiana Constantinovna were staying. He read Xenia the text of the family's letter to Nicholas, calling it an 'unfortunate move' which discredited the family in the Tsar's eyes. Dmitri 'suggested to go to Stavka [military headquarters] when *she* is away, otherwise there is *no point*. One *can't argue with her.*'[4]

On 19 February, leaving her younger sons at Ai-Todor, Xenia returned to her Petrograd palace. Two days later she wrote to her mother that Nicky was leaving that afternoon for Stavka. 'Perhaps you can now travel to him and see him alone.'[5] Unfortunately, the time for action was fast running out. By remaining in the capital with Andrei and Feodor throughout the disturbances, Xenia was on hand to see and hear the mounting problems. In her diary she charted the increasingly ominous chain of events:

24 February: 'There is disorder in the factories, they are demanding bread, there were some clashes with the police and Cossacks, they say there are some dead. . . .'[6]

Winter shortages of food and fuel provoked street demonstrations, and by 25 February more than 200,000 workers were on strike, marching defiantly through Petrograd shouting anti-war and anti-government slogans.

Xenia continued:

25 February: 'There are disturbances in the city, there was even shooting into the crowd, [they] say, but everything is quiet on Nevsky. They are asking for *bread** and the factories are on strike.'[7]

26 February: 'The disturbances are taking a bad turn. The workers in the factories are on strike and walking around the streets. There was shooting into the crowd again and there are a lot of wounded and killed. Terrible!'[8]

Late one afternoon, as the elder boys were being driven back to the Moika, a band of ruffians recognized the Grand Duchess's car.

---

* Words and phrases in italics in Xenia's diary entries are in English in the original. The rest are translated from Russian.

Running after it, they hurled snowballs as they shouted, 'Down with the dirty bourgeois.'[9]

It was a sign of things to come.

27 February: 'It is terrible what is happening. The shooting is already everywhere. They looted the armoury factory on Liteiny. They freed life-imprisoned criminals, . . . many regiments joined the revolution and are already mixing in the crowd. The guns were taken from many officers and some have been killed, many policemen were killed yesterday. . . . A Provisional Committee was formed in which are: Shingarev, Miliukov, Chkheidse, Kerensky, Shulgin . . . Rodzianko at the top!'[10]

By the following day things were taking a turn for the worse. 'We are sitting locked indoors', Xenia wrote:

'It seems that all Petersburg garrison took the side of the revolution. The 4th Infantry Regiment came from Tsarskoe and also joined the revolution. . . . The appeal came out and was pasted around to call for order and forbid shooting. . . . All political petty thieves etc are released from Lidovskoi Castle, they managed to . . . free everybody and they burned it down . . . so in the evening there was a massive glow. All day we heard shooting, they say that they tend to shoot more with blank cartridges. But in our garden and in the courtyard something is clicking all the time. In spite of all moods the crowd is in good spirits and does not want to rob anybody but the police continue . . . to shoot into the crowd with automatic guns from the roof! Of course they . . . wanted to burn the Maryinsky Theatre because the gun was on the roof and also it was on the Synagogue. I wrote a note to Rodzianko begging him to do [illegible]. . . . Petrov went to the Duma at 3.00 and came back at 10.00 with the answer. . . .

. . . We have the gates open and the public go through. . . . Mitia Dn [Dmitri Daehn was living at Xenia's palace] is languishing here but cannot go to Tsarskoe. The officers are disarmed on the streets so he and Papochka* do not go out from the house and all of us are wandering around all day and

---

* Unidentified, but possibly Prince Dmitri Orbeliani, Sandro's ADC, or one of the children's tutors.

languishing terribly. . . . I did not think and did not predict that we would have to live through such shame and horror' It would be great if Rodzianko could hold everything. . . .[11]

As the Imperial Guards joined the revolution and Cossacks refused to fire on the crowd Tsar Nicholas II, 500 miles away and unaware of the seriousness of the situation, refused to grant a ministry responsible to the Duma. Too late, he tried to return to the capital but his train was stopped on the way and he diverted to Pskov.

Xenia's diary entries for the next few days show how totally unprepared she was for the devastating news to come. On 1 March she wrote:

There is no end of the nightmare and there are such rumours going around I do not know whom to believe. There is talk that Nicky's train has been stopped in Bologoe, by whom? And after on Dno station he has been forced to abdicate!! I found out about it from Rumenski. . . . My God I cannot believe it, is it the truth? I am not going to cope . . . *Gave vent to my feelings and wept furiously.* Kind Vera [Orbeliani, wife of Sandro's ADC] caught me in this way and sat with me calming me down. I did not even have any dinner because of the headache.[12]

A day later, the family were becoming increasingly desperate:

It is a terrible horror that you can't wake up from! Talk continues all the time that Nicky has *abdicated* to the advantage of [Alexis] . . . and will be given to Mama and Misha will be Regent. God knows what it is all about and how it is all possible! How poor Misha could do it and at the same time (if it is all this way) how not to accept it for the sake of Russia? All this does not go into my head (I have a splitting headache all the time!) There is talk that the Social Revolutionaries want to have a Republic. . . .

Misha wrote to me two words in answer to my letter but does not write anything about what is going on but only the rumours that Nicky is in Pskov. The Mayor of Pskov is saying that he is in Tsarskoe! I do not know what and who to believe.

Buchanan was here in the morning . . . but does not know anything. . . . Started to receive telegrams. Received one from poor Mama asking what is going on with us and where is Nicky. Also from Irina. . . .[13]

As Rodzianko and the Duma assumed power, Nicholas, far away in Pskov, finally realized that it was now too late for concessions. Unwilling to plunge his country into civil war, he took the course urged on him by the Duma and the generals, and abdicated in favour of Alexis on 2 March. Within hours, afraid that he and Alix would be separated from their sick son, he changed the deed of abdication in favour of Michael.

Xenia's worst fears were confirmed the following day:

'Of course they got what they wanted – Nicky abdicated from the throne. My God! . . . give him strength to go through all this. Poor, poor one, what he has gone through, only God knows! . . .'[14]

Aware only that he was to be regent for his nephew, Misha was staying at Princess Olga Poutiatine's apartment on Millionaya, near the Winter Palace. Next day the ministers arrived to inform him he was to be Tsar. With anti-monarchist feelings high, and aware that his safety could not be guaranteed, Michael signed a manifesto stating that he would not accept authority until invited to do so by an elected Constituent Assembly.

Later that same day, Xenia's brother-in-law Grand Duke Nicholas Michaelovich, who lived near the Winter Palace, informed her that Misha was staying with Princess Poutiatine.

'Misha refused the throne and was supported in his decision by the Provisional Government,' Xenia noted in her diary on 3 March. 'He could not do any different. His manifesto has not come out yet. They were sitting with him from 10.00 till 3.00. Nikolai [Michaelovich] came to tea and after took me to Misha. . . . What a meeting! I was so happy to see him at last. In these days he lost some weight, looks older and . . . says all the time for what sins he has got all this.

. . . Unfortunately Nicky could not understand the danger. . . .' If Nicholas had reacted sooner and granted the concessions requested by the Duma he could have saved his throne. 'These few hours made all the difference!' Xenia added.[15]

Michael told his sister about the day's events. 'The interview was very moving,' Princess Poutiatine recalled. 'The Grand Duchess embraced her brother with tears in her eyes, not being able to control her emotion.'[16] When they said goodbye, Nicholas Michaelovich accompanied Xenia home. It was probably the last time she ever saw Misha.

The Provisional Government had asked Sir George Buchanan, the British Ambassador, not to call on members of the imperial family. Sir George refused to comply, visiting Xenia's palace on 3 March, where he found her 'in a great state of mind'.[17]

Despite her obvious distress, the diary continued the following day:

'Stayed late with Papochka and Vera [Orbeliani] while everyone went to bed, till 2.45 am. We were talking and crying, so heavy and painful in our hearts, I cannot help it. There was a snowstorm, everything is covered and it is difficult to go around the streets. . . . Horror!

'Received a telegram from Mama, she went to meet Nicky, I do not know where, thank God they will be together. Poor Mama! God help them! So sad and painful!

'The abdication of Misha came out. He says that he "keeps his strong decision and will take supreme power only if this is going to be the will of Our Great People who must establish this through a national election and a Representative Council of Constituent Assembly to decide the way of ruling and new laws for the Russian State".

'At last there is a telegram from the children [at Ai-Todor]. Thank God they are all in good health. . . . We had many people for tea.

'. . . I talked to him for a long time. He saw Guchkov (Military Minister) [actually Minister of War] . . . about the meeting with Nicky in Pskov and how calm he [Nicky] looked. . . .

'So difficult and painful, it is impossible!

'Went to evening service, when they presented the Cross there were no prayers for him [Nicky]. How terribly painful. . . . Everybody around me chatted and argued – *gave vent to my feelings*.'[18]

From her mother's letters Xenia gradually learnt the full details of the Dowager Empress's last heartbreaking meeting with Nicholas at Moghilev, to which she had been accompanied by Sandro. The old Empress was deeply upset by the experience, and by the distressing sight of her son departing for Tsarskoe Selo as a prisoner on his own train. 'I still can't believe that this dreadful nightmare is real,' she told Xenia. 'I hear *nothing* from poor Nicky, for which I suffer horribly. . . .'[19]

Increasingly disturbing stories reached Xenia's ears. 'Went to midday service,' she recorded on 5 March. '. . . Poor General Baranov has been pulled around and they injured him seriously hitting his head with the rifle butt. . . .

'Viazemsky, husband of Asia Shuvalova, was also killed . . . by accident. He was riding in the cab with Guchkov and an accidental bullet shot into his back, he died in [illegible] Community.

'It is all so disgusting.

'. . . The Stock Exchange news came out, they write nasty things . . . something is happening in the Duma, rows and masses of people. God knows. . . .'[20]

A few days later Xenia's aunt, Queen Olga of Greece, then living at Pavlovsk, travelled to Petrograd in a packed first-class carriage full of troops. She told Xenia how eighty soldiers had arrived at the palace a few nights previously to conduct a search. Persuaded not to wake the Queen, they stole some valuables as they left. Queen Olga was desperate to send a letter to her sister-in-law, the Dowager Empress, in Kiev. Xenia told her that a courier was leaving the following day, but the letter was not ready. It was finally given to Xenia, to send to her mother when and how she could.

From Kiev, Xenia heard from her sister. 'I shan't say anything of all we feel because it isn't to be expressed,' wrote the latter 'Such changes that I thought I was going mad & can't sleep till now and when I do – all the events go on in dreams.'[21]

From a friend, she received news of Nicky. 'He writes, "*he is wonderful, my heart bleeds, all quite unbelievable*".

'Poor Mama!'[22]

Xenia was becoming more and more depressed. Her cars had been requisitioned and she now had to travel by horse drawn cab,

On 6 March she wrote: 'Chatted with Vera until 2.00. [about the Duma and the new people in it]. . . . My God, how cruel it all is!

'Very heavy snow, it is real winter. . . .

'Good and touching Davidov came and he only asked me to tell Nicky one day that he will always love him and be devoted to him and it is only him . . . and nothing else in Russia. . . . He touched my heart, I had tears.'[23]

7 March: 'Got up about 10.00. In the evening chatted with Vera for a long time. Nikolai [Michaelovich] came over . . . an article came out with correspondence from Nicky, his letters to him. . . .

'Mitia Daehn went to Tsarskoe and in the evening they told him that he would be staying there because he gave a promise about not leaving Tsarskoe! Sonia [his wife] wants to go there tomorrow.

'I heard that the factories are working again, apart from those without fuel.

'. . . Visits from Lombard [Revd Bousfield S. Lombard, chaplain of the English church], Irina and Bimbo [Nicholas Michaelovich]. Everybody is bringing different news. There is talk that they want to bury those . . . "who died for freedom" on Dvotsovaia Ploschad [Palace Square].

'There is talk that a lot of officers were shot [killed] in Kronstadt.'[24]

8 March: '. . . Mitia D [Daehn] has been arrested in his own flat!'[25]

9 March: 'Got up at 9.00. Talked to Vera till 1.00. Still lie in bed.

'Nikolai [Michaelovich] appeared in the morning. He saw Kerensky [Minister of Justice].'[26]

Sandro had been forced to resign his commission. He telegraphed his intention of leaving for Ai-Todor and asking the Provisional Government to hasten the Dowager Empress's departure. 'Poor, poor Mama,' Xenia wrote in her diary, 'still that trial, the Crimea.'[27] The Dowager Empress was reluctant to return to the scene of her husband's death. 'Naturally I will be both happy and thankful to be together with you at Ai-Todor,' she told Xenia, 'but that is so difficult and sad. . . .'[28]

In her grief for her brother, Xenia wrote to him a few days later of her hopes that everything would end well for Russia and that the war would end in victory. 'We have to believe and pray and put our faith in God's mercy. Please God we shall meet again in better circumstances – but where, when and how?'[29] It was many months before Nicholas received her letter. To her mother she could only express anger at recent events, 'simply ashamed and embarrassed that everything crumbled *so quickly* and that *nobody* resisted or stood up for Nicky. Poor, unhappy man, what must he endure and think of his "loyal subjects"?! I am seized by rage at the thought of *those who destroyed him.*'[30] Knowing that Nicholas's children were ill with measles and desperate for news, she made one last appeal to the Provisional Government, asking to see her brother, but permission was refused.

With a heavy heart Xenia left for Ai-Todor on 25 March, her forty-second birthday, accompanied to the Nikolaevsky station in Petrograd by Andrei and Feodor, the lady-in-waiting Sophie Evreinoff, and Sandro's ADC Prince Dmitri Orbeliani. 'Grand Duchess Xenia, who I saw only a week ago, is quite well though naturally depressed,' Buchanan reported to the Foreign Office. 'She wrote to me before leaving for the Crimea . . . and said how much she had felt not having been allowed to see the Emperor before starting.'[31]

At Ai-Todor news of the revolution had already reached Xenia's younger sons when a servant came running up to the house shouting, 'they're coming to congratulate you!' Shortly afterwards a crowd of people wearing red ribbons and singing 'La Marseillaise' gathered outside. Monsieur Niquille, the Swiss tutor, led the boys on to the balcony, together with two-year-old Bébé in the arms of her nurse. He quickly defused the situation by making a speech. Switzerland, he said, 'had been a republic for three hundred years, everyone there was perfectly happy and he wished the same to the Russian people. . . . I hope everything will be as nice as it was before,' he added, to loud applause.[32] The crowd then departed, still singing revolutionary songs.

Xenia arrived on 28 March to find Sandro already there with her mother and Olga. They had left Kiev secretly at night on 23 March. Although Sandro had managed to organize a train, the Petrograd Soviet was demanding the arrest of all the Romanovs, and the local communists would never have let them leave openly. During the four day journey refugees tried to come on board at each stop but were repelled by a small unit of loyal sappers, who guarded the doors of every coach with fixed bayonets. At Sevastopol the train stopped outside the town and the imperial party transferred to cars provided by officers of the Military Aviation School who had served under Sandro. As they left the train, the Romanovs saw the hatred on the faces of a band of local sailors standing nearby. Xenia's diary described her own journey and the family reunion:

At last we are all together – such happiness. But what a meeting! Awfully painful for Mama, to see, to hear, to answer. . . . Got up at 6.00 because we had to be in Bakhchisarai at 3.00 [or 7.00? the figure is not clear] but instead we arrived at 10.30!
. . . Mama sent her own [car] . . . I travelled in it with S.D. [Sophia Dmitrievna Evreinoff] and Nikita. . . . sometimes there are a lot of birds singing, everything is going green and flowers. . . . and I cannot think about how bad everything is.
They met us on the Square in front of the house. The only . . . comfort is that we are together. They waited for us for breakfast. After that we sat on the balcony. Everything is like a dream, everyone is here: Mama, Sandro, Olga, all together. It is cozy in Mama's place. She lives 2 km from us. . . . We talked a lot about poor Nicky and about her meeting with him and about the entourage . . . and about Ruzsky [General Ruzsky] who was rude to him and disgusting. . . . In turn I told everything that happened in P. [Petrograd] and all that we lived through. Mama is indignant that I was not allowed to see Nicky.
Olga with Kulik [Kulikovsky] is living in rooms belonging to Papochka next to D and R [Dmitri and Rostislav] and Nikita and Feodor with [Stewart?] . . . temporarily the grand-daughter [Bébé] is with us. She is so sweet. . . .[33]

Dagmar and Olga had settled into the New House, while their retainers occupied the Suites House nearby. The Dowager Empress's party included her lady-in-waiting Countess Zenaide Mengden, the Cossack bodyguard Jashchik, and Prince Sergei Dolgoruky with his wife Irina, who stayed at his family estate of Miskhor, a potentially explosive situation which was to have tragic consequences. The devoted Prince Schervashidze had returned to Petrograd to sort out the Dowager Empress's business affairs.

With the younger boys' rooms in the New House occupied by her mother and sister, Xenia shared Sandro's bedroom. For several years now they had led entirely separate lives, and the enforced cohabitation put increased strain on the already fragile state of their marriage. According to a former lady-in-waiting to the Dowager Empress, long, uncomfortable periods of silence were now interspersed with prolonged scenes in front of their startled sons.

Other members of the family were at their estates nearby: Irina, Felix and his parents were at Koreiz, Nicholasha at Tchair and his brother Peter at Djulber. It was hard to believe there had been any change. The Crimea was peaceful, Tartar regiments were still loyal to the imperial family and some officers provided a voluntary guard. Xenia told her brother-in-law Grand Duke George that they were living very quietly and not seeing anyone.[34] Nevertheless, the strain of recent events had affected them all. 'Mama feels weak with a kind of chill,' Xenia wrote on 30 March.[35]

The Romanovs in the Crimea were now cut off from their relatives abroad.

Immediately after the revolution Sir George Buchanan and the Danish Minister Harald Scavenius had requested permission to stay in touch by telegraph with the Dowager Empress via the Russian Foreign Ministry. Fearing a counter-revolution by the Romanovs, the Soviet forbade this, and would only allow contact through official, censored, channels. To circumvent this all telegrams to, or on behalf of, Dagmar were sent through the Youssoupovs at Koreiz. Correspondence sent via the Danish Foreign Ministry or the Legation was returned, and the Provisional Government asked Scavenius not to send correspondence out of Russia for the Romanovs. Several people had offered to carry letters secretly to Ai-Todor, but Scavenius did not want to involve the servants.

Queen Alexandra had received letters, but hers to Dagmar, though received and read by the Provisional Government, were not delivered. Some of the Queen's language was so impassioned that the Foreign Office finally asked her not to send even simple messages of sympathy, which could be misconstrued as political interference. Dagmar's loyal friends, like Princess Julia Cantacuzene, continued to smuggle her correspondence to Petrograd but Buchanan was unable to forward anything, as the Minister of Justice, Kerensky, was afraid of the extremists.

This was particularly frustrating for the Dowager Empress, who did not realize that Buchanan was powerless to intervene. When Felix and Feodor returned briefly to Petrograd in April, Xenia took the opportunity to approach Sir George. 'Prince Felix Youssoupov brought me yesterday a letter from . . . Grand Duchess Xenia,' Buchanan reported to the Foreign Office on 25 April [NS], 'asking me to forward letters from her and Empress Marie to England and saying that the latter was in despair at not hearing from Queen Alexandra. She had . . . not dared to tell the Empress, as I had asked her to do, that I was not allowed to forward letters . . . and she begged me to try once more to obtain permission.'[36] None of the imperial family yet realized what a difficult and dangerous position they were in.

Dagmar was furious at what she saw as the British Embassy's refusal to help. Sir George finally arranged for the Queen to telegraph a message which Felix delivered verbally, hoping this would calm Dagmar. They were still receiving letters from inside Russia. On 29 April General Sergei Evreinoff, an eminent retired military officer and former director of Sandro's court, wrote expressing his allegiance to Xenia and promising to keep her up to date with news. He was as good as his word. Several long letters from him have survived, in increasingly bad handwriting as his health declined, giving a very personal view of the deteriorating situation around Petrograd.

In April all court property, including the palaces and private estates, was transferred to the State, and Xenia's palace on the Moika was requisitioned. The guards and the steward were shut in a closet while the contents of the wine cellar were removed. Pictures and carpets were stolen, but all the linen and silver had been taken almost as soon as Xenia left. Some of Xenia and Sandro's less faithful personal servants were involved in the thefts. Feodor Golovin was now appointed Commissioner for the Ministry of the Court. Xenia recorded the deteriorating situation in her diary: 'They say that in Sevastopol the disorder among the sailors is terrible and [admiral] Kolchak is totally in the hands of the sailors. Nobody has any civic fortitude. Very sad . . . they have renamed all the craft that formerly carried the names of Emperors. . . .'[37]

One of the major changes they had to face in their new situation was financial. All the members of the imperial family now ceased to receive their income from the Imperial Appanages,* and thus had to take stock of their position. Xenia had received a dowry of 1 million roubles (£100,000) on her marriage; Sandro had an annual income of 210,000 roubles (£21,000), of which 150,000 roubles was paid by the Tsar and the rest came from investments carefully made during his childhood,[38] all of which now suddenly stopped. The practical Xenia therefore drew up a list of the pensions and charities to whom she gave money out of the Appanages grant. Her business manager then took it to Prince Lvov, the Prime Minister, and explained that all these people and institutions would now be destitute. The prince agreed that Xenia should receive enough money to maintain these payments.[39] Nevertheless, Xenia and Sandro were forced to send many of their servants away, as they could no longer afford to keep them. 'There is chaos overall,' Xenia wrote. 'The revolutionaries are "*svinehund*" [sic].'[40]

According to Sandro they were under unofficial house arrest, though Xenia's diary gave the impression that they still had comparative freedom over the next few weeks, as they were able to pay visits to friends nearby, go to a notary at Yalta, as well as walk, garden, go fishing, play tennis and have picnics.[41] Every day Xenia went across to have tea with her mother and Olga, then they took a walk and discussed events, particularly the Empress's last meeting with Nicholas. It was reported in the newspapers that the Dowager Empress and Olga visited the White Palace at Livadia and that the Empress had begun to grow asparagus, although a request for extra sugar for jam-making had been refused.

Sandro had been asked to put a stop to his archaeological excavations. Soon he became taciturn and depressed, deprived of his work and with nothing important to do. He tried to occupy himself with his coin collection, astronomy and wine growing. His books on the navy and numismatics held no interest for him any

---

* Land purchased by Catherine the Great to provide incomes for the imperial family.

more. His wardens and would-be executioners were sailors, which brought home to him how little he had learnt about human nature from his library, while the numismatic works reminded him of Turkey, Asia Minor and other countries where he had spent some of the happiest hours of his life. He and the boys sawed firewood for the winter, or walked down to the sea. Sometimes as they crossed the lower road they met Prince Roman, the son of Grand Duke Peter who lived nearby. 'I didn't know my cousins very well,' Roman recalled. 'We only exchanged a few words.'[42] The whole family met for meals and they would always be found together in church on Sundays. Irina brought Bébé over to see her grandmother every day, and the owners of neighbouring estates came in the evening to play dominoes.

'It is the Birthday of my Sandro . . . 51 years old,' Xenia recorded on Easter Saturday. 'I was ready quite late and was sitting with Mama. 11.00 o'clock service. . . . It was good in the morning, a bit of fog and damp. Dima sat with the children painting eggs in N's [Nikita's] room. . . . I had tea with Mama. After that I slept and read and everybody thought about (?) . . . Mama, Olga and I had dinner together at Mama's. It is all not the same. . . .

'The service lasted for 1.5 hours. On the return home we were earnestly disappointed – there was nothing to break the [Easter] fast. It turned out that Kechurov did not understand Sandro and thought that he should not say anything, *nobody knows why?*'[43]

Xenia then recorded 'a major scandal with the cook and the food's unrestrained theft'. The cook, who had been called up for the Army, was leaving that day, so he refused to cook and departed, leaving them without any sugar or flour. The household was placed under the direction of Sophie Evreinoff and Sandro's ADC Captain Nicholas Foguel.[44]

On 10 April Grand Duke Peter's daughter Princess Nadejda married Prince Nicholas Orlov but, as they were afraid of repercussions if they held what the revolutionaries would describe as 'a family assembly', Xenia and her family were not invited. She and her mother waited discreetly outside the tiny St Nina's Church at Harax. Sandro and his sons resorted to hiding nearby, and as bride and bridegroom left the church they were startled to hear them rustling in the bushes.

The revolution had now reached the Crimea. Soviets had been established at Yalta and Sevastopol and both claimed jurisdiction over the Romanovs.

At 5.30am on 26 April Xenia and Sandro were awakened by loud banging on their bedroom door, followed by demands for them to open up immediately. Sandro was confronted with 'a monster in the uniform of a volunteer', who said he had come to arrest them all 'in the name of the Provisional Government and the Soviet of Workers & Soldiers' Deputies', and to search the house. Another sailor appeared brandishing a rifle and Xenia was told to put her hands outside the bedclothes.[45]

Sandro was then ordered to show the men around the house. Faced with this gang of armed revolutionaries, Xenia showed great courage. Sitting up in bed, she asked their leader if he was a Christian, as he did not remove his headgear when he saw the icons on the wall. Shamefacedly, he removed his cap. Meanwhile, a 'horrible looking female came and rummaged about in Xenia's things, stole a few of her jewels from the dressing table, and retired'.[46]

After the cupboards and drawers had been ransacked, Xenia was told to get up and dress. She said she had no stockings and sent the guard to fetch a pair from the next room. Making him turn his face to the wall, she dressed hurriedly 'in a great state of anxiety'. The bed was then searched and the pillows turned inside out. Personal correspondence was seized, and a ruby ring that Sandro had given to Xenia on the birth of one of their children was stolen. Xenia had no idea how the other occupants of Ai-Todor, particularly her mother, were faring. The Dowager Empress was subjected to the same treatment, being forced to sit undressed for hours while her rooms were searched. All her personal correspondence and diaries were taken. As she poured invective on the sailors, only Sandro's intervention prevented her from being taken away.

Later Xenia, her sons and the band of dirty, unshaven, long-haired sailors assembled in the dining room. Pointing to Nikita, Xenia told them: 'You see this son of mine was to become a sailor, because we all loved the navy, but we took him away [from the Naval College on Vassilievsky Island] for him not to become a scoundrel like you.' This was greeted with dead silence.[47] When the sailors finally left, the house was in a state of total destruction and everyone was traumatized. All edible food was taken from the kitchen. Later that day the Dowager Empress's chauffeur defected to the Soviets. Not long afterwards the gardener discovered a parcel underneath a tree; it contained gold cutlery which the sailors had stolen but, evidently thinking better of it, had thrown away as they left.[48]

Sandro lodged a formal complaint to the Provisional Government and a commission was sent to Ai-Todor to interview them. The inquiry took place in the Suites House. 'Poor Xenia was twice obliged to explain and give a description of the ring that was stolen,' the Dowager Empress told her sister-in-law.[49] None of the letters and diaries was returned and Xenia's ring was never recovered. The Dowager Empress's old Danish bible, seized as a 'revolutionary book', was returned a few weeks later.

The Provisional Government's Special Commissar now moved in with twenty heavily armed Soviet sailors. Sentries patrolled the entrance and the Romanovs were subjected to endless petty humiliations. If they wanted to go for a drive they had to say so in advance, otherwise the doorkeeper refused to let them out. Once, when they forgot to ask permission, they were stopped by the guard and told to give their full names. They were not allowed to get out of the car or go outside, even into the garden, after 10pm. Letters received either had the title crossed out or the word 'former' inserted – Xenia now found her correspondence addressed to the 'former Grand Duchess Xenia'.[50]

Feodor complained to his Uncle Bimbo, Grand Duke Nicholas Michaelovich, of the 'intolerable boredom' and how he would like 'to go away from here':

Papa has changed very much this past month, he is short of temper, terribly taciturn and one seldom sees the smile on his face, which he had in earlier times. . . . Mama is cheerful, but also dispirited. At dinner she sits in her own room and stays there the whole evening. . . .

My brothers are still healthy and behave as children do, and even Andrusha, who plays war with them on the table with wooden toys, acts like a child. It seems to me that Andrusha is not bored here. . . . He loves physical activity and works well, but he doesn't use his head and doesn't read or write. . . .

The other day, while travelling from Miskhor, I met the Princess [Irina] Dolgoruky . . . she is a terribly dear and wonderful person. I haven't seen him [Irina's husband, Sergei], he does not come here any more.[51]

By late May Irina Dolgoruky was ill. 'Later in the evening I talked with her on the telephone,' Xenia wrote, 'and found out that she has pneumonia! She coughs a bit when moving and groaned during the conversation.'[52] The weather was very hot and by the following day the temperature had risen to 40 degrees centigrade. 'In Korciz they brought in a new hideous 8-hour working day and are demanding that in all estates everybody including house servants must not work more than that! It means we will have to let go many temporary workers – *see if they'll like it!* It is in force from yesterday.'[53]

Irina's condition continued to deteriorate. 'Poor Irina D. It cannot be any worse. It was +40.3C today, it is terrible! Yesterday evening . . . +39.7C.

'From time to time the heart is getting weaker . . . and about 4.00 o'clock she was really bad so we all thought it was the end. She does not eat the milk and the stock given to her. They say she is very thin and she has some sort of spots on her face.

'In the morning I talked with Seriozha . . . I met him by accident. Poor thing!

'There was a bit of rain through the day. Irina [Youssoupov] came down for *breakfast.* . . . We all sat there with Mama and Papochka who was there as well. . . . *Picked a few roses here and there!*

'Irina brought the granddaughter [Bébé] and we were walking in the garden. . . . Olga was here and the granddaughter was sitting on my lap.'[54]

Although it was not unexpected, the imperial family were still shocked to hear that Irina Dolgoruky had died. Her first marriage, to Count Ilarion (Larry) Vorontzov-Dashkov, had ended in divorce. Only too late, according to at least one source, did it dawn on her that her second marriage to Sergei in 1914 was a mere screen for his discreetly conducted but long-standing affair with Xenia. Unable to live with it and the general misery any more, she took an overdose of sleeping tablets.[55]

The Romanovs were given permission to attend her funeral at Koreiz, and after the service everyone set out on foot for the cemetery a mile away. The Hon. Albert ('Bertie') Stopford, 'the Scarlet Pimpernel of the Revolution', who worked for the British Embassy (and also probably the Secret Intelligence Service), noted in his diary that he thought the Dowager Empress, whom he had not seen for more than a year, was better than he expected, albeit thinner, but Xenia 'appeared ill, tired, and very sad'. Irina Youssoupov told him that 'she was in indifferent health and much upset by recent events'.[56] According to Stopford, Princess Dolgoruky, 'an intimate friend of Grand Duchess Xenia', took 'a mistaken overdose of veronal'.[57]

Hardly had they arrived at the cemetery when there was a thunderstorm. All the cars had been left in the high road, except the Empress's which had gone to the lower road at the bottom of the vineyard. A hired carriage came to take the Empress, Xenia and her two youngest sons back to the car, and the burial was postponed. Soon afterwards Prince Dolgoruky moved into the Suites House.

Speculation some years later that Xenia was having an affair with her mother's devoted attendant must be treated with extreme circumspection. Her wan appearance and ill-health have been ascribed to a guilty conscience, but could just as well have been the cumulation of months of pressure and increasing anxiety. One source of information for the gossip about Xenia, including specifically the suicide of Sergei's wife, was Mrs Zenaide Burke, whose mother was a first cousin of Felix Youssoupov. She knew Xenia well in Russia and in London, and her mother was among the guests at the wedding of Felix and Irina. As a girl Zenaide had often played with Xenia's sons but disliked them, finding them too disorderly. She was, therefore, hardly an unbiased witness.

In a long letter to her brother-in-law Bimbo, Xenia, still under the stress of recent events, poured out her feelings:

I just have to mention how everyone misses the wonderful Irina D. and how dreadful and sad it is to realise that she is gone. We cannot get accustomed to this thought! – Poor Seriozha, I feel terribly sad, he doesn't allow anyone to come near him, how he suffers and how lonely he is now. He visits us here almost every day and often comes for breakfast – probably with pleasure as he is also very depressed.

Never will I believe that it was intentional that she took poison – she loved children too much and she was never an egoist. Terrible for them, dreadful and sad – they were deprived of a wonderful and exceptional mother. . . .[58]

Xenia also railed about the current state of affairs – how the Dowager Empress was allowed few letters, the 'crime' that the government had allowed 'those crooks, Lenin and company' into the country, and all the restrictions. Although Sandro and the children went swimming every day they were forbidden to leave Ai-Todor without telling the guards where and to whom they were going. On top of everything else, the dogs Dushka and Chifay were taken ill and the latter, which had belonged to the Dowager Empress, died. 'Everything is so sad and difficult,'[59] Xenia lamented.

In June Dagmar finally received some letters from Queen Alexandra. The Dowager Empress could now send letters through the British Embassy and the Danish Legation but, by early August, the only letter the Queen had received was one smuggled out of Russia by Stopford. By July Prince Lvov had resigned and Kerensky was Prime Minister and Minister of War. Alarmed by developments in the Crimea, Irina and Felix went to Petrograd so Irina could try to see Kerensky, who was living in some style at the Winter Palace with all the old servants, the guards and a red flag flying when he was in residence. Sandro was worried and had given Felix a letter for Kerensky, to see if he could gain concessions by a personal interview. Felix and Irina stayed at the Moika Palace for two months, and eventually Kerensky received Irina in the study of Alexander II, her great-grandfather. She asked him to ensure that her grandmother, the Dowager Empress, was well treated, then she left the Winter Palace for the last time.

Through Monsieur Niquille, Dagmar sent a message to Buchanan to say she was nervous about her safety. When Felix told him the Dowager Empress was under arrest, the Ambassador protested to the Minister of Foreign Affairs about the treatment of the British King's aunt. The Minister replied that, thanks to the pleas of Princess Irina, Kerensky had promised to improve the Dowager Empress's conditions. When Irina and Felix returned to the Crimea, they were careful not to tell Dagmar that Kerensky was living in Alexander III's rooms at the Winter Palace.

Xenia had noted in her diary that Irina and Felix were expected to return with the family's valuables. They had mixed success; the Dowager Empress's jewellery had already been taken from the Anitchkov to Moscow, but Felix managed to cut her favourite portrait of her husband from its frame. Xenia had been more fortunate in being able to bring most of her main pieces when she travelled to Ai-Todor. In the Moika Palace and the Youssoupov house in Moscow many of the family's treasures were concealed under Felix's supervision, in the hope they would be able to retrieve them in better times.

Irina had returned to the Crimea with letters from Queen Olga of Greece, whom she had visited at Pavlovsk at the end of July. 'Your dear letter, full of compassion for the recent events which have affected our lives, touched my very soul,' Queen Olga told Xenia. '. . . I pray that this terrible time should pass, that we shall see better times in our beloved Motherland and that some happy experiences should blot the disgrace of recent days from all our minds. . . . All kinds of vile acts are being committed in the name of liberty, national self-determination and justice and they are being substantiated by using pompous, meaningless words. Comrade Xenia, I hope that you have become self-determined and that you stand on a firm platform without any annexation and reparations for the good of the people and international love of your enemies and the world proletariat,'[60] she concluded, tongue firmly in cheek.

With Monsieur Niquille's departure for Petrograd on his way home to Switzerland, the children's normal schooling stopped. Their studies became superficial and irregular as Sandro tried to get others in the household to give lessons before finally taking over the task himself. Xenia spent most of her time with the children, but they had become as bored as everyone else, fractious, unruly and impossible to discipline, and she was in increasing despair. They knew all their books by heart, and there was no possibility of them obtaining any more. The attendants played dominoes with the children, Sandro laid down endless games of patience and the Dowager Empress knitted gloves for everyone until her wool ran out.

Sewing materials had become too expensive to buy, and what money they had brought with them was now gone. Clothes had to be darned and patched, and linoleum was used as soles for shoes when they could not obtain leather.

All the family were becoming shadows of their former selves, desperately worried about their deposed sovereign, his wife and their children. The servants, who shared their anxieties, were similarly frustrated, and became insolent and lazy. Foguel's daily consultations with the agent were complicated, as food became more expensive and difficult to buy. The butter looked like Vaseline and tasted like petroleum, the bread was coarse and dark, coffee was made from roasted acorns and tea from hips. Foguel suffered many sleepless nights.

The Provisional Government's hold was becoming increasingly shaky and in July the Bolsheviks nearly pulled off a successful coup. Soon afterwards the news that the Tsar's family had been moved to Tobolsk in Siberia came as a great shock to all the family. Nicholas, Alix and the children had been prisoners at the Alexander Palace at Tsarskoe Selo since March.

'Masses of emotions,' Xenia recorded in her diary. 'Vera brought letters from Tsarskoe and a lot of information, more of which is sad. . . .'

It is impossible to imagine what they lived through. . . . They'd been told a week before that they would have to go from Tsarskoe in case of possible evacuation. . . . They were hoping to come to the Crimea. Of course they were happy about that and made plans etc. But . . . found out that it was not the Crimea that they were going to but another place not telling them where. Only a few moments before the departure they announced they are going to Tobolsk. What monsters! My God! Misha found out about that from Vera O. [Orbeliani, presumably] who managed to get permission from Kerensky to meet Nicky. Misha came together with Kerensky who came in first and sat in the corner, after him came M. [Misha]. . . . In this manner started the meeting of the two brothers! What could they say to each other? Nothing of course! Both of them were very nervous and did not have any thoughts *put into words*. They talked about general things and N. [Nicky] could help M. to understand what had happened. M. said to him that he was not here earlier because he did not have permission and that Xenia asked a lot but they did not let her in. (I am glad he said that). Later . . . they had to leave at 12.00 midnight but they waited for it [the train] till 5.30 in the morning because it was not ready! The whole night they were sitting without going to bed.

. . . [illegible] writes that N. [Nicky] was a real saint and suffers everything with such obedience. . . . Olga very nervous (and he is the same) and Marie cannot recover from the February day when she was the only one to see everything happening.* All of them [the four girls] have had their heads shaved after the illness [measles]!

. . . I brought Vera to see Mama. . . . Mama was very sad and cried, poor one, but was glad to see and listen to Vera. She received a letter from poor Nicky, so nice, and from Misha and from Alix and the others. I also had two letters from Misha and one from Tatiana . . . but a lot of their letters and cards have disappeared. . . . Alix writes to Olga how difficult the packing is. All of it is so cruel and I do not have any words.[61]

While they were all in the depths of despair, Olga's son Tihon was born on 12 August. The Dowager Empress described the event as 'the only good news'.[62]

Xenia recorded the event in her diary. 'Olga gave birth to Tihon. It is a big joy. . . . All went well. . . . There was pain yesterday evening but in the morning she came to Mama and it was impossible to notice anything and . . . at 10.00 the boy was already born. . . .'

Because of Olga's age (she was thirty-five), they decided not to tell the Dowager Empress when labour commenced, so as not to cause any further anxiety. Only when the baby was safely delivered was she informed. According to Xenia, there was a great deal of conspiracy in the family to keep news of the impending birth from Dagmar, but luckily events happened very quickly. 'I went with S.D. [Sophia Evreinoff] thinking I was going for the

---

* She saw the soldiers ready to defend the Alexander Palace from the revolutionaries, heard the sounds of the shooting.

night but suddenly Tania [probably Tatiana Gromova, one of Olga's maids] congratulated me with a nephew! The doctor was 20 minutes late. We sent Molchanov to fetch him. . . . The little boy is a very nice, big baby with a long-shaped head. Olga said – *I'll do it again!* Incredible person!'[63]

The following day Xenia wrote:

I sat with Olga a whole hour and was late for midday service. She is stupidly happy. She is delighted with the little boy (and I feel it). She is feeding him (even she does not have enough milk yet). He is big. . . . Irina and Felix had breakfast. Mama still does not feel very well (I as well feel dejected) I slept badly. Slept during the day but it did not help. I read newspapers and sat with Nikita. He feels much better. It is warm in the evening, +37C. . . .

[?] had dinner with Sandro and I . . . talked about S. who he often saw and about his feelings towards Nicky and how he suffered for him. He took Sandro's letter himself to Kerensky in the Winter Palace. But he did not see him. But . . . he receives in rooms belonging to Nicky (rascals!) and S. went to a reception where he was on duty for many years and a man told him about Nicky's rooms.[64]

Xenia had managed to send a letter to her cousin Ducky, who had escaped with her husband Cyril and their children to Finland. 'Jelly dear, it was such a joy to hear from you. . . .' Ducky replied. 'And now that "they" have been moved what must your Mama's and your feelings be. Where have they gone, did they wish it themselves and what does it mean? Day and night we wonder. . . . That they saw M [Michael] before starting is a good sign, perhaps it means the beginning of something new. How tormenting and awful. I know nothing.

'The way you are all treated I call such a screaming shame that I can't bear to think about it. If only we had you here for a time of rest and complete change what good it would do you, such complete calm and lovely weather and seems such miles away from all that is going on, an untouched corner of this earth. . . .'[65]

Soon they were all confined to the limits of Ai-Todor. Entry was restricted to Felix, Irina and the doctor, who gave them news of their relatives on nearby estates. They were often hungry, but sometimes crabs and butter were sent over from Koreiz. As they had so much room people were occasionally billeted on the estate. When Xenia and Sandro dared to protest, they were given a blunt lecture on the common workers' duty.

Because she was married to a commoner, Olga was in the fortunate position of not being considered a Romanov by the guards. The Dowager Empress could not accept Nicholas Kulikovsky as a proper member of the family, and pointedly excluded him from family councils. Olga and her husband went to live in the flat over Sandro's wine cellar, taking with them all Dagmar and Xenia's jewels concealed in cocoa tins (which, at the first sign of trouble, they hid in a hole in the bottom of a rock by the sea).

In September General Kornilov attempted to rout the Soviet and replace it with a military dictatorship. Kerensky turned to the Soviet for help. The attempt failed when Kornilov's men fraternized with the Bolsheviks, who then refused to return the weapons issued to them by Kerensky. In the wake of this incident Xenia and her family were placed under arrest, with nobody allowed either in or out for almost a month.

By mid-October the imperial family's guard was removed, as many of the sailors were becoming restive about guarding people who were neither criminals nor involved in propaganda.[66] Prince Schervashidze arrived from Petrograd and told them that Kerensky had declared a republic.

The Russian Cabinet now met secretly and agreed which of the Romanovs were to be allowed to go abroad. It was decided that the Dowager Empress would be first and, when approached by Buchanan, the Foreign Office stated that there would be 'no objection' to her being accompanied by Grand Duchess Xenia.[67]

Soon afterwards letters arrived from Nicholas in Tobolsk, and Xenia had letters from Tatiana and Alix. Perhaps because the letters had to pass through a censor, Alexandra wrote in Russian:

My darling Xenia,
My thoughts are with you, how magically good and beautiful everything must be with you – you are the flowers. But it is

indescribably painful for the kind motherland, I cannot explain. I am glad for you that you are finally with all your family as you have been apart. I would like to see Olga in all her new big happiness. Everybody is healthy but myself, during the last 6 weeks I experience nerve pains in my face with tooth-ache. Very tormenting. . . .

We live quietly, have established ourselves well [in Tobolsk] although it is far, far away from everybody – turned away. But God is merciful, He gives us strength and consolation. . . .[68]

Xenia had a dispute with the local commissar about post control. Eventually he refused to send the letters to Tobolsk and advised her to address them to the local commissar there.[69]

The Dowager Empress, who had been unwell ever since she heard that Nicholas had been moved to Siberia, was now seriously ill. Xenia, Olga and Sandro were constantly at her bedside. The British Embassy and the Danish Legation were kept fully informed of her condition. By October she had recovered, but was still very weak and unable to leave the house. A new commissar had arrived and conditions had improved.

That month Sergei Kostritsky, the imperial dentist, returned from Tobolsk with first-hand news of Nicholas, letters and a few small gifts. Xenia was overjoyed to see her brother's writing again. She was able to send at least one letter with Claudia Bitner, former director of the Girls' Lycée at Tsarskoe Selo, who travelled to Tobolsk soon afterwards, but all correspondence had to be submitted to the commissar for censoring.

There was another way. With the aid of two loyal officers, a young girl and various friends along the route, letters and parcels that did not go through the hands of the censor were smuggled to and from Tobolsk at no little personal risk to those involved. In this way they were able to maintain contact with both Nicholas and Michael, who was at Gatchina, for some months.

But matters were about to get considerably worse. In Petrograd the Bolshevik Central Committee voted for an immediate insurrection, and in response the Yalta men tightened their grip, carrying out daily searches for bourgeoisie and counter-revolutionaries, who were taken out and shot. At Ai-Todor there was a mood of uncertainty.

'We are locked in again and it is unexpected and annoying,' Xenia wrote on 16 October. 'Everybody was sitting quietly at Mama's when suddenly Poliakov [the Empress's Cossack bodyguard] came and told Sandro that the commissar was asking for him. He has just come back from Sevastopol and announced that the mood is very alarming in Petrograd and that Bolsheviks are coming out everywhere.'[70]

The fall of the Provisional Government could only be a matter of time.

8 (1918–19)

'It all seems like a terrible nightmare'

On 25 October 1917 the Bolsheviks seized power and Lenin became master of Petrograd. Banks were nationalized, private bank accounts were frozen, and the Romanovs were left with nothing. At Ai-Todor they were placed under strict house arrest, under threat from the Sevastopol and Yalta Soviets who were arguing over whose right it would be to execute the family.

'*Novoe Vremya* [The New Times] for 26 October published a full description of everything that happened in P. [Petrograd] on 24 and 25', Xenia wrote. 'The Bolsheviks occupied the National Banks, Telegraph (but they've been thrown out from there), and Telephone. Everywhere indescribable chaos prevailed. . . . There are no directions from above.' The Winter Palace was under fire from the *Aurora*. 'In the end the Winter Palace was taken. . . . The Provisional Republican Council surrendered. . . . The meeting was scheduled for the next day in the Winter Palace and they all went there and nobody knows what happened there. Afterwards they tried to find Tereshchenko [Michael Tereshchenko, Foreign Minister in the Provisional Government] but nobody knew where he had disappeared!'[1]

The commissar, Vershinin, gave every appearance of being 'pleasant and kind' but was afraid to make any decisions without approval from the Sevastopol Soviet. Xenia and Sandro's home had effectively become their prison, and they were now completely isolated. Nobody was allowed in or out except Irina, much to Xenia's relief, and Dr Malama, and they faced being without light as there was no kerosene. They were guarded by fourteen men and Xenia found some of them prepared to chat and 'quite decent'.[2] Although during November both Paul and Sergei

Cheremetev wrote to Xenia about the uncertain and chaotic conditions in Moscow, the bombardment in the streets and the fact that nobody was allowed into the Kremlin, it may have been some while before these letters reached Ai-Todor.[3]

One of Xenia's greatest worries was the fate of their property. She was distressed at bad news about what was happening to their estates, and the constant thefts. Soon she feared they would all be destitute. 'Everything is so sordid and cruel and painful. It would be better if it came from the Germans, not our own people.'[4] They decided that when things settled down they would open a hotel. Sandro would be the manager, Sergei Dolgoruky the doorman, Sophie Evreinoff the housekeeper, Andrusha the chauffeur, Foguel the cashier, Xenia the housemaid, and the younger boys lift attendants and porters.

At the end of November Xenia wrote to the former Tsar to describe their total isolation and the privations they were going through. She commiserated with what he, Alicky and the children were suffering as well: 'The heart bleeds at the thought of what you have gone through, what you have lived and are still living! At every step undeserved horrors and humiliations. But fear not, the Lord sees all. As long as you are healthy and well. Sometimes it all seems like a terrible nightmare, and that I will wake up and it will all be gone! Poor Russia! What will happen to her?'[5]

Over the weeks conditions deteriorated. Vershinin was dismissed and replaced by Zadorojny, a representative of the Sevastopol Soviet. Trains were not running from the local station, and newspapers, letters and telegrams arrived very infrequently. Increasingly anxious, Prince Schervashidze asked that Harald Scavenius should help the Dowager Empress to leave Russia officially, accompanied by a member of the Bolshevik government and a member of the Danish diplomatic corps, but she refused to go without her family. 'To watch and realize that our country is being destroyed, and so senselessly, is unbearable, and you simply wonder how you can go on living!' Xenia wrote to Nicky. 'You want to believe that everything is not yet lost, that people will be found to lead Russia out of this chaos and terrible impasse. What have they done with our unfortunate people? Will they come to their senses one day?' Even worse was her anxiety about their mother: 'Why should she have to suffer, and put up with such adversity, privations and insults at her age?'[6]

New Year's Eve came, the end of an awful year. Xenia spent the day walking, eating ('dinner was very tasty') and talking. 'In the morning . . . went to Irina and Felix . . . did not sleep at night. . . .' Someone came from Sevastopol and told them that the Bolsheviks were approaching Ai-Todor.

'God help us that everything will be different and becomes better,' Xenia continued.

'I stayed later with Pr. Finikin [Prince Schervashidze], S.D. [Mlle Evreinoff] and Seriozha D [Dolgoruky]. We talked about our poor motherland perishing and where they are leading it to and us with it together.' She ended the year with a heartfelt prayer: 'God bless next year and help all of us and our poor Russia and bless our dear everyone in Siberia.'[7]

They had little news, and Xenia complained in January that they had not been out of Ai-Todor for three months. They were making a list of their gold, silver and valuables. The Dowager Empress agreed to allow Prince Dolgoruky to send a telegram to Lenin outlining their plight. In February Lenin changed the Russian calendar from the Old Style Julian Calendar to the New Style Gregorian Calendar, so that 1 February now became 14 February, in line with Europe.

In March the prisoners were assembled for a roll call. The Dowager Empress refused to come downstairs. 'A Committee from Sevastopol [arrived] consisting of two sailors. One of them is the very famous Pozharov, a good Bolshevik (very attractive face). There were two people dressed in civilian clothes. . . . They started to list all of us and all the other people. Zadorojny was going around with the list and not recognizing anybody. [He pretended not to recognize them and made them answer their names.]

'. . . Mama was very angry but later it all made her laugh and she was looking down on everyone from above. She said, "Do not forget to list the dog!"'[8]

On 3 March Russia signed a separate peace with Germany at Brest-Litovsk A quarter of Russia's territory, including some of its richest croplands, was surrendered as the Ukraine, the Baltic States, Finland, Poland, the Caucasus and the Crimea all came under German rule. The terms were harsh, but Lenin needed peace at any price. As German troops marched into Kharkov, Odessa and Tagenrog one-third of the population of Russia now found themselves in German-occupied territory. The Ukraine became an independent republic and the other areas were either incorporated into Germany or became German protectorates. Russia was left defenceless as, overnight, Germany trebled in size.

On 11 March the occupants of Ai-Todor were moved to Djulber, the nearby Arabian-style villa of Grand Duke Peter, his wife Militza and their younger children Marina and Roman. Their other daughter Nadejda, Grand Duchess Olga and Irina Youssoupov, all married to 'commoners', were allowed to go free. The decision was prompted by the rivalry between the Yalta Soviet, which wanted to execute the Romanovs immediately, and the Sevastopol Soviet, which wanted to protect them at least until Petrograd decreed otherwise. Zadorojny, who had served under Sandro at the Military Aviation School, was a secret supporter of the imperial family and felt he stood more chance of defending them inside Djulber's high, stout walls. They were joined by Nicholasha and his wife Anastasia ('Stana'), former Duchess of Leuchtenberg, with the children from her previous marriage. The Empress, Xenia, Dmitri, Rostislav and Vassili arrived in cars, the others walked over. While Militza welcomed the Empress, together with Xenia and Sandro, conspicuous in a pink shirt and black tie, Prince Roman took care of the boys. There were forty-five people in all, including servants.

Militza and Peter gave up their own rooms to the Empress. Xenia and Sandro moved into Peter's upper office next door. Nikita, Rostislav and Vassili were given Roman's two rooms, while he moved into the Arabian sitting room where mattresses had been placed on the floor for the other boys. Roman soon formed a lifelong friendship with Andrei, Nikita and Feodor. Sophie Evreinoff and Zina Mengden were allocated rooms on the second floor. Some of the servants from Ai-Todor were given the rooms of Peter's staff who had remained in Petrograd. Conditions were cramped and they all complained of their enforced proximity. Gradually their possessions arrived from Ai-Todor and they were able to settle into their new 'home'. To add to her troubles Xenia was suffering from toothache and later had to have the tooth

Tsarevna Marie Feodorovna (Dagmar) with her daughter Xenia, 1875. After the birth of three sons, a daughter was a welcome addition to the family. (*Det Kongelige Bibliotek, Copenhagen. Dept. of Maps, Prints and Photographs*)

Xenia aged 2, 1877. She inherited Dagmar's charm, but not her outgoing personality. (*Det Kongelige Bibliotek, Copenhagen. Dept. of Maps, Prints and Photographs*)

4. 'Best friends' – Xenia and Princess Marie of Greece at Fredensborg, mid-1880s. Xenia and 'Greek Minny' remained close throughout their lives. (*Det Kongelige Bibliotek, Copenhagen. Dept. of Maps, Prints and Photographs*)

3. The Anitchkov Palace. Xenia's birthplace was in the heart of St Petersburg. (*Private collection*)

A family gathering at Fredensborg, *c.* 1890. Back: Crown Prince Constantine of Greece; Grand Duke Paul of Russia; Prince George of Greece; Alexandra, Princess of Wales; Tsar Alexander III; Christian IX of Denmark. Middle: Queen Louise of Denmark; King George of Greece; Princess Alexandra of Greece; Princess Marie of Greece; Grand Duchess Xenia; Prince Harald of Denmark; Princess Maud of Wales; Princess Louise of Denmark. Front: Princess Thyra and Princess Ingeborg of Denmark. (*Ballerup Egnsmuseum, Denmark*)

Olga, Dagmar and Xenia on the imperial yacht, 1880s. All the family looked forward to the annual cruise in the Finnish Archipelago. (*The Imperial Russian Historical Society*)

Xenia with the Empress Marie Feodorovna, 1891. The Grand Duchess was her mother's constant companion. (*Det Kongelige Bibliotek, Copenhagen. Dept. of Maps, Prints and Photographs*)

Christian IX, Queen Louise and their family in the Cupola Hall, Fredensborg, 1891. Left to right, standing: Princess Thyra and Prince Gustav of Denmark; Tsarevich Nicholas of Russia; Prince Waldemar of Denmark; Tsar Alexander III of Russia; Alexandra, Princess of Wales; Prince William of Glucksborg; Queen Louise of Denmark; Prince George of Greece; Princess Ingeborg and Princess Louise of Denmark; King Christian IX of Denmark; Princess Victoria of Wales; Prince Nicholas of Greece; Grand Duke Michael of Russia; Crown Princess Louise of Denmark. Seated: Grand Duchess Olga of Russia; Queen Olga of the Hellenes; Empress Marie Feodorovna of Russia holding Prince Christopher of Greece; Marie, Princess Waldemar of Denmark; King George I of the Hellenes; Grand Duchess Xenia of Russia; Princess Marie of Greece; Prince John of Glucksborg. (*Royal Archives. Copyright © 2002, HM The Queen*)

Alexander III and his family at the Kejservilla, Fredensborg, c. 1890. The small villa was a favourite place for tea parties. Left to right: Tsarevich Nicholas; Prince Albert Victor of Wales; Grand Duke George Alexandrovich with Xenia in front; Prince George of Wales with Grand Duke Michael Alexandrovich in front; Princess Victoria of Wales; Alexander III. (*Det Kongelige Bibliotek, Copenhagen. Dept. of Maps, Prints and Photographs*)

Tsarevich Nicholas, Empress Marie Feodorovna and Xenia at Spala, Poland, 1892. Although Xenia visited the imperial hunting lodges, she was never taught to handle a gun. (*Sue Woolmans*)

Alexander III and his family at Livadia, 1893. Left to right: Tsarevich Nicholas, George, Empress Marie (seated), Olga, Xenia, Alexander III. On the ground: Michael. Xenia was in love with Sandro by this time, but her parents refused to hear any talk of marriage. (*Private collection*)

Sandro and Xenia, 1905. Although Sandro later strayed, he called her a 'great woman' and a 'wonderful mother'. (*Harold Brown*)

Xenia with her cousins, Denmark, 1890s. Back: Grand Duchess Xenia, Princess Maud of Wales; front: Princess Victoria of Wales, Princess Louise of Denmark. (*Ballerup Egnsmuseum, Denmark*)

Ropsha seen from the back. The palace where Xenia and Sandro spent their wedding night is now in ruins. (*Photo: Katrina Warne*)

A family group in 1896. Back: Grand Duchess Xenia holding Princess Irina;
Nicholas II; front: The Dowager Empress Marie Feodorovna holding Grand
Duchess Olga Nicolaievna; Grand Duchess Olga Alexandrovna; Empress
Alexandra Feodorovna. (*Det Kongelige Bibliotek, Copenhagen. Dept. of Maps,
Prints and Photographs*)

The Farm, Peterhof. Xenia and Sandro moved here for the birth of their first
child, Irina, in 1895. (*Photo: Sue Woolmans*)

A family group, Cannes, 1898. Left to right, standing: Princess Alexandra of Cumberland; Countess Torby; Grand Duchess Elena of Russia; Prince Christian of Denmark and his fiancée Duchess Alexandrine of Mecklenburg-Schwerin; Marie, Grand Duchess Vladimir of Russia; Crown Prince Frederik of Denmark; Grand Duchess Xenia of Russia; Ernest Augustus, Duke of Cumberland; Grand Duke Michael Nicholaievich of Russia; Princess Marie Louise of Cumberland; Anastasia, Grand Duchess of Mecklenburg-Schwerin; Grand Duke Alexander Michaelovich of Russia. Seated: Princess Olga of Cumberland; Princess Thyra of Denmark; Prince George William of Cumberland; Duchess Cecilie of Mecklenburg-Schwerin with Prince Ernest Augustus of Cumberland behind her; Crown Princess Louise of Denmark; Thyra, Duchess of Cumberland. Front: Grand Duke Michael Michaelovich of Russia; Duke Frederick Franz of Mecklenburg-Schwerin; Prince Christian of Cumberland; Grand Duke Andrei of Russia; Prince Harald of Denmark. *(Royal Archives. Copyright © 2002, HM The Queen)*

Xenia with Irina, Andrei and Feodor in 1899. The birth of Xenia's second son emphasized the need for Empress Alexandra to give birth to a male heir. *(Det Kongelige Bibliotek, Copenhagen. Dept. of Maps, Prints and Photographs)*

Xenia and Sandro's palace at 106, Quai de la Moika, St Petersburg. The palace is now the Lesgaft Sports Institute. (*Photo: Katrina Warne*)

Princess Marie of Greece, the Grand Duchess George of Russia. In 1900 'Greek Minny' married Sandro's brother and became Xenia's sister-in-law. (*Private collection*)

Princess Xenia Georgievna of Russia, Mrs William Leeds. Grand Duchess George's younger daughter was the god-daughter of Grand Duchess Xenia. (*Private collection*)

Sandro with his dogs, early 1900s. The Grand Duke made his career in the navy. (*Imperial Russian Historical Society*)

Xenia and Sandro with their children, *c.* 1908/9. Nikita, Irina, Andrei, Dmitri, Xenia holding Vassili, Feodor, Rostislav and Sandro. Irina grew into a dazzling beauty, but the boys had the reputation of being 'rather wild'. (*Private collection*)

И. В. Вел. Кн. Александръ Михайловичъ и Е. И. В. Вел. Кн. Ксенія Александровна съ Августѣйшими дѣтьми.

Ai-Todor, Xenia and Sandro's Crimean estate. More buildings were added as their family increased. (*Jacques Ferrand*)

Nikita, Xenia's third son, in the uniform of the exclusive Corps des Pages. (*Private collection*)

Andrei, Xenia's eldest son, at Ai-Todor, 1914. All the children appreciated the freedom of the Crimea. (*Private collection*)

Xenia with Irina and Vassili in her boudoir at Ai-Todor, 1914. (*Jacques Ferrand*)

Xenia at Ai-Todor, around 1914. (*Private collection*)

Xenia and Sandro outside Ai-Todor,
c. 1914. (*Jacques Ferrand*)

Xenia outside Ai-Todor, c. 1914. That
summer was the family's last stay
during peacetime. (*Jacques Ferrand*)

The Dowager Empress Marie Feodorovna photographed by her daughter Olga in Kiev, October 1915. (*Private collection*)

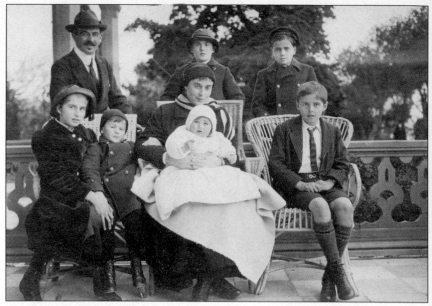

Princess Irina Dolgoruky holding her daughter Olga. Miskhor, January 1916. Beside her sit some of the children of her first marriage: Marie, Larry and Alexander Vorontzov-Dashkov. Prince Dmitri Romanoff stands behind Alexander. Marie later married Xenia's son Nikita. (*Private collection*)

Xenia's diary, 3 March 1917. The entry begins: 'Of course they got what they wanted – Nicky abdicated from the throne. My God! . . . give him strength to go through all this.' (*The Hoover Institution Archives, Stanford. By kind permission of Prince Andrew Romanoff*)

Xenia and Sandro. Biarritz, 1919. By now they had effectively separated. (*Imperial Russian Historical Society*)

Djulber, Crimea. Grand Duke Peter's Arabian Nights style palace where the Romanovs were imprisoned in 1918. (*Photo: Coryne Hall*)

Xenia and Sandro's Silver Wedding anniversary, Biarritz, 1919. Felix Youssoupov, Nikita, Andrei, Xenia, Sandro, Irina, Feodor, Elisabeta holding her baby Princess Xenia. (*Imperial Russian Historical Society*)

San Antonio Palace, Malta. Xenia and her sons stayed here on their journey into exile in 1919. (*Photo: Coryne Hall*)

A stylish portrait of Xenia, taken probably in the 1920s. Xenia spent little on herself, in order to give more to her sons. (*Private collection*)

Xenia with her granddaughter Princess Xenia, Biarritz, 1919. By the time of her death Xenia had thirteen grandchildren. (*Private collection*)

Grand Duchess Olga and her husband, Col Nicholas Kulikovsky, with their children Tihon (front) and Guri. Photographed soon after they escaped from Russia in 1920. (*Ballerup Egnsmuseum, Denmark*)

Xenia with her children, London, 1920s. Standing: Feodor, Nikita, Andrei, Dmitri; seated: Xenia, Rostislav, Irina; on floor: Vassili. As the family dispersed, these reunions became all too rare. (*Private collection*)

Princess Victoria of Wales, one of Xenia's closest friends in England. A similar photograph stood on Xenia's desk at Ai-Todor. (*Private collection*)

Princess Irina, Xenia's only daughter, 1920s. Irina and her husband Prince Felix Youssoupov made their home in France after the revolution. (*Private collection*)

Nikita and Countess Marie Vorontzov-Dashkov on their wedding day, Paris, 1922. After the Second World War they settled in America. (*Private collection*)

Vassili, 1920s. (*Private collection*)

Rostislav, 1920s. Both later made their homes in America. (*Private collection*)

An unusual photograph of Irina and her brother Nikita, taken in the South of France, 1920s. (*Private collection*)

Xenia and Olga, 1925. Neither of them believed in the identity of the 'Anastasia' claimant. (*Imperial Russian Historical Society*)

Xenia's grandchildren Andrew, Xenia and Michael Andreievich, London 1924. The three children of Prince Andrei and his first wife Elisabeta Ruffo de Sant' Antimo ('Elsa'), who lived with Xenia at Frogmore. (*Private collection*)

Frogmore Cottage, Windsor. King George V gave Xenia this 'grace and favour' house in 1925. (*Photo: Coryne Hall*)

Grand Duke Alexander Michaelovich, 1928. In the late 1920s, Sandro embarked on several successful lecture tours of America. (*Private collection*)

Xenia's grandchildren Irina Youssoupov (Bébé), Nikita Nikititch and Michael Feodorovich, 1927. The photograph was given to the Dowager Empress on her 80th birthday. (*Private collection*)

Дорогой Прабабушкѣ
отъ Ирины Никиты и Михаила.
14/27го ноября 1927г.

Хорошей Маме —
Ирина и Михаил Феодорович
Март 1926г.

Princess Irene Paley, wife of Prince Feodor, with her son Michael Feodorovich, March 1926. Although Feodor and Irene later divorced, she contributed to the cost of his medical treatment for tuberculosis. (*Private collection*)

Xenia and Olga, 1928. In the drawing room at Hvidøre, after the death of their mother. (*Imperial Russian Historical Society*)

Princess Irina Youssoupov, Corsica, 1926. In 1924 Felix and Irina bought a house in Calvi. (*Private collection*)

Irina, Olga, Xenia and Andrei. Hvidøre, 1920s. In the 1920s Xenia's life was divided between London, Paris and Denmark. (*Private collection*)

Countess Marina Golenitschev-Koutouzov. Marina married Xenia's son Dmitri in 1931, but they divorced in 1947. Both later remarried. (*Private collection*)

Vassili and his wife Princess Natalia Galitzine, 1939. The couple met and married in America. (*Private collection*)

Princess Irina Youssoupov modelling a dress for the Youssoupovs' *couture* house, 'Irfé', late 1920s. (*Private collection*)

The Villa St Thérèse, Carnolés. The home of the Tchirikoff family, where Sandro died in 1933. (*Photo: Sue Woolmans*)

Olga and Xenia dining with Russian friends at Domus Medica, Copenhagen, 1930s. A house owned by the Danish Medical Association, it was near the Amalienborg Palace. (*Ballerup Egnsmuseum, Denmark*)

Grand Duchess George of Russia, Rome, 1937. Xenia was devastated when her best friend died in 1940. (*Private collection*)

Xenia and her children at Frogmore, 1936. Back: Rostislav, Irina, Nikita, Vassili, Dmitri, Andrei. Front: Feodor and Xenia. (*Paul Edward Kulikovsky*)

Wilderness House, Hampton Court, Xenia's final home in exile, seen from the back. (*Photo: Coryne Hall*)

Olga and her family at Knudsminde, just before they left Denmark to make a new life in Canada, 1948. Back: (left) Tihon and his wife Agnete; Olga and Col. Kulikovsky; (right) Guri and his wife Ruth. Front: Guri's children Leonid and Xenia. (*Paul Edward Kulikovsky*)

Prince Alexander, King Umberto of Italy and Mother Martha, 1950s. The devoted Mother Martha was jealous of Xenia's visitors. (*Private collection*)

Xenia and Olga (seated second row, third and fourth from left) at a party at Domus Medica, Copenhagen, in the 1930s. (*Ballerup Egnsmuseum, Denmark*)

Xenia with her grandson Alexander at Wilderness House, 1950s. Prince Alexander lived with his grandmother from 1953. (*Private*

Xenia (right) with her daughter Irina (left) and daughter-in-law Marie (Princess Nikita) at Wilderness House, 1950s. Xenia loved to walk round the gardens of Hampton Court with Marie's son, Alexander. (*Private collection*)

Xenia with Andrei's second wife Nadine, Andrei and Nadine's daughter Olga and Mother Martha, Wilderness House, 1950s. Although by now Xenia seldom went out, she received many visitors. (*Private collection*)

Xenia's coffin in the church at Carnolés, South of France. April 1960. Mourners included King Umberto of Italy, Prince Roman Romanov, and Xenia's grandchildren Alexander, Xenia and Marina. (*Private collection*)

Xenia in her drawing room, late 1950s. She spent hours writing letters every day.
(*Private collection*)

Xenia's burial at Roquebrune, 29 April 1960. Irina stands with her head on Andrei's shoulder, beside her is Dmitri. Slightly to the right, in the light coat, is Prince Felix Youssoupov. (*Private collection*)

Xenia and Sandro's grave at Roquebrune, 'in a wonderful position overlooking the sea'. (*Photo: Sue Woolmans*)

removed. Although everything was very pleasant, it was not the same. 'I want to go home madly!'[9] she wrote.

They all more or less led their own lives. 'Mama is very depressed and spends most of the time in the garden,' Xenia wrote on 20 March. 'Nicholasha came to her and stayed until dinner. In the evening as usual I sat with D. and later with S.D. It seems that Petrograd is already in the German Occupation zone. But it is not known whether they entered the city or are moving between P. and Berlin. The daughter of Prince Dolgoruky [a neighbour] received a letter from a man who was there and started wars himself. . . . Urcenson [?] left P. at last but we could get nothing from him. There are some movements in Yalta. . . . The soldiers are demanding to know where they are going to be sent to and against whom they are going to fight! But there are talks that mobilization has already been noticed. In Cevet the Council made a decision to defend it against the Germans, but how? Nikimov was taken without any shots.'[10]

Soon they were not even allowed into the small garden and Xenia complained that they had nowhere to walk. The only visitors allowed were Xenia's granddaughter Bébé, who toddled in and out with letters sewn into her coat, and Dr Malama. These visits from little Irina helped to lift Xenia's spirits. 'We had so much joy to see our granddaughter,'[11] she recorded. Apart from the Empress and Xenia, everyone ate together in the large dining room. Sometimes Xenia had tea with the others, or the Empress invited someone to join her at 5pm. At first the food was tolerable enough, its monotony enlivened on occasion by wine from Djulber's cellar. Whenever something special was cooked for the Empress, she divided it among her grandsons. She was also allowed a bottle of milk, and afterwards the bottle was used to smuggle letters in and out.

By such means Prince Schervashidze was able to send a desperate plea for help to Harald Scavenius. The letter was taken to Petrograd by Herr M.A. Jurgensen, who seems to have taken over as tutor to the children. He remained in Petrograd awaiting the reply. Scavenius sent a string of telegrams to Copenhagen, stressing that the Dowager Empress and her daughters were in acute danger and suffering all sorts of privations. Their situation was relieved slightly by the arrival of a French governess with

25,000 roubles [approximately £1,700] sent by Count Benckendorff.

'The yearning for Ai-Todor grows stronger,' Xenia wrote to Nicky on 5 April. 'I'm drawn back there and it seems to me that we aren't even in the Crimea, but in some utterly different place, which only resembles the Crimea. In Ai-Todor . . . it was terribly uncomfortable. They all turned against us there, and were most unfriendly. I truly don't know what we did to them! It was unpleasant to see how other people's belongings were dealt with, which happens here and there. Here we are more under lock and key than at Ai-Todor.'[12]

Prince Schervashidze's desperate appeals had achieved a positive result. In March Dr Carl Immanuel Krebs, a 29-year-old former Guards officer and member of the Red Cross delegation, arrived at Yalta. He had travelled from Petrograd without authorization. After handing over provisions and 50,000 roubles (about £3,300) to Jurgensen, who smuggled them into Djulber, Krebs asked if he could see the Empress. Permission was granted on condition that only Russian was spoken, that the guard commander was present and that any letters given to, or received from, the Empress were censored. The interview took place on 20 March. While the Empress sat by the window with Krebs, Xenia and Sandro distracted the guard commander so that they could have an undisturbed conversation – in Danish.

On Xenia's forty-third birthday the family were allowed to go to Nicholasha's nearby property, Tchair, for the christening of Nadejda's baby daughter, and Irina and Felix were permitted to visit for two hours. Xenia was worried as to how they would prepare for Lent, as they were unable to go to church. She took her religious duties very seriously and, several years earlier, when Feodor had become cynical about religion and, in the Grand Duchess's own words, 'unkind and corrupted', she was in despair.[13]

They passed the time with musical evenings, when the young people sang and played the piano, or endless card games. Sandro gave the younger boys lessons in ancient history and Greek mythology, and one of his teaching charts still exists.[14] Stana's secretary, Boldarev, wrote witty verses about everyone. Only the Empress and Xenia were exempted – they were given tributes, comparing them to flowers. Some of his poems have survived.

Early in April they all suffered a severe shock when Prince Schervashidze, who had been in poor health for some time, was found dead in bed. His body was taken to the little chapel in the park at Ai-Todor, and the Empress was permitted to attend the funeral.

The treaty of Brest-Litovsk brought more danger for the Romanovs, as the Germans began to march towards the Crimea. Zadorojny was warned that the Yalta men planned to execute the Romanovs before the arrival of the Germans. Bands of Yalta men now descended on Djulber under the pretext of acquiring gold for the revolution. Luckily Dagmar and Xenia's jewels were still with Olga at Ai-Todor. Zadorojny refused to let the Yalta men in and they departed, threatening to return. Unbeknown to the Empress, a horse and carriage stood ready outside the door to whisk her to a neighbouring estate if they tried to force their way in, though Xenia and Sandro doubted if she would go.

As the days of suspense and uncertainty dragged by, the family were at last permitted to go into the courtyard. All around them, houses were searched and ransacked, their inhabitants arrested or murdered. Seriously alarmed, Olga and her husband fled from Ai-Todor with their baby and begged to be admitted to Djulber. Seeing Olga through the window, Xenia and her mother were overjoyed, thinking she was coming to join them. The guards refused to let Olga in, but Foguel was permitted to take a mug of milk out for Tihon.

'All morning I was watching the passing ships,' Xenia wrote on 30 April. '. . .There was a submarine far on the horizon. What does this mean? . . . Early in the morning some battleships passed. It is very warm. We were watching from my balcony. Mama came. . . .

'. . . Not very happy news was brought by Zadorojny from Yalta. . . . Oh dear . . . – I cannot believe we will have to see Germans? Poor Yalta finally got rid of all rascals, murderers and robbers. . . .'[15]

The Yalta contingent was now expected to arrive at any moment. Every gate and exit was locked and machine-guns were positioned. Zadorojny knew he could not defend Djulber against armed bands and he suggested he drive them all to Alupka and hide them in a wine cellar. The Grand Dukes decided they would remain at Djulber. All day they prepared for a major attack. Zadorojny returned their weapons so that they could defend themselves and Sandro helped to position the searchlights. It could only be a matter of time before the men returned from Yalta, and Zadorojny decided he would go to Sevastopol to summon help. It would be a race to see who reached them first – the firing squad from Yalta, or their reinforcements from Sevastopol. That evening Nicholasha personally guarded the Empress's door. A night watch was organized in five shifts. Sophia Evreinoff slept in the corridor outside the room of Xenia's younger sons and Zina Mengden stayed with the Empress, a small knife under her pillow.

They were saved by an advance party of German soldiers, sent personally by the Kaiser. The Romanovs had been freed by Russia's enemies. Later they discovered that the transport bringing the Bolsheviks from Yalta during the night had missed a bend on the road and crashed. Although their lives had been spared, none of the family was happy about the circumstances of their liberation.

'Magical day,' Xenia recorded on 1 May. 'Hyacinths are in full bloom. . . . Everything is so beautiful and everything is spoiled by the German invasion. This is some kind of terrible dream, I cannot take it into my head.'[16]

Both the Empress and Nicholasha declined the Kaiser's invitation to go to Germany and they refused to receive the German officer who had saved them from death. Sandro was angry, fearing they would all be killed when the Germans left. He wanted to know if he and his family could travel to Switzerland and he spoke to von Stolzenberg at Ai-Todor, a move that caused a rift between Sandro and the Dowager Empress. It appears that some journalists tried to gain access to Djulber.

'He wanted to see [illegible, possibly Nicholasha] . . . but he did not receive him. Later we found out that it was a correspondent [journalist] so it is good that he was not received . . . he wanted to find out if everything is good with us and if the team who are guarding us have been put there by Bolsheviks with aggressive goals.'[17]

The Empress refused to be guarded by Germans, so instead the family were protected by a band of local Tartars. The Germans were surprised, however, when Sandro pleaded for the release of Zadorojny.

Xenia reported the current situation. 'One regiment is still in Yalta. The comrades did not even believe that the Germans were coming. There was talk that they are Ukrainians. . . .' During the tense time that had recently elapsed the family had become quite fond of some of their guards. 'I pity them and they have become closer and dear!' Xenia continued. 'Three of the Red Guards have been killed. In the morning, during the day and in the evening we heard shooting when we were in the garden. Now they will have to have revenge for everything. After tea we went to confession to the church with Father Vassili. He was talking very well and it was very pleasant. 12.30 was Midnight Service. . . .'[18]

Soon afterwards Irina, Olga and Nadejda visited Djulber. Gromov, Militza's cook, was finally able to go to the little town of Koreiz for provisions and that evening they were treated to a magnificent dinner. Although it was close to the end of the Lenten fast, nobody refused a course. As soon as they were liberated, Sandro moved back to Ai-Todor. Xenia remained at Djulber with her sons, where they celebrated Easter and Gromov once more excelled himself with the Easter feast. Xenia's sons took full advantage of their new-found freedom, walking in the grounds and going to the beach. To Vassili's delight, he was able to drive his friends around without a groom.

On 8 June Xenia and the boys joined Sandro at Ai-Todor. Although at first the relations between the Dowager Empress's party and the family of Peter and Militza had been strained, after so many shared anxieties and experiences they were all sorry to part. 'Again we came back home,' Xenia wrote in her diary. 'Everything seems like some sort of dream where I do not remember what happened. . . . There was a big farewell breakfast with our hosts. There were 12 people at one table and 15 at another. . . . Exchange of mutual greetings and invitations to each other etc. Thanking the hosts for the hospitality and cordiality . . . and it is even sad because we spent 3 months here! At the end it was good. Left about 3 o'clock.'[19]

The Empress moved to the main house at Harax, while Olga and her family lived in one of the small houses on the estate. 'Everything is so good and cosy,' Xenia continued. 'Mama is very happy. Beautiful tea, There were lots of very tasty things that the kitchen lady prepared and everything was served nicely. . . I am so happy that Mama likes everything [at Harax]. . . . I am very happy that Papochka is living with us.'[20]

The Germans decided to remove the family's Tartar guards. 'In the morning Germans came to Djulber and received an order to position their own guards and disarm ours. The negotiations were taking place on the road near the gates. The Commander with two assistants was invited, together with the Head of Security. There will be a patrol on the road.'[21]

The family now settled down to a more peaceful existence of tennis parties, fishing, gardening and picnics. Xenia, Rostislav and Vassili visited Harax. 'Olga and Kukushkin came with Tihon. We were sitting on the balcony. Came back on the horses. . . . At 1.00 o'clock D. picked me up and we went . . . to Yalta. We were running around the stores and Mama and I became tired because D. was unusually rummaging everywhere. . . .

'. . . Members of the Ukrainian Regiments were very happy to see each other.' One had recently arrived. 'He is very thin because he was in prison in Taganrog for a long time. Poor man.

'. . . Found everybody in the *Hall*. We sat for a while but S.D. was not in his best mood. *Why?* There are a lot of Germans in Yalta.'[22]

The younger people published a newspaper, which was edited by Olga Vassilievna, a nurse from Olga's hospital in Kiev who had accompanied them to the Crimea.[23] Some of Zina Mengden's relatives arrived. Xenia gave them a house at Ai-Todor, which friends helped to furnish. A postcard came from Xenia's former tutor Ferdinand Thormeyer ('Siocha'), who was working for the Red Cross in Switzerland, asking for news of the family. All his letters had remained unanswered and he hoped they were in good health. 'Poor old Thormeyer's' pension had stopped with the revolution.[24]

'Kukushkin came and met D. with Mama. Everyone went to church but I stayed behind with D. and went there at the end of the service. We were sitting in George's study [George Michaelovich, who owned Harax] and were chatting. Magical weather. There were too many people in the church. Had breakfast at Kukushkin's . . . sitting on the balcony afterwards. . . .

'. . . On the way he told me lots of interesting [things] and most of all from Tobolsk. One day a General came from Reval through Berlin and he saw Mama. Henry of Prussia was in Reval and had given an order to secure Nicky and the family. Henry wrote from there to Mama. . . .' Someone else told them what had been happening in Gatchina and described how he was nearly killed.

'Horrible in Yalta . . .', Xenia continued. 'Sitting on the balcony. It is a beautiful evening. There is a rumour that Lenin has been arrested.'[25]

14 June: 'All morning I spent with Olga. She is 36 years old. It was thunder and strong rain early this morning. It is very hot and stuffy but later it was a little windy. Mama came and brought roses to her. D. brought her different presents like sugar, butter, vodka! Tihon was crawling and climbed onto the chair without any help. We came back on ponies to breakfast with Irina. . . .

'We were cutting dry roses with Papochka and D. . . . I came back with Mitia and Sonia, they gave me a lift. . . .

'In Yalta they put out an announcement that anybody who speaks badly about the Germans will be deported from the Crimea! *Stupid.*'[26]

15 June: 'Collecting roses in the morning. There are a lot of them. . . . They are not as good as they could be. The best ones are in the nurseries around the *tennis court.* . . .'[27]

Life carried on as normal and only the occasional rumour from the north disturbed the tranquillity of Ai-Todor.

16 June: 'Beautiful weather. Walked around the garden and sat in the Hall with S.D. [Mlle Evreinoff] and Papochka. About 11 o'clock went with Andrusha to Harax on ponies. . . . Afterwards we all went to the service. Sandro and the children came . . . Kukushkin, Mitia, Felix, Andrusha and Odi [Feodor]. At home we sat and chatted on the balcony and in one of the rooms. Mama is very happy and feels at home. Yesterday she had Orlov [Prince Vladimir Orlov (1869–1927), Princess Nadejda's father-in-law] for dinner and he told a lot of interesting things about the Germans.

'. . . What is happening in Moscow? . . . unknown but there was a rumour about Lenin's arrest and it is not correct. The Slavs group blew up a bridge. . . . A big mess is happening and movement . . . they demand disarming but the Allies are opposed and supporting them and gave an ultimatum.

'After dinner sat around on the balcony. It is a magical evening. . . .'[28]

Then bad tidings began to arrive. Michael and his secretary Johnson had been living in comparative freedom in the Korolev Rooms, Perm, since March. Shortly before dusk on 12 June they were taken away by a group of men. Nothing had been heard from them since.* For months rumours spread that Misha had been rescued by monarchists and was in hiding. Many believed that his disappearance from Perm was a deliberate move by the White Army to spirit him out of Bolshevik hands and thwart Germany's plans to set him up as a puppet Tsar, while other reports said he was living in Omsk. Although plots for his restoration continued during the autumn of 1918, Xenia and her family never heard from him again.

Soon afterwards rumours began to circulate that Ella, Princes Constantine, Igor and Ivan Constantinovich, Prince Vladimir Paley and Sandro's brother Sergei, who had been imprisoned at Alapayevsk, had all vanished. Two more of his brothers, Nicholas and George, were in a Petrograd prison with Grand Duke Paul Alexandrovich and Grand Duke Dmitri Constantinovich. Xenia received news of them all from her cousin, the younger Grand Duchess Marie Pavlovna, who had reached Odessa. Marie had married Prince Sergei Poutiatine in 1917 and, after telling Xenia about the birth of her son Roman on 15 June 1918, the Grand Duchess continued:

I am terribly tormented by Papa's fate, since I learnt that the Bolsheviks held him in custody after our departure and put him in the house of preliminary imprisonment. There is no news from there. . . .

In February all the Romanovs definitely had to register and all the men were deported except Papa, who was left behind exclusively thanks to the energy and enterprise of Princess Paley.

. . . little Volodia [was] deported at the same time [Marie's half-brother, Prince Vladimir Paley] with the Constantinovichi and Sergei Michaelovich to Viatka, from where they passed through Ekaterinburg and then to Alapayevsk . . . in the Urals. With them also was . . . Aunt Ella. Where she is now I absolutely don't

---

* Michael and his secretary were executed by the Bolsheviks shortly afterwards.

know, but all the others disappeared without news and you can imagine how concerned we are about Volodia.

Georgie, Nikolai and Dmitri Constantinovich are also with Papa in the house of preliminary imprisonment and have been there for six long weeks already. They say that Georgie does not feel very well, but this is not reliable information.[29]

By the time this letter reached Ai-Todor, Xenia had probably heard that the Romanovs at Alapayevsk had been killed. The most dreadful news was yet to come. In April Nicholas, Alix and Marie had been moved to Ekaterinburg in the hostile Urals. The other children remained in Tobolsk until Alexis recovered from a haemorrhage, when they were sent to join their parents. Conditions in their new 'home', the shabby Ipatiev House, ominously renamed 'The House of Special Purpose', were squalid, with rude and slovenly guards who demonstrated their contempt for the former sovereign, his family, their physician and last remaining faithful servants at every opportunity and permitted them no privacy whatsoever. In May the family's courier disappeared en route between the Crimea and Tobolsk, and since then there had been silence from Nicholas and his family. No letters had been received from them since March. The outbreak of civil war in Russia sealed their fate. To avoid the possibility of their capture and liberation by the anti-Bolshevik White Army, the local Soviet decided to eliminate them.

On the night of 16/17 July 'Citizen Romanov', his wife, children and servants were awakened, told they were going to be sent away, and herded into a room in the basement. One of their captors then told them that their friends had tried to rescue them but failed, and read out an improvised statement of execution. He and his fellow jailers shot them all at close range, then took their bodies to a mineshaft a few miles away and destroyed them. Rumours were slow to filter out and at first there was uncertainty as to whether they had all been killed, or whether it was only the Tsar, with the rest having been sent away to captivity elsewhere. The imperial family had completely disappeared, and nobody, least of all Xenia, knew what to believe.

20 July: 'It is cooler weather today and a bit wet. At the end of the day it was very strong rain and thunder. In Odessa there is a strike. The reasons are economic – they are not being paid their salaries. . . . The sadness continued. . . .

'In the newspapers there is a small excerpt from Nicky's letter to some General telegraphed from Stockholm, that they are all alive thanks to Commissar [Chkognevich?] and that it is a better life over there . . . and that maybe Alix will be going into the Convent! But where are they?'[30]

As more and more rumours circulated that Nicholas was dead, Xenia and Sandro tried to prevent a memorial service from taking place, in order to spare the Dowager Empress further heartbreak. They also made every effort to stop her from learning about memorial services held in the European capitals, but they could not prevent her from hearing what was in the newspapers, and similar news came from Thyra or other relatives. Dagmar refused to attend the requiem at Ai-Todor and, out of deference to her, no other members of the family attended. She asked them all not to pray for the souls of her son and his family as long as she was still alive.

From Finland, her cousin Ducky wrote to Xenia of her incredulity at such a heinous crime:

Since two days we are living with such a profound & overwhelming despair in our hearts that life itself seems to be over. They all try to make us believe that it is really true that Nicky is gone. That his martyrdom is over. But we still refuse to believe it. This terrible news of his death has been spread several times before and it was not true then. Why can't it be untrue now? They want to believe that such a crime would come true.

God cannot have meant you all to suffer like this. Or did He find that Nicky had suffered enough and that for a kind & pure heart like his, eternal rest might be granted sooner. Perhaps He knew that that poor heart had born it's [sic] trials to breaking point. He took him out of this world of suffering & wrong doing, that he, who had never meant harm to any body, should no more be at the mercy of the wicked. . . .[31]

On 25 July, nine days after the massacre, the advancing White Army took Ekaterinburg and found the Ipatiev House empty. On 4

August the Spanish Ambassador in London wrote to Madrid regarding Spain's approach on behalf of the Tsar's widow and daughters, whom they believed to be still alive, and asking if it would be possible to include the Dowager Empress in the proposed negotiations. As she was a sister of Queen Alexandra, any intervention in her favour would make the Russian imperial family more acceptable to the British royal family and British public opinion, even though the move was being prepared to obtain the release of the Empress Alix.

King Alfonso XIII of Spain offered to maintain the Dowager Empress for the rest of her life, and was understood to have requested German assistance to help them all leave Russia. King George and Queen Mary were anxious for Alfonso to use his influence. Pope Benedict XV made a humanitarian appeal to the Austrian and German governments and also offered Dagmar a life annuity. Then it was learnt that the family had almost certainly died with the Tsar and that Dagmar was in no hurry to leave Russia. On 7 September Dagmar was visited by Waldemar Spare, a Finnish former officer in the Russian Imperial Guards, who now worked for the Finnish War Ministry. He returned to Copenhagen on 27 September and reported that the Dowager Empress was well, living in relative freedom and guarded by Germans. She did not believe the Tsar was dead, and expected Empress Alexandra and the children to be sent to the Crimea. Moscow and Petrograd were now under the reign of the Cheka and there were wholesale massacres of the aristocracy. Civil war raged between Reds and Whites, and Xenia recorded developments in her diary.

'In Murmansk there are about 30,000 French and Czechoslovaks. Judging by some newspapers there is a battle going on in Yaroslavl between the Bolsheviks and the White Guards and nearly all the towns are burned to the ground.'[32]

Meanwhile, Ducky's elder sister Missy, Queen of Roumania, worried endlessly about her cousins and their family. Her alarm was compounded by being cut off in Roumania, then under German occupation, and by being unaware that Ducky had escaped to the comparative safety of Finland. She sent several letters by courier to the Crimea as the Bolsheviks steadily approached from the north. Missy begged Xenia.

If possible do send me an answer to tell me something about yourselves. . . . The thought of Nicky fills me with boundless indignation and grief and what *has* happened to that unfortunate mistaken Alix? who was in *so* many ways cause of all your misfortunes! and is little Alexi [sic] still alive? How and where are all the girls? It's all so fantastic that sometimes one thinks one must be able to wake up out of it all to get back to the old days of happiness.

Xenia dear, how can it all be true! . . . Please answer if anybody offers to take a letter. I have a safe friend helping.[33]

Xenia was now able to pass on news of Missy and her family to Ducky, cut off in Finland. In return, Ducky had news of two of Sandro's brothers, brought by a man who had briefly been held in the same prison:

Jelly dear, what a joy to receive your letter. . . . To know you and your Mama are well and don't believe any of those dreadful things one hears, gives one new courage to live. . . .

Poor Georgie and Nicolai M [Michaelovich] are still shut up in prison in Petersburg. Uncle Paul and Dmitri C [Constantinovich] also, also Gabriel [Constantinovich]. They must have suffered too dreadfully . . . no-one allowed to talk to them and each of them kept separately, too unthinkable. Nicolai . . . talked . . . and joked with his guards . . . but the others are completely broken. . . .[34]

The occupants of Ai-Todor tried their best to carry on as normal. 'The Name-day of Dmitri and Papochka,' Xenia wrote on 8 November. 'We presented him with some things.'[35] This presentation, in which everyone participated, helped to take their minds off other matters. Missy and her husband King Ferdinand of Roumania had received information of a Bolshevik uprising in the Crimea, timed to coincide with the German withdrawal. The Romanovs would then be killed. A courier was sent from Roumania to the Crimea, carrying the King and Queen's proposals to send a ship to bring their relatives to safety.

9 November: 'Papochka called me from Harax asking me to come with *belle-mere* [Princess Zenaide] and *to meet* Kaznakov who returned in the evening. I came to Zenaida who was sitting on the balcony. Felix killed me by offering me what he wrote concerning Rasputin!! And he replied – "Yes, this is true, it is a little bit horrible! They won't understand his psychology!"'

At last Xenia reached Harax and met the messenger:

He sat with M. Goncharova and Kaznakov but left discreetly when I noticed that he wanted to talk to me. The things he told me killed me terribly – one thing after another! He left Jassy on Monday with a letter to Mama and [Nicholasha?] from Missy . . . and Colonel Boyle – some Canadian* who did some big favours to Missy and the King during difficult times and is himself a very good man. Three of them . . . decided to send a transport ship here to take Mama and the rest of the family away to Roumania and hopefully to go further on to England! Kaznakov says that he has a very good knowledge of what is going on here and he is positive that it will get worse when the Germans become an ally. . . . The ship could arrive here any day next week . . . he was persuading me that departure is necessary.

In the newspaper was an appeal for . . . [?] from the Will [sic] of Nations and about fighting the Bolsheviks.[36]

Missy sent a dramatic plea to Xenia to leave Russia while there was still time. The Queen said she was sending Colonel Joseph Whiteside Boyle, 'a Canadian, a remarkable man, one in ten thousand. . . . Put yourself entirely in his hands, his methods may be somewhat surprising but they are always to the point. . . .'[37] Xenia, or more probably the Empress, reassured by the presence of Allied ships in the Crimea, refused. Later that month Missy sent another desperate letter:

. . . we are anxious for you all because there may be a very dangerous moment when the Germans leave and before the allies arrive. . . . You must trust [Boyle] and listen to him – and if he persuades you to leave please leave and come to us and from there if possible we shall have all arranged so that you can

* Boyle was actually American.

go to England. . . . Trust Col. Boyle utterly, you will never regret it, he is one of those strong men as one seldom meets. . . .[38]

Meanwhile, the collapse of Germany was imminent.
10 November: 'There is a rumour that Wilhelm has abdicated and that a Constituent Assembly will be called again. The Germans did not talk about that'.[39]

The rumours turned out to be true, as next day Xenia wrote:
Wilhelm has abdicated, his son has abdicated all rights to the throne and they will be calling a Constituent Assembly. . . . A few days ago an officer came with some soldiers. . . . They made it look like a search and took away the revolver and stole the clock and something else! Kuchurov brought Conditions for a peace deal from Yalta. This is something terrible. . . . I can imagine the rejoicing of the allies, especially the French . . . this exceeded all their expectations'.[40]

After the signing of the armistice on 11 November, defeated Germany now had to evacuate the Crimea. 'What a huge downfall for Germany,' Ducky wrote incredulously. 'Could one believe that they would collapse like this. . . . Our position gives us nothing any more, so if we are ever worth anything again in this life it will be thanks to ourselves. . . .

'Nobody cares for us abroad, nasty selfish brutes! I tried to get help for your Mama a year ago from England at the time when you seemed to have neither money nor food, but they refused and said perhaps Roumania would help. It fills my heart with boiling wrath. The Danes have all through been the kindest and the best. . . .'[41]

'The Germans are leaving from here,' Xenia wrote in her diary on 13 November. 'How everything flies!'[42]

Andrusha had become friendly with Elisabeta Ruffo di Sant' Antimo, a divorcee with two children. Now, as the Germans withdrew, Xenia had to contend with a delicate family matter. 'Andrusha told us that Elsa is expecting a baby due in February and that she is coming from Odessa on Monday and the wedding will be on the first available day!' she wrote on 13 November. 'This is the last thing we need! What a punishment and I feel sorry for

Andrusha. . . . It is impossible to demand that he waits or that he not marry at all. She caught him. . . . I do not know what to think.'[43]

Other royal relatives also feared for the Romanovs' safety. The Red Army was closing in, and though the Soviet government had already made peace with Germany, the situation was confused, with Germans preparing to move out of Russia and the Western Allies preparing to intervene to help the Whites in the civil war. Andrei, Feodor, Nikita and Felix wrote to General Denikin, Commander-in-Chief of the White Army, but their request to join up was refused. As Romanovs they were considered 'undesirable'.[44]

King George V now sent Commander Turle to the Crimea. The Admiralty telegram described Ai-Todor as 'running back from the sea, a yellow building with greenish tiles and occupied by the late Emperor's sisters'.[45] When Turle transmitted the King's offer to take the Empress by warship to Constantinople, she laughingly refused. But as the German Army withdrew, it was feared that the Bolsheviks would take their place, and her sang-froid was not shared by others.

Boyle, who had already rescued Xenia's cousin Grand Duchess Marie Pavlovna from Odessa, arrived in the Crimea on 24 November with an armed force of 200 soldiers, a hand-picked crew, guns, provisions and a car. The Empress believed it was her duty to stay and Boyle returned to Roumania with letters for Queen Marie from Xenia and her mother. There had been great debate in the family over what they should do. The Empress and Xenia thought it was unnecessary to leave. Sandro disagreed and was angry with Xenia. 'Feel sick with myself and life and everything altogether,'[46] she wrote on 22 December.

By now Sandro was anxious to go to Paris and see the heads of the Allied governments, in order to impress upon them how serious the situation had become in Russia. On 24 December the family received a telegram from Aunt Alix saying that Sandro really was going on a British cruiser. The ship would sail straight to Taranto, which would be very convenient. 'Sandro had tea at Irina's and announced to all the children that he is leaving [for Europe].'[47] Xenia vividly expressed her feelings at this news.

25 December: 'I was with Sandro at Harax and he announced to everyone and Olga about his decision to leave – "I came to say that I am going the day after tomorrow!" Olga started laughing and Mama pretended to faint . . . but I still cannot understand how he can do this! Nothing to do about that – "*what can't be cured must be endured!*"'[48]

In England Queen Alexandra was desperate for the whole family to leave Russia. '. . . yesterday we had a telegram where she replies – *Long to see you* but I cannot and . . . "*need*" to go now,' Xenia continued.

All day there was not a very comforting feeling, very sad and Sophia was very supportive talking about Sandro's leaving.

I was talking to Sandro about his relationship with D. and asked to talk to him about this matter and he did this. Also I asked him to pull himself together.

O.K.* terribly disappointed about Sandro's departure. She still has a temperature. . . . Made a bed on the couch in my bedroom. Sandro went to sleep on the settee. There are persistent rumours in Yalta about the taking of Petersburg [*sic*] by the English.[49]

Sandro arranged with Admiral Calthorpe to leave on HMS *Forsythe*. Grand Duchess Olga and her husband also decided to go, heading for the Caucasus where the Red Army had been pushed back.

26 December: 'That is it – Sandro has left! So sad and difficult but I think I am happy for him. I went with him to Yalta. . . . There were a lot of people on the Mall, Nikolas was here [possibly Nicholai Orlov] and one military regiment. I followed Sandro to the torpedo boat (*Acorn*) and the commander offered me a cabin as he thought I would be going too. It is very comfortable, as usual with the English.

'Very, very sad to part – *such a wrench* – and most surprising is his full independence. Where did he get that from?' Sandro was accompanied by Andrusha and his bride Elisabeta. 'They departed very quickly and disappeared. . . .'[50]

---

* Olga Konstantinova Vassilievna, later Mme Tchirikoff.

During the bitterly cold winter of 1918/19 Xenia and some of her sons caught Spanish 'flu, and one of the boys nearly died. Then the Empress was taken ill and a professor had to be called in from Yalta.

Xenia received a telegram from Sandro, dated 17 January. He was in Taranto, Italy, about to go via Rome to Paris and then London. He stressed again that they must leave.[51] Her next news of him came in February, via Thormeyer, who heard that Sandro had arrived in Paris at the end of January. The old tutor wanted to go and see him, but it was too difficult to leave Switzerland. Xenia was in despair that Thormeyer had no news of her brother Misha, who had completely disappeared.[52]

Meanwhile Danish efforts to free the four Grand Dukes imprisoned in Petrograd had failed. From Cotroceni Palace, where she was staying with Missy, Marie Pavlovna wrote that they had just learnt that 'Papa [Grand Duke Paul], Nicolai, Georgie & Uncle Mitia were killed. Gabriel was let go and he is in Finland. This news came to us from . . . London, from Georgie's secretary. Unfortunately, we can not doubt this . . . news. You will understand what a nightmare it is for me. Everything, everything disappears into the past, everything which is good, everything which is bright and the only thing that's left is the terrible reality. . . .'[53]

From Georgie's widow, Greek Minny, who was living in London, Xenia heard more:

. . . those fiends came to tell them in that prison that they would be free next day . . . instead of which they were driven to the Peter & Paul Fortress and shot. . . . There was a long article in the Journal by a reliable Frenchman . . . but it is too painful for me to go over it again. Such irony, to be buried two steps from the place they had a right to be buried. This man says they were perfectly calm and died with the greatest dignity and courage! Poor old Bimbo made a long speech to his executioners which impressed those inhuman monsters! Poor Paul seems to have collapsed, being so weak from want of food. He was so thin and ill that they did not recognize him. The truth came out only a few days after when a man was boasting in the streets that he had a pair of boots on belonging to a Romanov he had shot the day before. To think that people like that can exist! . . .

'I have heard from Sandro several times,' she continued, on a more cheerful note. 'He says [the] Andrushas have a comfortable flat. As Sandro lives at the Ritz he sees Nancy Leeds quite often. . . .'[54] It was from a newspaper in the Paris Ritz that Sandro found out about his brothers' deaths.

On 19 March Elisabeta gave birth in Paris to a daughter. 'On behalf of Grand Duke Alexander congratulations grand-daughter Xenia [.] all well,' a member of Sandro's staff telegraphed to the Grand Duchess, giving the news.[55]

In the Crimea the Bolsheviks were closing in. The French had pulled out of Odessa after their sailors mutinied and only the poorly trained volunteer White Army now stood between the imperial family and disaster. The Romanovs were celebrating Xenia's birthday when Capt Charles Johnson of the battleship HMS *Marlborough* was announced. He stressed the seriousness of the situation and produced instructions to evacuate the Dowager Empress and her family that very evening. He also brought an offer of asylum from King George V, and a letter from Queen Alexandra begging her sister to leave while there was still time. Even now, with hope of escape overland cut off, the Empress refused to leave and without her nobody else could go. It took several hours of persuasion to change her mind. Finally she gave in, insisting that all the family, the retainers and scores of refugees who were in danger from the Bolsheviks should be evacuated with her. Xenia was told 'that they are going on board the *Marlborough* at 5.00 and that everyone should be there. What grief and desperation,'[56] she wrote in her diary.

As *Marlborough* was hastily rearranged to accommodate many more people than originally envisaged, the Romanovs began to pack. In this respect Xenia was luckier than her mother and sister. As she was leaving from her own home, she was able to ensure that the most valuable possessions, including her jewels and 54-piece set of solid gold plate, were packed ready for loading at Yalta the next day. Among the hastily packed possessions were several cases marked 'Fragile – Belaoussoff', which belonged to Xenia's old laundress. Later they were found to contain mainly useless rubbish.[57]

Vassili recalled later the sadness of leaving, and of having to decide what to take with them, mingled with the excitement of boarding a battleship. Everyone wanted to get on the ships. 'The

Russian custom in making long journeys is to take lots of cooks along: in exile, especially, chefs took priority over chancellors,' Xenia explained many years later. 'So suddenly everybody was claiming to be a great chef. . . . Quite a few generals and engineers got aboard that way.'[58] Xenia sent a hasty telegram to Sandro, receiving in return an acknowledgement from the French Vice-Admiral saying it would be immediately transmitted to Paris.[59] Then, after a final lunch at Harax, they went to say goodbye to friends at Djulber.

The Empress had asked to embark at secluded Koreiz cove and the ship's carpenter hastily improvised a jetty. Marines and sailors landed on the beach to defend it from the approaching Red Army and escort them to the ship. Speed and secrecy were vital. Any move that betrayed the evacuation to the Bolsheviks could be fatal.

Xenia and the Empress arrived by car with their dogs and Vassili's pet canary. Clutching her dog, Xenia took her last steps on her native soil and boarded the pinnace behind her mother. Vassili's bicycle was given to his tutor, then he and Feodor walked down towards the sea, sadly seeing all their favourite places for the last time. Meanwhile, his favourite pony pulled the cart carrying their luggage.[60]

Lieutenant-Commander Pridham had been deputed to welcome the Empress and her daughter on board. Just as he was enquiring when they were expected, he spotted two unaccompanied ladies walking along the deck and was suddenly confronted with the Dowager Empress and Grand Duchess Xenia. Pridham escorted the Empress to the captain's cabin. Just as he was about to leave, Xenia offered to help him allocate the cabins. 'I found myself closeted with an extremely charming and capable woman,' Pridham recalled, 'who knew exactly what was entailed and had a very clear idea as to how the details should be settled. . . .'[61]

While her sons argued over who had the hammocks in the cabin they shared, Xenia sorted out accommodation and gave orders to the Russian servants. She insisted that her mother's maid Kiki should occupy the cabin next to the Empress, and for herself took one of the smaller, darker cabins on the deck below. After dark they sailed for Yalta, where under cover of the ship's guns the evacuation continued for a further three days. Extra bedding was hastily brought from the imperial estates and spare

145

mattresses were arranged in the officers' cabins for the older people. The younger passengers crammed themselves in as best they could. Nineteen members of the imperial family were on board with their maids, menservants, governesses and officials of their households, in addition to 1,170 evacuees and crew and a fortune in jewels.

For Xenia's five sons it was an exciting experience. Vassili soon became a great favourite with the crew, while Dmitri watched the British battleships keenly from *Marlborough*'s deck. He already had a great knowledge of British warships, and later admitted that he never travelled without his copy of *Jane's Fighting Ships*.[62] Xenia summed up her own feelings in her diary, written on board HMS *Marlborough* that evening. '. . . *to have to sever oneself – from one's own people*, to say nothing of the grief of departing from Ai-Todor – 'home', the motherland. . . .'[63]

HMS *Grafton*, four British destroyers and one French ship arrived to help with the evacuation. The rumour that the Empress was leaving caused panic, as people abandoned all their possessions and hurried to the waterfront in a frantic effort to board the allied ships. Many families became separated in the chaos and others had only the clothes they stood up in. As the embarkation neared completion, a desperate appeal reached Xenia on board the *Marlborough*. It was written in pencil by her childhood friend Dmitri Cheremetev, who had arrived in Constantinople:

Refugees from Miskhor, Koreiz, Alupka & Gaspra are arriving in Constantinople. . . . The second [ship] brought some of our ladies and . . . the *Princess Ena*, also carrying some of our people, is expected today. But on arrival in Constantinople, we have come across unexpected obstacles in the form of not being given leave to disembark following an order by . . . the French General. They say, tomorrow everyone will be reunited, but our further fate remains unknown. . . . All the refugees are asking for you to intercede . . . so they will be allowed to *remain under English protection* and not be left at the mercy of the French. They want to end up on the *Grafton* and in this way to be left in the sphere of your influence on the *Marlborough*.

For God's sake help us![64]

Whether Xenia was able to do anything is unknown.

On 11 April 1919, as HMS *Marlborough* slipped quietly, almost imperceptibly, into the Black Sea, nearly all of the family stood on deck. 'What fools we are,' Vassili heard one of his grown-up cousins murmur.[65] The Captain handed Xenia his binoculars so that she could have a last look at the coastline.

'What are those little black things all along the shore?' she asked.

'Madame', he replied, 'that is your silver.'

The servants had been so afraid they would be left behind that they had not loaded the chests.[66] In all, about fifty-four cases were left on the quay. Xenia said it did not matter, but over the coming years there must have been many times she regretted it.

As they sailed along the Crimean coast past the familiar landmarks – Livadia, Kishkine, Djulber – their last sight was the Ai-Todor lighthouse. When Sandro was a child, for him and his brothers it was 'a symbol of happiness'.[67] To Xenia and her sons, it was a last glimpse of home as they sailed into exile. Never again would they see Russian soil.

9 (1919–24)

'Any mark of sympathy in times like these'

As HMS *Marlborough* steamed across the Black Sea to the Bosphorus, Grand Duchess Xenia, daughter of one Tsar of Russia and sister of another, was now a stateless person. Like the other refugees she was given a certificate: 'I certify that H.I.H. Grand Duchess Xenia Alexandrovna left Russia in HMS *Marlborough* on the 11th April 1919. (Signed) Capt. Johnson.'[1]

At Constantinople they anchored off Halki Island. Provisions were taken on board and Admiral Calthorpe came to discuss their future. The immediate destination for Xenia, her sons and her mother was Malta, en route to England where they would be granted asylum. The British government would not permit Grand Dukes Nicholas and Peter to reside in England and, probably out of a desire to avoid embarrassing her future hosts, the Empress did not want them to accompany her to Malta. While arrangements were made to transfer them to another ship, life on board continued in as normal a manner as possible, given their straitened circumstances. There was even some lighthearted banter, and at dinner one evening Xenia's staff saw her laugh for the first time in ages. To relieve the monotony the officers organized a picnic on Halki Island for the children, while some of the adults visited Hagia Sophia in Constantinople. Vassili amused himself by playing deck games with Prince Dolgoruky's niece Sofka, and Felix entertained the company with his guitar.

On 16 April the two Grand Ducal parties transferred to HMS *Lord Nelson* bound for Genoa. Other exiles came on board to take their place, and again Xenia helped to allocate the cabins. Some of the refugees were destitute and Xenia asked Pridham if he could provide two pairs of shoes. He had to hint that it was impossible to keep handing out stores and begged her to take them to the unfortunate people as a gift. Xenia nicknamed Pridham 'Job', as he was 'beset with many afflictions', his duties even including arranging limited laundry facilities for the ladies. At one point Xenia had to save the harassed Lieutenant from the embarrassment of trying to decline the Empress's dinner invitation, explaining to her mother that he still had to deal with many things.[2]

The vessel was due to return to the Black Sea after discharging her passengers but this upset Dagmar, who immediately telegraphed to King George of her gratitude for the 'hospitality and remarkable kindness from everybody here on board', and that her sole wish was to go in the *Marlborough* to join him as soon as possible in England.[3] The Admiralty informed Admiral Calthorpe that HMS *Lord Nelson* would convey the Empress to England, if she wished; but she should be warned that another opportunity might not come soon – if at all.

They left for Malta on Good Friday. Easter was celebrated in traditional manner with a service in one of the larger cabins, specially decorated with pictures and candles. Hand-painted Easter eggs were provided for the Empress to give to the children, and in gratitude Pridham received a pearl Easter egg from her and a gold and ruby one from Xenia. Pridham recalled that, despite the sadness they felt in leaving their country, all the family were in good spirits. None of them believed in rumours that the Tsar had been killed, and he thought Xenia and her mother were unaware that the news had been published in *The Times*.[4]

News of the family's imminent arrival in Malta was kept with 'strict military secrecy'.[5] A 'secret' telegram instructed the Governor to 'receive them with as little ceremony as possible, and unofficially, and you had better not meet them yourself. They will arrive practically destitute without clothes or money. . . . Do not allow arrival or any reference to it to appear in the local papers. All proper expenses of maintenance and clothing will be refunded to you.'[6] These instructions were later changed, and in the end they were received with all due honours.

HMS *Marlborough* anchored in Valletta harbour shortly before 5pm on 20 April. They disembarked the following morning as the Royal Marine Band played the Russian national anthem and were welcomed by the Governor, Lord Methuen. The Empress, Xenia and her sons were driven to the San Antonio Palace with Aprak, Zina Mengden, Sophie Evreinoff, Sergei Dolgoruky, the cook and the Cossack bodyguards. The ADC was amused when Prince Dolgoruky immediately pinned up several rather risqué pictures from *La Vie Parisienne* in his room. The Youssoupovs and other retainers were lodged in hotels around the island.

San Antonio Palace, the Governor's lovely summer residence at Attard, had been hastily refurbished for the royal visitors, even to the provision of an Orthodox chapel. Though the Russian servants had been insolent and had done as little as possible when the baggage was being unloaded, Xenia insisted on making sure they were comfortable before settling into her own rooms. In contrast her sons cheerfully helped everyone, refusing to allow Miss Coster to carry even the smallest of her bags. 'I'm afraid you must think these menservants of ours very lazy and that they have bad manners,' Feodor said to the ADC, 'but what is one to expect after two or three years of revolution?'[7] After welcoming the Empress, Lord and Lady Methuen returned to Valletta leaving a young ADC, Robert Ingham, in charge.

Xenia soon took to chatting with Ingham after dinner. She made him tell funny stories and they talked about the latest, rather scanty, fashions. Xenia said her husband had recently attended a ball in Paris where the ladies were 'beautifully undressed'. When Ingham explained it gave greater freedom for dancing she replied, 'Oh! then they'd better come naked altogether, with a few feathers round.'[8] One evening they discussed Malta's new compulsory education scheme and the Malta Boy Scouts. 'In Russia we also had Scouts, but now – nothing,' Xenia remarked sadly. She was delighted with the palace and its beautiful gardens, and overjoyed to have proper food again after living on whatever they could obtain. 'But you English are so good,' she added. 'But the French: Oh! the French have been so foolish and it is all through them that all this trouble was started, and Odessa had to be given up.'[9] Ingham could only mutter a diplomatic reply.

Xenia asked Ingham to keep an eye on the boys. One day two of them persuaded him to take them to the races at Masa racecourse, in strict defiance of Lord Methuen, who said he was not to leave the Empress. This put Ingham in an awkward position.

In the freedom of Malta, Xenia's sons had become very high-spirited. They tickled the servants' legs at mealtimes, tugged at the guards' rifles so that they came crashing to the ground as their grandmother walked past, and one evening a couple of the elder ones slipped off into Valletta. Somehow they had persuaded the chauffeur to bring the open car into the road behind the high garden wall, and then they climbed a tree and dropped into the seats. Late that night there was a commotion at the palace as they returned and started chasing the guards. Ingham, clad only in pyjamas, had to chase one of the boys up to his room to make sure he went to bed. Though he tried to cover up the escapade, Xenia soon found out. 'I thought I told you not to give the boys any money,' she said, 'so how they had such a noisy night of it I simply don't know.'[10]

Another night Feodor and Felix Youssoupov made a tour of Valletta's night clubs with some of the *Marlborough*'s sailors. With so many offers to buy them a beer, they had to return home quickly before they became too drunk. Even the Empress was in despair when two of the younger boys began throwing bread pellets across the table during dinner. Every morning, however, they respectfully greeted their grandmother with a bow and kissed her hand.

During their eight-day stay Xenia and her mother went for drives around the island, had tea with Lady Methuen at Valletta Palace and received many visitors. They quite 'lost their hearts' to Malta and its people. Years later, when Ingham visited her in England, Xenia told him that 'she had asked the King if she and her mother could make Malta their home'. The King replied that he had already made other arrangements.[11] As they left San Antonio on 29 April Xenia picked four ruby and diamond studs from her white silk blouse. Pressing them into Ingham's hand, she said simply, 'for you to remember me by'.[12]

Meanwhile Sandro was in Paris, desperate to leave Europe behind him for good. He shook his head wearily when statesmen told him that Russia would soon surely turn the clock back, with all the Grand Dukes returning to their palaces in St Petersburg, and declared emphatically that he would not accept the whole of Russia as a gift. With regard to his own personal future, the only possible alternatives were the United States, where he had made several good friends, and Fiji, which he had visited in his bachelor days and where he considered a large family could live comfortably on very little money. He wrote a long letter to Xenia and their sons supporting the project, describing the beauties of Pacific life, and imploring them to move to a part of the world 'where one is given a munificent chance to assemble the bits and pieces of a life cut by the scissors of history'.

Her reply dashed his hopes, as she told him bluntly that he must be out of his head to want them to take refuge 'in a God-forsaken spot when the coming six months may see the reestablishment of a legitimate regime in Russia'.[13] Bored with Paris, where none of the senior allied statesmen would receive him, and relieved to hear of the safe arrival of Xenia, the Empress and the others at Malta, he left for Biarritz to try to rekindle and relive the happier days of some twelve years previously. From there he telegraphed to Lord Hardinge at the British Embassy: 'Hear from my wife that after short stay at Malta all going to England. Will you enquire if I will be able to go too?'[14] Hardinge forwarded the message to Lord Stamfordham, asking how he should reply, and the telegram was passed to the King.

The royal family still had to contend with a certain degree of embarrassment. After the Tsar's abdication King George V had been anxious to help cousin 'Nicky' and his family, and when asked if they would offer them asylum for the duration of the war Prime Minister Lloyd George and his Cabinet assented. At first the Provisional Government in Russia pressed for the imperial family's departure, but later they feared hostility from the extremists and made no effort to accept the British offer. Moreover the Tsar's children had measles and could not be moved at the crucial moment. By the time they were better, the chance had passed. For years it was believed that the King had done his best to rescue the family but was prevented by Lloyd George, who was generally regarded as less sympathetic to the monarchical cause than any other holder of the office during the century.

The truth was rather different. Fearful of reaction from the growing republican movement if the autocratic Romanovs were given asylum in England, and the subsequent threat to his throne, King George requested his government to withdraw the offer.

Now, in 1919, neither King George nor Mr Balfour, the Foreign Secretary, wanted the Russian Grand Dukes to come to England, where their presence would be blamed on the King's influence. Thus Sandro's request was refused; he could join his wife later in Copenhagen if he wished. The Grand Duke, reported Hardinge, did not seem in the least worried at the refusal, even though he rightly pointed out that he had left Russia 'under British protection'. Hardinge added tersely that he was not 'much impressed by [the] explanation of H.I.H. having left his family'.[15] On 28 April Sandro telegraphed to Xenia: 'Approve plan, sorry can't come my request refused, life agreeable, quiet, what day Irina Paris. Love Alexander.'[16] The 'plan' was for Xenia, Dmitri, Rostislav and Vassili to accompany the Empress to England; Feodor and Nikita would go with Irina and Felix to Paris; and Bébé would accompany the elder Youssoupovs to Rome.

The Home Office had been requested to grant the Romanovs 'all possible facilities for disembarkation'[17] but there had been some difficulty over the entourage. Finally, seventeen males and twenty-six females were permitted to accompany them to England. None of them was sure what sort of a welcome they would receive. Xenia was so concerned about money that she telegraphed to Toria asking her to 'take seven bedrooms, two servants' rooms, one sitting room and dining room; cheapest possible hotel'.[18]

The final leg of Xenia's journey to England was made on the older, slower HMS *Lord Nelson*. All the crew noticed how animated the Empress's party were, even organizing dances on the quarterdeck. The children played 'everlasting games of quoits' and exercised the dogs, including Xenia's black dog Toby, acquired from the Dolgorukys.[19] Unfortunately, the owners of these animals were informed, the dogs would have to be placed in quarantine on landing. 'No exceptions will be made,' the Admiralty telegraphed.[20] Before they left the ship, Xenia collected another certificate giving the dates of her departure from Malta and arrival in England.

When *Lord Nelson* docked at Portsmouth on 9 May 1919, Xenia, with her mother at her side, moved forward to embrace her aunt Alix. Then, after an emotional reunion alone, the party boarded a special train for the journey to Victoria station, where King George and Queen Mary were waiting.

'The Dowager Empress Marie of Russia . . . arrives in London today, accompanied by her daughter the Grand Duchess Xenia,' announced the Court Circular. 'The Dowager Empress will go to Marlborough House . . . while the Grand Duchess and her sons will stay, for a time at least, at Buckingham Palace.'[21] At the palace Xenia's servants fell on their knees before King George, mistaking him for the Tsar, miraculously resurrected from the dead.

Over the next few weeks the Court Circular faithfully recorded Xenia's movements – drives with Queen Mary and Princess Victoria; lunch with Queen Alexandra; lunches at Buckingham Palace. Queen Mary, not the most maternal of figures, was kind to Xenia's sons. Among those who visited Xenia was Sandro's brother Miche-Miche, who lived in England with his wife Sophie and their children, Zia, Nada and 'Boy'. Miche-Miche had lost everything in the revolution; with no money or capital in England he was forced to sub-let Ken Wood and move to a house in Cambridge Gate. King George and Queen Mary offered a loan of £10,000, with Sophie's jewels as nominal security. Luckily, his daughters married well – Zia to the extremely wealthy Sir Harold Wernher; Nada to the Marquis of Milford Haven. The birth of Nada's daughter in 1917 caused something of a sensation. When the King and Queen received a telegram saying 'Tatiana has arrived', their instant, if momentary, reaction was that the Tsar's daughter had escaped from Russia.[22]

Other visitors to Xenia included Colonel Boyle, who took letters back to Missy in Roumania, and Robert Ingham, on a brief visit to London. She also received some photographs taken on board HMS *Marlborough*, sent by one of the crew.

Xenia was concerned about the plight of the hundreds of Russian refugees still stranded in Malta. British policy was to 'refuse all Russian Refugees unless they have strong business reasons or their presence is required here for the purpose of British trade'.[23] Yet, although the restrictions had been explained, the Empress and Xenia were continually pressing the Foreign Office to allow exemptions for 'various loyal subjects of the late Imperial regime',[24] including Herr Jurgensen, the tutor who had done so much to help them when they were all under arrest in the Crimea, and Olga Vassilievna. 'I have impressed upon the Empress and the Grand Duchess Xenia the difficulty of admitting Russian refugees here in any numbers – no matter what class – they quite realise it, The Empress is most grateful for the consideration shown to them,' Sir Arthur Davidson told the Foreign Office. 'The Empress feels bound to try and help these people as far as she can, as they have done all they can to help her in the anxious time through which she has passed since the revolution.'[25]

The Home Office's policy was to take only refugees considered capable of supporting themselves. When the matter of refusal to admit 'certain members of the Russian Imperial House either to visit or reside in Great Britain', despite their loyalty to the allies during the war, was raised in the Commons in 1921, the government replied that they were anxious 'not to admit refugees from Russia who were and are anxious to come here in very large numbers'.[26]

On 14 June Xenia and her sons moved to the Savoy Hotel, while her maids remained at Buckingham Palace. 'Any mark of sympathy in times like these . . . is a comfort but you and Georgie have shown and given me *so much* and have both been a great moral help to me and I do feel it *so* deeply . . .', Xenia wrote to Queen Mary. 'We are quite comfortable here and have rooms overlooking the river, two bedrooms and sitting room all very nice and airy. We shall move to our house Friday.'[27]

This house was at 28 Draycott Place, Chelsea, a four-storey terraced property with a basement and bay windows just behind King's Road. Xenia, Grand Duchess Marie Pavlovna recalled, 'lived in a small house smothered by a large family of boys and numerous female servants who had followed her out of Russia. Smiling, always perfectly enchanting and a little bewildered, she moved about the house in search of a little privacy.'[28]

Xenia's most pressing concerns were financial. With the help of Herbert Galloway Stewart, her sons' former tutor, she opened a current account at Coutts, the royal family's bankers in the Strand. With £1,000 to her credit she immediately wrote out a cheque for £98 in Harrods. She went shopping in Piccadilly, buying her favourite rose water perfume in a shop near Fortnum & Mason's which was probably Penhaligon's, founded in 1870, who later confirmed that their Bury Street branch had a large Russian clientele. One of these even gave Mrs Penhaligon a sable coat.[29] In July Irina arrived with Felix, and they moved to his Knightsbridge apartment.

In the summer Xenia and Sandro were briefly reunited in Biarritz, where they posed for photographs on the occasion of their silver wedding anniversary. Xenia was also able to see Andrusha and Elisabeta's daughter Princess Xenia. It had originally been Xenia's intention to settle at her house on Villa Said, a small road in the Russian Quarter of Paris. Situated just off Avenue Foch, it was full of large, prestigious villas. Yet perhaps by this time she and Sandro had drifted too far apart. As the British government would not grant him a visa for England, there was no question of him moving there, even had he been thus inclined, and he decided to make his home in France. King George V also thought that his cousin would be safer in England and persuaded her to stay. Most of Xenia's family had come to England, and she thought the boys would receive a better education there. Such a decision was also influenced by the advice in one of Ducky's letters; commiserating with Xenia on her homesickness, she added by way of consolation that 'at least it may be good for your children, & England is good for boys, even if they are a little miserable at school at first, it will teach them certain things that they would never learn in Russia'.[30]

Xenia returned via Paris. For someone of high rank, accustomed to coming and going as she pleased, it must have arrived as something of a shock to learn that she now needed a visa. On 7 August the British Ambassador in Paris telegraphed a request to the Foreign Office from Sandro that 'permission be obtained for Grand Duchess Xenia to return to England on August 13 accompanied by her two sons Theodor [sic] and Nikita'.[31] Instructions were awaited from Buckingham Palace and Marlborough House.

The King, Lord Cromer replied, 'hopes the necessary visas will be granted'.[32] Sir Arthur Davidson confirmed that Xenia's return was 'in fulfilment of permission given by the Foreign Office and Home Office to Her Imperial Highness to go to France for a short visit to her husband and to return to England on its completion'. His further remarks throw an interesting light on the official British attitude to Xenia's husband and sons:

Her three sons who came with her from the Crimea are at school in England, and her object in bringing over Princes

Theodor [sic] and Nikita is probably to place them also at School or College.

There does not appear to be any objection to their being allowed to accompany their mother *as they do not possess Grand Ducal Title or Rank.* [authors' emphasis]

The Grand Duke Alexander is aware that he himself is not permitted at present to come to England.[33]

Xenia and Nikita finally left Paris on 15 August, travelling via Boulogne. It had been arranged that Feodor would follow later. There was a measure of urgency as on 19 August the Dowager Empress left England to make her home in Denmark, and Xenia doubtless wanted to say goodbye.

In London Feodor and Nikita helped Felix in his work for the Russian Red Cross. He established a workshop to give employment to Russian refugees, as well as a centre in a house at Belgrave Square where emigrés could go to seek help and advice.

With no experience of looking after herself, at the age of forty-four Xenia was now alone in a very different world. Sandro's former ADC Prince Dmitri Orbeliani lived nearby, but his death in 1922 removed any moral support from that quarter. Although Andrei was married, and Feodor was later to make his home with Irina and Felix, Xenia still had the well-being of her other sons to worry about. Among the retainers following her to England were her chambermaid Alexandra Pavlova; Anastasia Grigorievna, ('Na'), her old nurse; Miss Coster, the governess; the old laundress Belaoussoff; Kalominoff, the manservant; and Sophie Evreinoff, the lady-in-waiting, with her maid, all of whom now had to be supported.

The stress of recent events had taken its toll on her health. 'I feel much better but the weakness and headache continue and I still stay in bed,' she told Feodor, who was with the Youssoupovs in Paris, on 29 January 1920. 'I hope you will come soon. Yesterday Dmitri departed to his island and today Vassili. Rostislav has a duty cold and is staying until Monday. It is a very great pity that you did not meet. Today is . . . the anniversary of the death of poor uncles [Nicholas and George Michaelovich]. There is going to be a service and requiem [funeral mass] in our church here. God knows what is happening in Russia. How unbearably painful and hard this all is. . . . Nikita is very happy with his life in Cambridge, he writes every day! . . . Do not forget the perfume. . . .'[34]

On Good Friday 1920 Olga and her family arrived in Copenhagen. Their journey out of Russia had taken them to Novorossiysk, Rostov and then Novo-Minskaya in the Caucasus, where Olga gave birth to their second son Guri on 23 April 1919. Forced to flee from the approaching Red Army on a bitter November night, they sheltered at the British Consulate in Novorossiysk, where a British officer Olga had known in better days put them aboard a ship bound for Prinkipo, Turkey. Within a few weeks the British High Commissioner arranged their passage to Constantinople, and then to Belgrade, where King Alexander offered them a home. The Dowager Empress had other ideas, and the family were soon on their way to Denmark.[35]

Seventeen of the fifty-two Romanovs living in Russia disappeared during the revolution or the subsequent Red Terror. Survivors included Queen Olga of Greece; the indomitable Grand Duchess Vladimir ('Miechen') and her sons Cyril, Boris and Andrei; Grand Duke Dmitri Pavlovich, whose exile after the murder of Rasputin had saved his life; and Dmitri's sister Grand Duchess Marie. Of Sandro's family there remained only him, his brother Miche-Miche and their sister Grand Duchess Anastasia of Mecklenburg-Schwerin, who died in 1922.

As the Romanovs surfaced one by one, and with no definite news of Nicholas and Michael, rumours flourished. Ducky told Xenia: 'Etter said he had news from [Neratoff?] in Paris about Misha. "He is alive and well and I know where he is" were his words to Etter, but unless you know something certain I am afraid [Neratoff?] was saying more than he really knows. But it filled us once more with hope – about the others Xenia dear unless you can give us hope . . . I have none.'[36]

It might be wondered how much Xenia and the rest of the Romanovs knew about the failure of King George V and Queen Mary to save Nicky, Alix and the children, but once the King had given her a grace and favour house she had every reason to stay, particularly given her impecunious state. Nevertheless some relations were prepared to speak their mind. From St Cloud, Prince George of Greece wrote of his utter disillusion with the state of affairs:

Morals, principals [sic], heart and every Christian feeling has been done away with by this infernal war and those who are guiding the nation today are all without religion. There is *one*, who might have stuck to principal and to nobel [sic] acts, only one, and this is English Georgie, but he, hiding behind the words 'constitutional King' allows the evil to conquer over everything that is good and right, so as to stick to his d–d throne, which now a days is no better than a W.C.[37]

In 1920 Xenia was appalled to learn that some of Nicholas and Alexandra's intimate letters were about to be published in London. She had already seen some newspaper cuttings, following publication of the correspondence in America. Olga, who received similar information, warned her mother and they decided to leave the matter with Xenia in London. Xenia told the King, who put her in touch with Sir Charles Russell, the royal family's solicitor. Sir Charles applied for a 'grant of administration' over the Tsar's property in England, including literary rights. On 17 May 1920 Xenia was granted Letters of Administration to Nicholas's total estate in England, as the Tsar's elder sister and heir.[38] In a letter of 15 June Sir Charles also informed her that he had obtained an Order from the Supreme Court 'injuncting Sir George Thompson Hutchinson & his Company from dealing in any way with the letters'.[39]

The gross value of Nicholas's estate in England was £500. This comprised the damaged jewellery and bones found at the Four Brothers Mine and brought to Europe in 1920. Nicholas Sokolov, a monarchist officer, had conducted an investigation into the events at Ekaterinburg and established that the Tsar, Tsarina, their children and servants had been shot, their bodies loaded into a lorry and taken to the Four Brothers Mine, where they were stripped, burned, dissolved in sulphuric acid and thrown down a disused mineshaft. Jewellery, remnants of clothing, bones, false teeth and the body of Tatiana's dog were discovered in the mine, but the bodies of the family and servants were never found.

General Dieterichs wanted the relics, Sokolov's dossier and the family's personal possessions to be kept by the British government until they could be returned to him or handed to Nicholasha. The Foreign Office preferred the relics and the dossier to remain in

Russian hands, while the personal possessions were to be sent to Grand Duchess Xenia.[40]

Xenia then received a letter from Nicholasha in Rome, who had just received a copy of the dossier. He was passing these documents, which were of 'extraordinary state importance', to Michael de Giers, the 'doyen of the Imperial Russian Diplomatic Corps in Europe',[41] so they could be checked for legal authenticity under 'an official body appointed to General Wrangel'.* Nicholasha continued:

> Once the legal checking has been done, I will know its result and I will let you know, together with sending you a copy of the documents and material evidence which will legally not be needed. Then it will all have to be sent to your august Mother. It can be done only through you, as you alone can prepare her for these minutes – a nightmare that cannot be described – if the investigation confirms the legal authenticity.
>
> May God help you and all of us to bear such a heavy trial which has been sent on to us from above. . . .[42]

Early in 1920 fifty-four cases of the imperial family's personal possessions were sent to Vladivostok for onward transmission to England in HMS *Kent*. Only twenty-nine cases reached the British ship and subsequently London, where they had to be fumigated. When the boxes were opened in the presence of Xenia, the King and Queen Alexandra at Marlborough House, they were found to contain nothing but rubbish. They were taken to Xenia's London home and soon forgotten. A few months later Xenia received a letter from Baroness Buxhoeveden asking whether she had found Empress Alexandra's jewels, which were concealed in a roll of cloth in one of the boxes. Armed with the exact location, Xenia went back to the boxes and found the jewels. She also received all the small items found on the Romanovs killed at Alapayevsk, which she distributed among the family, and some religious books belonging to the Empress Alexandra and Grand Duchess Tatiana.

---

* Commander-in-cheif of the white Russian forces in the Crimea during the civil war.

Towards the end of the year Xenia learnt of the death of her aunt Marie, Dowager Duchess of Coburg. It was said that the Duchess, who had been living in straitened circumstances in a shabby hotel annex in Zurich, had died from apoplexy after receiving a letter addressed merely to 'Frau Coburg', though she had been suffering from a weak heart for some time. Some three weeks later Xenia received a depressing letter from Ducky. A breakdown in communications had evidently caused some ill-feeling on the embittered Ducky's part:

Many loving thanks for your letter. You really understand the complete and hopeless grief Mama's death means to us. I feel quite as if life were over. . . . All these years have been one long straining to reach her again and hardly had I found her only to be separated for ever. Nothing matters to me any more now only to live for the children, educate them well and give them as happy a life as possible.

Also many thanks for your letter after Aunt Miechen's death. That was quite another kind of grief and such terrible sufferings and remorse but I miss her also. I never disliked her as much as she did me. I never wrote to you all this last year, as you never answered my last letter from Finland sent through Messrs Reuters in which I so much implored you for news of Nicky and Alix. I felt so hopeless when you did not answer that letter. Gradually one feels as if it was no more worthwhile crying for anybody. Nobody seems to stick together any more and all one's family feelings and struggles become utterly . . . useless. Indifference and ingratitude all round. Most of the members of our family behaving as badly as possible, giving an ugly picture to the world of what remains of the Romanoffs. Our own brothers [sic] the worst example of all.

I am utterly discouraged and disgusted – have no more wish or hope for anything.[43]

Throughout the 1920s, Xenia's life was divided between London, Paris and Copenhagen. In October 1921 she attended the wedding of her goddaughter, Princess Xenia Georgievna, to William Leeds in Paris, the bride being given away by Sandro. Later she went on to Denmark, to attend the seventieth birthday celebrations of her aunt, Dowager Queen Louisa, on 31 October. London was her main home, while Sandro remained in Paris. It seems that he still hoped Xenia would change her mind, pouring out his feelings in an emotional letter from Paris in January 1922:

> Sweet Xenia
> I write again with hope to touch your soul and your heart! Tomorrow you will celebrate New Year [the Russian New Year] and maybe will think about me and that with your refusal you pushed me away forever.[44]

In his memoirs he gave the impression that any initiative to try to end what had become a marriage only in name came from him, but this letter suggested that maybe Xenia had finally reached the limits of her tolerance. Occasionally he visited the Youssoupovs. 'Papa had breakfast with us today,' Irina wrote to Xenia from Paris that autumn, 'also I was at his [place] a few times. He is in a good mood. He is . . . nearly the same as he was before. . . . Staying in Thesin [?] in my view was good for him. . . .

. . . We would like to come to London at the end of next week or the beginning of the week after. Will you have space for two of us?

. . . I could not come earlier because I did not have a warm coat – we took it for alterations. Now I can!'[45]

By August 1922 Xenia had moved to 18 Lennox Gardens, SW1, a terraced house a few streets away from her previous address. On 3 September she lent the house for the wedding reception of Princess Nina Georgievna and Prince Paul Chavchavadze. Despite court mourning for the Duchess of Albany, a large turnout of royals attended the religious service including Xenia, in a grey velvet gown with a sable stole and a grey satin-swathed toque; Queen Alexandra and Princess Victoria; Queen Olga of Greece and her son Christopher; and Princess Alice of Greece with her daughters Margarita and Theodora. Nikita, Dmitri, Rostislav and Vassili were among the groomsmen and the choir consisted of former members of the Imperial Theatre in St Petersburg. The bride's mother, Xenia's old friend Greek Minny, who had boasted 'she would marry the first Greek she met',[46] had recently married Captain Pericles Ionnides ('Perks'), captain of the destroyer which had brought the royal family back from exile to Greece.

Among the other guests was Natasha Brassova, whose marriage to Misha had caused so much trouble. When Michael was arrested in March 1918, Natasha contacted Harald Scavenius, who accordingly arranged for seven-year-old George to leave Russia forthwith. As the son of a Grand Duke, albeit a morganatic one, young George's life was in considerable danger. The boy and his English governess Margaret Neame hid for five weeks in the house of Colonel Cramer, a Dane who had been charged with overseeing the exchange of prisoners of war. On 25 April George, with Miss Neame posing as his mother – her passport showed her to be the wife of a repatriated Austrian officer – and Captain Sorensen, a Danish officer, boarded a Red Cross train packed with German prisoners of war. Neither Miss Neame nor George could speak German but, to their relief, they were passed through the Russian frontier at Pskov without incident. At Berlin they stayed in the British Embassy while discreet enquiries were made as to whether they could pass through Germany. Kaiser Wilhelm then intervened personally, ordering that they were to be permitted to proceed straight through the German border. A first-class carriage took them to Copenhagen, where they were escorted to Amalienborg Palace and stayed until Natasha was also able to escape from Russia. George joined his mother in England shortly after Easter 1919.[47]

It has always been thought that 'Countess' Brassova and her son had no contact with the exiled imperial family. This does not appear to have been the case, as they were also present at a dinner on 20 April 1923. The menu, written under a crowned monogram with 'KA' in the corner on the back, included references to Xenia's Russian estates – *Fruites de Gatchina au Bleu, Cotelettes de Volaille Ai-Todor, Creme Moika 106*'. Sergei Dolgoruky was also among the guests.[48] Xenia's fondness for her brother Misha may have prompted the invitation.

At the end of 1920 General Wrangel's forces in the Crimea were finally beaten by the Bolsheviks. For the emigrés this was not only the end of the civil war in Russia, but also the end of their hopes of an imminent return to their homeland. In the meantime, they had to survive. With no income and no independent financial means, Xenia, like all her Russian relatives, was thrown back on the only resource she had – jewellery to sell through third parties, in what has been described as 'a series of somewhat unfortunate transactions'.[49] Unfortunately, the jewels were immediately recognized. When the dealers realized that the Romanoffs were selling their jewels, Xenia and her relatives received only a fraction of their true worth.

Although a pearl pendant was sold to Lydia, Lady Deterding, wife of the Dutch oil magnate, buyers recalled the rather sinister significance attributed by some superstitious people to Xenia's necklace of black pearls. Nevertheless, it was her pearls which were to cause the biggest sensation.

With no real experience of handling money, Xenia was easy prey for unscrupulous opportunists. In December 1921 a self-styled financier, Maurice Sternbach, came to England with a letter of introduction which he claimed to have obtained in Copenhagen, to seek and obtain an interview at Claridges Hotel with Prince Dolgoruky. A meeting was arranged with Xenia, and Sternbach spun her a long and convincing story about himself and his commercial activities. He told her that he was in a good position to get her a fair price for her jewellery, and she entrusted him with a considerable amount. He signed a document to confirm that he was holding the jewels as her property, and not until several pawn tickets were recovered was she aware that he had parted with them. Next he contacted his business partner Albert Calvert, and between them they devised a scheme under Calvert's company, the General Exploration and Finance Syndicate, registered in 1898, its aim being 'to purchase or otherwise acquire and deal in real and personal property of all kinds, to advance or lend money, and to guarantee the payment of money and the performance of obligations of all kinds'. Calvert was introduced by Sternbach to Prince Dolgoruky at the Carlton Hotel as 'a financier of high position in London', though he was already the subject of eight bankruptcy notices presented against him.

Xenia was persuaded to part with her jewels to produce capital for a venture which, she was assured, 'would bring her wealth beyond the dreams of avarice'. In February 1922 Sternbach induced her to pawn a rope of pearls for £4,000, out of which she handed him £3,500, and he paid £2,000 to Calvert. The following month Xenia pawned a further rope of pearls for £5,000,

Sternbach was handed £3,500, and he paid Calvert £3,000. Later that month Xenia pawned a pearl necklace for £5,000, the whole of which was handed by Sternbach to Calvert.

It was the return of these three sums of £2,000, £3,000 and £5,000 that Xenia claimed in a court action in April 1923 in which she appeared as plaintiff and Calvert as defendant.

Sternbach and Calvert had devised a scheme by which they would pretend to take out an option for the Exploration Syndicate to purchase certain patent rights of a photographic printing process, involving payment of money from Sternbach to Calvert. In all, £10,000 was required from Xenia to make substantial profits from this invention; too trusting for her own good, she believed Sternbach's statements implicitly. There followed several interviews between both men and Dolgoruky, and he told Calvert firmly that if the investment was not a good one it would ruin the Grand Duchess. Calvert assured him repeatedly that the investment was sound, that there was no possible risk, and that he would ensure the Grand Duchess was in no danger of losing her money. On the basis of these assurances, the pearls were handed to Sternbach and pawned. Later Xenia was given a document declaring that Sternbach was holding her profits from the option on trust – a document not worth the proverbial parchment it was printed on.

On 14 March 1922 Sternbach wrote to the Grand Duchess to say he firmly believed that within a week the deal would be closed, and the first deposit or option would then be paid to him, of not less than £50,000. The balance, he added patronizingly, he would discuss 'when you are a little better, because even a Grand Duchess might get excited, if she is not well, if I mention the sum of three million seven hundred and fifty thousand dollars, or maybe more, and fifty per cent interest in all royalties. It is hard to write. It is easier to explain.'[50]

By the time he was called on to make his next explanations he was in court, having been arrested in London soon afterwards for defrauding another woman out of her watch. Further offences were taken into consideration, including fraud for dishonoured cheques and the theft of hairbrushes from a hotel in Paris. He was sentenced to three months' imprisonment and then deported back to his native United States of America.

When the case came to court Xenia, giving evidence, said that Sternbach, telling her about the printing process invention of which they had the option, assured her that it would 'upset the whole world and bring in large sums of money'. After describing how she handed over her jewels, she received his letter about the huge profits to be expected, and at this stage she still believed him. Dolgoruky told the court that Sternbach had told him that Calvert had an option through a German firm in Hamburg for 'a very beautiful invention' on which profits were estimated at £50,000 plus royalties. Even so, the Grand Duchess had received nothing. Without retiring, the jury returned a verdict for the plaintiff for £10,000, and judgment was entered accordingly with costs.

After this débâcle, King George V decided to take a hand. On the advice of Sir Frederick Ponsonby, his Keeper of the Privy Purse, he appointed Peter Bark as Xenia's financial adviser. As the Tsar's last Minister of Finance, Bark was therefore well acquainted with the monetary affairs of the imperial family. When the White Army collapsed in 1919 he was in Paris seeking financial help for the White government. His family was rescued from the Crimea by the British and they moved to London later that year. Immediately on his appointment as Xenia's adviser, for which he apparently received no salary, he began to reorganize her financial affairs. With no regular income, he recommended she sell the house on Villa Said, although this dragged on into 1926. The King then granted Xenia an allowance of £2,400 a year.

According to the recollections, some fifty years later, of King Olav of Norway, the family were unanimous that Queen Alexandra and the family in England should pay the greater part of the allowances granted to Xenia and her mother. In fact, King George paid part 'and the rest was paid by us others'.[51]

Bark 'tried to find out what other liabilities there were,' recalled Ponsonby, 'but she was so delightfully unbusinesslike that he was never sure he had cut her off from all her entanglements'.[52] One of the problems as far as Bark was concerned was that Xenia insisted on helping those less fortunate. She was heavily involved in charity work, in England and France, often visiting the *Maison Russe*, an old people's home on the rue de la Cossonerie at St Genevieve-des-Bois. Founded at the instigation of Princess Vera Mestchersky in 1927 and baptized with the name of the Empress

Marie Feodorovna, it housed 250 people. The first Director General had been one of the heads of administration at Tsarskoe Selo before the revolution.[53] Xenia was also sending food and money to friends in Russia.

'Thank you *ever* so much for all your dear letters and food parcels,' said 'Anna', in a note written in English with no sender's address and year. '. . . it was so delightful to get your letters full of kindness and love. You cannot imagine what it means here. . . .' She went on to give news of her family living in the country, 'near the place of the mother-in-law of your daughter . . . it is quite all right but rather sad, the estate is occupied by strangers and the winter house is burnt'. 'Anna' said she often thought of Xenia, who was so kind to her 'all these years'. In another undated note, she thanked Xenia for the £5 Christmas box and asked if it was true that all Xenia's children were getting married.[54]

It was true of Nikita, who married Countess Marie Vorontzov-Dashkov on 19 February 1922. Marie's mother Irina,* who had died in 1917, had married, after her divorce from 'Larry' Vorontzov-Dashkov, Xenia's admirer Prince Sergei Dolgoruky. Marie was thus the granddaughter of the former Minister of the Court, Count Ilarion Vorontzov-Dashkov, and the niece of Xenia's childhood friend Sandra Vorontzov. Xenia attended the wedding in Paris, followed by the reception at Felix and Irina's house at 27 rue Gutenberg, Boulogne-sur-Seine. They had bought the house a couple of years previously and still managed to maintain some style, employing a gardener, chauffeur, cook and several servants.

Despite outward appearances, Irina also found it necessary to acquire new skills. 'Thank you for your letter,' she wrote to Xenia. 'I did not answer you because I was very busy. I am taking lessons in stenography with Irina B. Three times a week we go to school. Apart from that we study to type on the typewriter.'[55]

---

* Irina Dolgoruky was said to have committed suicide because of her distress at learning of her husband Sergei's affair with Xenia (see chapter 7, pp 113). That Marie would have been unlikely to marry one of the sons of the woman who bore such a heavy responsibility for her mother's tragic death has been taken as a further argument against any truth in the rumours of an affair between Sergei and Xenia. However, the two families were close. Marie's godfather was Sandro's brother Grand Duke Nicholas Michaelovich.

Irina remained close to Sandro, and one of her letters to Xenia apparently refers to him:

It is a terrible pity that I cannot come to you. If only I could live with you everything would be much easier but it is impossible. I will try to come soon. How long do you think to stay in London? So would like to see you and live with you. I have to stop. He is going away. I thought after his visit I won't be in the house. It was so nice to have him here. Pity he is going away.[56]

Another of Xenia's worries was her mother. In January 1922 the Dowager Empress was staying at Sandringham with Queen Alexandra and Queen Olga of Greece. Unfortunately the Empress was ill and the relationship between the two sisters, once so close, was not good. 'Tante Alix leaves early in the morning and does not get back until it's getting dark, by which time Mother is seriously tired out,' Queen Olga told Xenia. Alix complained from morning till night that she was going out of her mind, 'she keeps forgetting everything and is very confused and all this annoys Mother terribly. . . . Relations between the sisters have seriously deteriorated and the reasons for it are growing all the time. T. A's deafness and her normal bad habits are becoming much worse . . . and her and Mother's [habits] are very different.'[57] Soon after Dagmar's return to Hvidøre, Sandro told her that she should have stayed in England, as the separation was bad for her. Sadly she replied that she felt much closer to her sister when there was a distance between them. 'When I lived in London, I felt estranged from her.'[58]

Xenia was now established in a house at 2 Princes Gate, Kensington, near the Royal Albert Hall. On 26 April 1923 she and her mother attended the Duke of York's marriage to Lady Elizabeth Bowes-Lyon. Shortly afterwards she left for Paris for the wedding of her son Feodor, who married Princess Irene Paley at the Russian Orthodox Cathedral of St Alexander Nevsky on 31 May 1923. Irene was the daughter of Xenia's uncle Grand Duke Paul, by his morganatic marriage to Olga Pistolkors, created Princess Paley. It was one of the last real family gatherings in exile, and among those invited was King Alfonso XIII of Spain, who knew the Paleys from their stays in Biarritz, although it is not known if he was able to attend the wedding.

By 1924 Xenia and Sandro were grandparents several times over. Besides Bébé, still being thoroughly spoilt by the elder Youssoupovs in Rome, Andrei and Elisabeta (called 'Elsa' by the family) now had three children (Xenia, born 1919; Michael, 1920; and Andrew, 1923); and Nikita and Marie had a son, Nikita, born in 1923. When Feodor and Irene's son Michael was born in 1924, Feodor asked his mother to be with him during the birth.[59]

The Grand Duchess arrived at Hvidøre towards the end of 1924 to find her mother's condition slowly improving. Xenia occupied a spacious room at the front of the villa near the open veranda, with her maid Sasha Pavlova on the floor above. Vassili slept in the former billiard room downstairs, and soon became friends with his cousin Tihon Kulikovsky, who was ten years his junior. 'Poor Xenia doesn't feel well herself,' Grand Duchess Olga told the old nurse Nastya, 'and she is again experiencing pains in the stomach. The children (and us too) are glad that they're staying for the holidays in Hvidøre, still it will make the winter a bit shorter. I'm so happy that Xenia's here. Mother is taking our good old phosporene, iron and other disgusting things. Poor "Kiki" [the Dowager Empress's maid] hasn't been going to bed for 8 weeks, she would sleep on the divan for a bit next to the bedroom and that's it. But she's a wonderful person.'[60]

Her mother's health was not Xenia's only family concern at the time. 'Worried about Elsa, having heard about the forthcoming operation and I'm worried for her and poor Andrusha,' she told Nastya, 'but today we've had the telegram that everything went well.'[61]

In the autumn of 1924 an article in the *Handelsblad* caused a flurry of correspondence in The Hague and anxiety among the Romanovs. 'According to the *Handelsblad* certain merchants in Amsterdam have purchased jewels belonging to the former Russian Imperial family to the value of eighteen million florins,' Sir Charles Marling wrote from the British Legation in The Hague to the British Consul General in Amsterdam. 'This paper states that these stones are now on sale and may be seen at the Amsterdam Bank, in whose hands the financial arrangements for these sales have been placed. I shall be glad to learn whether this press report is correct and, if so, I shall be glad to receive such information as you may be able to obtain on the subject.'[62]

Sir Charles was the former British Ambassador in Teheran, and had brought Xenia's cousin Grand Duke Dmitri back to England in defiance of the ban on Russian Grand Dukes entering the country.[63] Enquiries soon revealed that the diamonds in question had been ceded to the Polish government by the Soviets as reparations after the war between Russia and Poland that followed the First World War.

Adding to their general anxieties was the uncalled-for gesturing of one of their senior cousins. In 1922 Grand Duke Cyril Vladimirovich, second husband of Ducky, who had unstintingly provided Xenia which such moral support over the last few years, had proclaimed himself 'Guardian of the Russian Throne'. Now, in 1924, with the presumed deaths of Nicholas, Alexis and Michael, Cyril proclaimed himself 'Emperor', thus breaking the unwritten rule that no member of the Romanoff family would claim the throne during the Dowager Empress's lifetime.

Queen Olga of Greece, still proud to consider herself a Russian Grand Duchess by birth, was among those who shared the sense of outrage: 'I am most grateful to you for the copies of the letters which probably were largely responsible for [your] dear Mother's illness,' she wrote to Xenia from Rome. 'I can hardly bring myself to write down the extreme indignation I feel in connection with K's [Kyrill's] actions – it is obvious that in his own mind all this passes for "patriotism" – what a terrible thing!'[64] Cyril's declaration had divided the Romanoffs and caused a rift in the family which would never heal.

10 (1925–8)

'The light of our life is gone'

By 1925 Xenia's financial state had again become desperate. King George V allowed her to settle in Frogmore Cottage as a grace and favour residence, and she felt she could never thank 'cousin Georgie' enough, writing to him from Hvidøre:

I can't bear this silence any longer (as I know too much!) & must write to you & express my feeling of *deepest* gratitude for all you have done & are doing for me. Really Georgie, it is *too* good & kind of you. I longed to write at once & have written & torn up many sheets of paper but felt shy! & didn't quite know what was going on – but now having heard from Bark I had to break the silence. I never dreamt that any one *would* trouble you with all my troubles – for had I known – I would have never let them do it – after what you had already done – to help me. I can't bear the idea that you are *been* [sic] worried on account of me & that something is going on behind my back. (Of course, I can't deny that I am in a fixture & a most unpleasant situation at the present moment – but I would stand anything rather than be a *burden* to others. Bark writes that you offer me a Cottage at Windsor. Words *fail* me to express all I feel – I am touched beyond words & thank you from all my heart. But . . . do you know *what* a lot we are!? I hope to be in Paris in about a fortnight – see to all the affairs concerning the house there – *how & if* it can be disposed of – & then come over to England with the full notion of things & settle the rest after having seen you & talked matters over with you personally. Being so far I am unable to *know* how things really are & that is why I must find out myself first – before I return to London. I couldn't leave Mama – else I would have been back since a

171

long time – Thank God she is much better at last though not feeling very strong yet & still keeps to her rooms.[1]

The Frogmore estate in the Home Park at Windsor, north-west of Frogmore House, is situated down a private drive leading from the Long Walk. The estate was acquired by King Henry VIII some four centuries earlier, and its boundary lay less than a mile from the castle. Queen Victoria, Prince Albert and the Duchess of Kent are buried in mausolea nearby. Frogmore House, whose gardens had once been a favourite place for Queen Victoria to work on her State papers, had been arranged by Queen Mary as a family museum, and the Cottage is nearby. Prince Nicholas of Greece described the white-painted house in a letter to Xenia as 'your pretty little home at Frogmore'.[2] Officially 'grace & favour apartment No. 9', it comprised about twenty-three rooms, including a large drawing room, dining room, study, butler's pantry, housekeeper's room, kitchen, scullery and store rooms. The only toilet 'was fitted out in a manner which suggested a stubborn devotion to the sixteenth century',[3] and the house was still lit by oil lamps and candles.

On her arrival Xenia found two large engravings of the Russian coronation ceremonies on the walls. The Ministry of Works had been given no notice that the Grand Duchess was moving in, and her occupation of the house was 'more or less secret', though Ponsonby later said that it was 'well-known in the vicinity of Windsor'.[4]

Ponsonby immediately engaged a clerk to look after Xenia's accounts and hand over the balance of the King's allowance after the payment of salaries and other household expenses. 'But I found she practically starved herself,' he recalled, 'and never spent a penny on her clothes, in order to give more to her sons.'[5] Andrusha, Nikita and Rostislav all received regular payments from her bank account. By the following year the Cottage was proving too small for Xenia's large household. King George therefore arranged for her to have Home Park Cottage, situated opposite, as well. 'Really it is *much too sweet* and good of you,' Xenia wrote from Hvidøre, 'and I can't say *how* much I appreciated this new most kind attention and *how touched* and grateful I am! Why should you do it? I feel *quite* shy . . . and don't deserve this kindness. . . . I just long to get back to my dear little house at Frogmore – it must be so lovely there at the moment. . . .'[6]

The King and Queen paid occasional visits, but Xenia's most frequent caller was the lifelong spinster Princess Victoria, who spent many years as a 'glorified maid' to her mother.[7] Her visits to Xenia's large family must have come as a welcome relief. The staff included a butler, the maid Alexandra Pavlova ('Sasha'), Nastya and Sophie Evreinoff who looked after Xenia, a secretary, and a cook who had trained at Maxim's in Paris. Old Belaoussoff was also living at Frogmore. If she met the King walking in the park, she insisted on plunging into a series of low curtseys and addressing him as 'Sire'. Felix recalled that she must be nearly a hundred years of age, thin and stooped with an aquiline nose, looking just like the Fairy Carabosse in *The Sleeping Beauty*.

Andrusha and Elisabeta also lived with Xenia, as did their children and the English nanny Edith. Russian was spoken in the household and Xenia's grandson recalled that she was always very strict at mealtimes. Grace was said first and the children had to sit up straight with their hands on the table, only speaking when spoken to. When they reached the age of fifteen these rules were relaxed, and they were then treated as adults and allowed to take part in the conversation.[8]

Frogmore Cottage was not only open house for Xenia's family, but also for their friends. Veta Zinoviev recalled taking her own children Andrew and Natasha, together with two of the Galitzine children, to play with the Grand Duchess's granddaughter Princess Xenia. Little Prince David Chavchavadze, the grandson of Sandro's brother George and Greek Minny, was also brought over to play with Xenia's grandchildren. When his nurse wheeled him over to Windsor Castle he tried to talk to the guards in Russian, his only language.[9]

Xenia was a frequent guest for lunch or tea at the various royal residences. She would dress up and say, 'I'm going to see my cousin the King.'[10] In June 1925, after lunch at Windsor, Queen Mary showed her the State Apartments, gardens and greenhouses and they had tea in the gardener's house.[11] In August Xenia stayed overnight at Buckingham Palace and the following day visited the Commonwealth Exhibition at Wembley with the King and Queen in spite of heavy rain.[12] In 1926 she was back in

Copenhagen, where her mother was again unwell. One subject was taboo in the Dowager Empress's household – the events at Ekaterinburg in 1918. But in 1925 rumours flying round the royal courts of Europe brought this unwelcome subject back into the limelight.

In 1920 a woman had been pulled from a Berlin canal, claiming to be Grand Duchess Anastasia Nicolaievna, sole survivor of the massacre at Ekaterinburg in July 1918. Ill-tempered, apparently deranged, single-minded, reclusive and unable to speak a word of Russian, she would divide the exiled Romanoffs for the next sixty years, until her death in America. Xenia, the Dowager Empress and most of the surviving family were convinced that Anastasia was a fraud, and long after they were dead they would be proved right. In 1994 DNA tests were carried out on a piece of tissue from Anna Anderson, as Anastasia was later to be known, found in a hospital laboratory after her death. As many had long suspected, they proved conclusively that she was no Romanoff, but a lowly born Polish imposter, her real name Franziska Schanzkowska. Nevertheless the campaign to recognize the *Unbekannte*, or 'Unknown' as she was soon named, gathered momentum in a campaign which bitterly distressed Xenia and her mother, the real Anastasia's grandmother.

At the time of the Anastasia controversy, the Dowager Empress was anxious to avoid publicity. In 1925, however, Grand Duchess Olga announced that she was going to visit the woman, who now called herself 'Frau Tchaikovsky', although Xenia allegedly sent her sister a strongly worded telegram telling her not to go.[13] Nevertheless Olga went, mainly at the insistence of her aunt Thyra, Duchess of Cumberland, 'just to clear up the case once and for all'.[14]

According to 'Anastasia's supporters, Olga at first seemed to recognize the young woman as her niece[15] but later changed her mind. In Denmark a statement was issued saying that Grand Duchess Olga had been to Berlin 'but neither she, nor anyone else who knew Tsar Nicholas's youngest daughter, was able to find the slightest resemblance between Grand Duchess Anastasia and the person who calls herself Frau Tchaikovsky'.[16]

But rumours of the survival of one or more members of the family continued to circulate. In late 1926 it was said in Bavaria that Grand Duchess Xenia and her daughter Irina were coming to see 'Anastasia', who was staying with the Duke of Leuchtenberg. Needless to say, no such visit ever materialized.[17]

In 1928, when the claimant was staying in America as the guest of Greek Minny's daughter Princess Xenia, Mrs William Leeds, it was said that 'the Tsar's sisters were prepared to support Anastasia for life "in some secluded spot in Europe"' – provided she renounced her claim to identity. Princess Xenia denied this, saying that her aunts' attitude was 'far too negative for them to have dreamed of such a thing'. Apparently, she rashly promised to take Mrs Anderson to see the Dowager Empress in Denmark, until she came up against 'the categorical opposition' of her aunts, whom she did not dare challenge.[18]

It was also an embarrassment as it drew attention to the family's finances. Ever since his abdication, there had been rumours about Tsar Nicholas II's missing millions, said to have been deposited in the Bank of England. In 1929 the *New York Times* estimated the amount at around $1 billion, although the money inherited from Alexander III was repatriated in 1900. There were also believed to be deposits with Baring Brothers in London, and considerable amounts in banks throughout the world. The Tsar's personal deposits in the National City Bank alone were rumoured to be around $60 million. In theory, no member of the family could withdraw any money remaining in these accounts until the matter was resolved.

Many people believed that, when Olga and Xenia learnt that Frau Tchaikovsky had spoken about coded bank accounts for the Tsar's children, this destroyed any chance she had of recognition as Anastasia.

Neither Xenia, her sister or mother had any financial motives in the Anastasia affair, their main concern being the honour and integrity of the Romanov dynasty. Most if not all of the Tsar's money had been withdrawn from foreign banks to help the war effort, and he had instructed his relatives to do the same. Any funds remaining belonged to the Tsarist government, not to the Tsar personally, and, as Olga had taken care to point out, her mother would certainly not have accepted a pension from King George V if they had possessed any money in England. In the 1920s many people had an interest in the affairs of the Dowager

Empress and her daughters and, as long as rumours flourished that substantial amounts were waiting to be claimed, they were determined to make sure that 'Anastasia' was never recognized.

The Romanoffs who escaped from Russia brought out some excellent jewellery which they refused to sell at first. They had never had any experience of dealing with money, seemed unaware of how much they were spending and complained of poverty. Even the long-suffering King George V found it a constant burden to support his often profligate Russian relatives. By October 1923 Dagmar's debts, which were guaranteed by Hans Niels Andersen and the East Asiatic Company, had reached almost one million kroner and were rising steadily. Count Ahlefelt and Andersen raised 200,000 kroner (about £10,000) by private subscription to enable her to continue living in Denmark. Though the Danish Foreign Ministry refused to allow a public subscription, other private subscriptions followed. The Great Northern Telegraph Company, another concern which Dagmar had done much to promote in Russia, paid her a small annual allowance of 15,000 kroner, but insisted the arrangement be kept secret, in case the Soviet government complained.

Where the state of the Romanoff finances was concerned, Xenia still had several allies. One of the most important was Prince Sergei Georgievich Romanovsky, 8th Duke of Leuchtenberg, the son of Nicholoska's wife 'Stana' by her first marriage to George, 6th Duke of Leuchtenberg; he had been under house arrest with his mother at Djulber in 1918 and was on board HMS *Marlborough* with the Dowager Empress when she left Russia. In 1925, after reports circulated that there was money in two of the city's banks, he applied for limited Letters of Administration in New York on Xenia's behalf and that of over thirty other relatives. Berlin banks also held deposits but, as the years ticked by without the family being able to make a claim, the fall of the mark considerably reduced their value.

In the autumn of 1925 Xenia spent a week at Sandringham, where she visited Queen Mary at York Cottage. Greek Minny and her husband Perks were among Queen Alexandra's guests at the Big House. The Queen Mother's health was failing; at the age of eighty, she was now almost stone deaf and becoming very thin. Although she always appeared for lunch and then took her afternoon drive, she spent most of her time asleep in a darkened room. Xenia was at Irina's house in Boulogne-sur-Seine, Paris, when she learnt of the death of Queen Alexandra at Sandringham on 20 November, and immediately sent her sympathies to the bereaved King:

> I just can't say how deeply I feel for you – this yr great sorrow & loss & mourn yr beloved Mother dear with you all. She is at peace at last after all her sufferings & one ought to be glad for her but for those who remain behind it is very hard & sad. . . .
>
> I am so distressed not to be with you all at such a moment & not to be able to come back but I must go to Motherdear who expects me now. I can't bear to think of her, her grief & all she is going through. . . .[19]

A few months later Xenia lost another of her aunts, Queen Olga of Greece. 'Please thank dearest Aunt Minny for her dear messages, I know and understand perfectly what she must be feeling,' Prince Christopher wrote to Xenia in July. 'Mama lately was constantly speaking of her and making plans for paying her a visit in summer.'[20] Prince Nicholas complained that the only English cousin who had made the effort to write to him on his mother's death was Maud. 'And when dear A, Alix died I wrote a letter to *everyone*. Such is life!!!'[21]

Xenia also sent condolences to her cousin Missy, whose husband King Ferdinand of Roumania died in the summer of 1927. 'Thank you Xenia dear for your kind understanding words,' Missy replied. 'All things seem torn asunder, but at least my people are good to me and consider me their mother – I think of you homeless and uprooted!'[22]

In a postcard to Nastya in 1924 Xenia mentioned that she had begun drawing again,[23] and some of her work was sold for charity. On 1 April 1926 the Mutual Charitable Society for Russian Officers in Denmark raffled some 'exceptionally beautiful paintings' done especially by Grand Duchesses Xenia and Olga, with proceeds going to disabled soldiers of the society in dire financial need. Letters were sent to several people on behalf of the chairman, the Grand Duke of Mecklenburg, asking them to arrange for the sale of tickets.[24]

Xenia was also patron of the Russian Red Cross. The old organization of the Russian Red Cross Society had remained in existence in Britain after the revolution. From the 1920s the society took care of penniless Russian exiles in England, maintaining two houses in Chiswick, West London, for the old and infirm and giving small grants or pensions to others. In the 1950s one of Xenia's former maids was a resident of one of these homes. The society also gave medical help, aid to children, paid funeral expenses of poor Russians and collected clothes for distribution.

Fundraising activities centred around the annual Christmas Bazaar, but plays, dances, lectures, recitals and concerts were also given. Xenia's sister-in-law Sophie, Countess de Torby, was regularly involved, organizing the annual Red Cross Ball and other functions which Xenia frequently attended. A typical example was the Red Cross Ball held at the Hotel Cecil on 10 July 1924, at which it was stated that 'H.I.H. Grand Duchess Xenia of Russia will receive the guests'. Even during the Second World War the society managed to remain open, despite the obvious fall in donations. In 1949 the society changed its name to the Russian Benevolent Society 1917, but the good work continued under Xenia's patronage and with the involvement of many members of her family.

July 1928 marked the tenth anniversary of Ekaterinburg, and Nicholas and his family were now officially presumed dead. As the Tsar's elder sister, Xenia stood to inherit any money belonging to him and his family which remained in England. She also began a claim on some of the Tsar's personal property in Finland. Peter Bark travelled to Denmark in 1928, his expenses paid by King George V, to take power of attorney from the Dowager Empress and Xenia to pursue legal action against the Finnish state.

Xenia tried to recover the Langinkoski imperial fishing lodge and property in the village of Halila near the Finnish/Russian border, including the Halila Sanatorium which she understood had been bought personally by her father in 1892 for 100,000 roubles. Since 1918 Halila and Langinkoski, confiscated from the Romanovs by the Bolsheviks and handed over to the Finns at the Treaty of Dorpat in 1920, had been part of Finland. The action initially failed, as the Finns claimed that Halila had been bought by the Russian Chancery and handed over to the Department of the Empress Marie by Nicholas II in 1900, and this foundation was supported by state funds. Both properties, they claimed, were therefore Russian state property.

With financial problems uppermost in all their minds, Xenia, Olga and Sandro hoped that the Dowager Empress would sell her jewels. Sandro wanted the family to open a paper factory, while her daughters merely wanted a keepsake. The reply was always the same, 'you will have all of it when I am gone'.[25]

By the time of her eightieth birthday in November 1927, the matriarch was very feeble, and by the following summer the old Empress was failing. 'Loving thanks, so happy to get dear letters [.] feel miserably weak. Kiss your children and dear Toria,' she telegraphed at the end of August.[26]

In the autumn Xenia was summoned from Paris. She arrived with Vassili and immediately sent a telegram to Sandro urging him to come at once. On Thursday 11 October the Empress went into a coma, as Xenia, Olga and the nurse Sister Caroline mounted a vigil at her bedside. By Saturday, when the doctor was summoned again at 4 o'clock, it was obvious that the end was near.

The Empress died at 7pm, surrounded by Xenia and Vassili, Olga with her husband and sons, and Prince Sergei Dolgoruky. As her mother and elder sister had been, she was in her eighty-first year. Later that evening King Christian, Queen Alexandrine, their sons Crown Prince Frederik and Prince Knud, Prince Waldemar and Thyra arrived at Hvidøre, where Father Koltcheff held a service in the bedroom.[27] Her coffin then lay in the Garden Room, watched over by her Cossack bodyguards, while arrangements were made for the funeral. Sandro arrived too late to see the Empress alive.

Evidently slow to forgive her for the petty differences between them that had marred her last years, King Christian X had decided there was no need to give a state funeral to someone who was technically a mere ex-Empress. Xenia and Olga were furious at this indignity and insult to their mother's rank, and their protests, added to public opinion, forced him to think again.

The Empress's coffin was taken on the royal hearse, escorted by the Guards in full-dress uniform, to the Russian Church in Copenhagen. There she lay in state for three days, surrounded by a mountain of wreaths and flowers.

The funeral took place on 19 October, in a church filled with Russian exiles and the largest gathering of the Romanoff family since the revolution: Xenia, Sandro and four of their sons, Andrei, Feodor, Nikita and Vassili; Irina and Felix; Olga and Colonel Kulikovsky; Grand Duke Dmitri Pavlovich and his sister Marie; Princes Gabriel and George Constantinovich with their sister Tatiana; and Princess Albert of Saxe-Altenburg. Xenia and Olga found the sudden appearance of all these relatives in poor taste, especially as many had taken little notice of the Dowager Empress since their exile, claiming defensively that her pride had prevented them from coming to her aid in the past ten years. The appearance of Cyril, whose claims as pretender had so annoyed her, was particularly resented and they were even more indignant when it was learnt that he was lodged at the King's palace of Sorgenfri with the King of Norway and other distinguished guests. King Christian X and Queen Alexandrine of Denmark, Crown Prince Frederik, Prince Waldemar and his family, King Haakon of Norway, Crown Prince Gustav Adolf of Sweden, the Duke of York, the Grand Duke of Mecklenburg, Thyra and her son the Duke of Brunswick with his wife Victoria Louise, were all there. After the service all the Russians, led by Xenia and Olga, kissed the icon on the coffin lid before a special train took them on the 20-mile journey to Roskilde Cathedral, burial place of the Danish royal family.

At 8pm there was a large banquet for all the visiting royalty and dignitaries at the Amalienborg. Afterwards Xenia and Olga joined Sandro at Hvidøre. Sadly, they realized that after all these years they had nothing to say to each other. With the death of the matriarch whose mere presence had kept the family united, at least on the surface, it was a closing of the final chapter on the old Russia which they had known and loved and was now no more.[28]

To Queen Mary, Xenia wrote:

I can't tell you how touched I am by yr kind words of sympathy in our sorrow. . . . You know how we loved our Mother, & how we clung to her always & now in these cruel years of exile more than ever! She was *all* that was left to us – everything was centred in her – our home our country all the dear past. We all looked up to her & it was through her & in her that we, her children & our countrymen found courage to bear our heavy burden. She was so wonderfully brave & such a help in every way. The light of our life is gone & we feel so miserably lonely & miss her quite terribly! . . . It was a real agony to see her getting weaker & weaker day by day & often in pain & not be able to help her!

And now we are going through another ordeal – looking through all her letters, papers & belongings dividing them between us & picking to pieces with our own hands our last 'home' – & then in a month Olga & I will have to part![29]

11 (1928–36)

'As the Grand Duchess
is very poor . . .'

After the Dowager Empress's death, the family's most pressing concern was to read the will and settle the estate. Everything was left to Xenia and Olga, with nothing for Michael's widow or his son George, though Dagmar had made provision for her servants and Cossack bodyguards. King George was still paying pensions to the Russian suite and servants the following year. The sisters received so many letters of sympathy* that they had to express their thanks in the newspapers. In grateful remembrance they gave Father Koltcheff, the Empress's confessor, a Fabergé icon of the Exaltation of the Cross. The Russian Orthodox Church abroad received three items which had belonged to the Dowager Empress – an Icon of the Virgin, a relic of the Cross, and a relic of St John the Baptist. A deed from Berlin Cathedral dated 9 November 1928 acknowledged their receipt from Xenia and Prince Dolgoruky and a second, dated 29 April 1932, recorded that the items had been given to King Alexander of Yugoslavia, whose Minister received them on his behalf.[1]

Shortly before the funeral the Empress's jewels had been spirited out of Denmark, to forestall any possibility of their being claimed by the Bolsheviks. They remained her most potent legacy, and King George was anxious to avoid any repetition of Xenia's unfortunate experiences which had led to the embarrassing 1923 court case. Aware that other relatives had their eyes on the jewels, and alerted to rumours that a gang of international jewel thieves planned to steal them, he sent Bark to Copenhagen. The jewel box

---

* Over 200 of these letters are preserved.

was sealed in Xenia's presence and taken to Buckingham Palace while arrangements were made for their sale.

With all the jewels now safely out of the way, Xenia and Olga had to go through the contents of both Hvidøre and the Kejservilla at Fredensborg to decide which items they wanted to keep. Everything else was to be sold at auction. Among items that fell to Xenia's share were the gold and nephrite Hvidøre seal; a pink cornelian rabbit with diamond eyes; and the 1916 Cross of St George egg, the only Fabergé Easter egg to leave Russia with its rightful owner.

On 27 November Xenia and Olga held a final reception at Hvidøre. As a souvenir, all the guests were presented with a card bearing the flags of White Russia, Denmark and England, with the signatures of both Grand Duchesses. Then the sisters went their separate ways. A request from the Belgian legation in Copenhagen for Xenia to be allowed to pass unhindered through Belgium to France was dated 28 November.[2] Still feeling her mother's death keenly, Xenia stopped in Paris. In March she wrote to Nastya about a wound that had not healed yet, 'and there is a deep scar left'.[3]

King George appointed Bark as Trustee of the Empress's estate in England, while King Christian X appointed Esbern Trolle, Solicitor of the Supreme Court, and Vice-Admiral Andrup, who had recently looked after the Empress's finances, as executors for the Danish estate.

Twenty-four hours after the Dowager Empress's death, a statement signed by twelve of the Romanoffs and three of the Tsarina's family, believed to have been drawn up by Sandro, was released to the Associated Press by the Grand Duke of Hesse's Court in Darmstadt. It set out their 'unanimous conviction that the person currently living in the United States is not the daughter of the Tsar'. The other signatories included Olga, Xenia and her six sons, Irina, Grand Duke Dmitri and Grand Duchess Marie Pavlovna, the Grand Duke of Hesse and his sisters Victoria and Irene. Grand Duke Andrei and Princess Xenia (Mrs William Leeds), who believed in the claimant's identity as Anastasia, were not consulted.[4]

Barely had their mother been laid to rest before Xenia received an intemperate letter from Gleb Botkin, the main supporter of the so called Anastasia. The son of the Tsar's personal doctor, who was shot with the family at Ekaterinburg in 1918, Botkin now living in New York, was quick to accuse the surviving Romanoffs of trying to defraud 'Anastasia' of her inheritance:

> Twenty-four hours did not pass after the death of your mother, the Dowager Empress Maria Feodorovna, when you hastened to take another step in your conspiracy to defraud your own niece, Her Imperial Highness Grand Duchess Anastasie Nikolaevna, by issuing a statement to the press declaring yourself 'firmly convinced that the woman bearing the name of Mme Tschaikowsky, living at the present time in the United States, is certainly not the Grand Duchess Anastasia Nikolaevna . . . you have established yourself through the British courts heir to the fortune of the late Emperor and his heirs; that you are trying for years by fraudulent methods to gain possession of that fortune and, judging by newspapers, have already succeeded in obtaining some real property estate in England.

'Anastasia', he insisted, remembered every detail of her childhood and had all her physical signs including birthmarks and the same handwriting as in youth, and this was surely enough to establish her identity. Angrily he concluded:

> Before the wrong which Your Imperial Highness are [sic] committing pales even the gruesome murder of the Emperor, his family and my father by the Bolsheviks. It is easier to understand a crime committed by a gang of crazed and drunken savages, than the calm, systematic, endless persecution of one of your own family.[5]

Botkin took care to promote his case by circulating copies of the letter widely in order to make everything as public as possible. He had found a powerful ally in Grand Duke Andrei Vladimirovich who, as a younger brother of Cyril, the self-proclaimed Tsar of All The Russias, had his own axe to grind. Just over a year earlier he had told Botkin that the woman who claimed to be Anastasia definitely resembled Xenia's children, 'the so-called Alexander III type'.[6] Now, after Botkin's furious letter, he was in despair, knowing that any hopes they might have of persuading Xenia, Olga and the rest of the family to take 'Anastasia' seriously were dashed. Botkin, he told Gleb's sister Tatiana, had *'completely ruined everything'* [original emphasis].[7]

Sandro made no secret of his feelings. 'Thank you for your letter,' he wrote to Xenia from Paris on 20 November:

Also for the vileness of Botkin, what a character, I am very ashamed for the Russian person. I will take advice from an American lawyer but in my opinion it is better not to do anything and wait for their attack. I am sure that some American lawyer wrote this letter and it is simply challenge and provocation.

I will make everything ready for your arrival but please do not take a hotel here. You have a lot of friends . . . who will be happy to have this opportunity to be fed. Korobasov [Sandro's major-domo] and the kitchen lady will take care of you and you will feel comfortable and good. I am very pleased that everything came out this way. Vasia [Vassili] can live with Feodor and this is better and comforting for you and for me because my house is quiet and full of peace loving people.[8]

It is doubtful whether Botkin's letter, which was still in Xenia's possession at her death, had any effect beyond hardening her resolve to have nothing to do with the woman who, she was already convinced, was a fraud. If some shadow of doubt ever crossed her mind, it counted for less than her view that the woman had been set up by those who were seeking the Romanov fortune for their own ends.

Prince Michael, son of Xenia's son Andrei and his first wife Elsa, who lived with his parents and grandmother at Frogmore Cottage and then Wilderness House until he joined the navy, recalled many family conversations on the subject. To him it was evident that everyone, especially his grandmother, was 'appalled by the claims being made by the hordes of impostors', and 'looked upon Anderson and the three-ringed circus which danced around her, creating books and movies, as a vulgar insult to the memory of the Imperial family'.[9]

Potential claims on the Tsar's money in a Berlin bank were also causing problems. 'Concerning your words about Mend. [the Mendelssohn Bank in Berlin],' Sandro wrote to Xenia on 20 November:

I do not understand what you mean by 'I am telling you this for your own good'. I do not need anything, but not you, nor I, nor Olga have the right not to care about their own children and leave the possessions of Nicky for plunder. I love Bark very much but you must not think that his words are the words of God. Although he knows a lot but cannot know everything. It offends me that you do not have even a little trust in my words and me. The gossip you are receiving does not have any grounds. This I had to tell you. Because you do not know what I have done for your prosperity but from my side it is understandable and normal.[10]

One month after his aunt's funeral King George became seriously ill. For several days he hovered between life and death, and spent the next six months convalescing. The jewel box was finally opened at Windsor in May 1929, to reveal the seventy-six items comprising the last of Dagmar's considerable collection, including the Diamond Star of the Order of St Andrew; ropes of pearls, 'the largest the size of a cherry'; and brooches, bracelets, hair ornaments and hatpins, all sparkling with diamonds, emeralds, rubies and sapphires. Her spectacular diamond necklaces and tiaras had remained in Russia. A week later Mr Hardy of Hennell & Sons, Bond Street, was asked to price every item provisionally and to take as long as he needed to sell the jewels discreetly. Xenia withdrew items totalling £11,415 but, because of the slump, the rest were not disposed of until 1933, and some were returned unsold. The final sale price of £135,624 15s was put in trust for Xenia and Olga. Some items were bought by Queen Mary who, contrary to popular belief, paid the full valuation figure. When she died in 1953 her jewellery, including pieces from the Dowager Empress's estate, passed to members of the British royal family. The original provisional valuation dated 22 May, just after the box was first opened, still exists, with its handwritten figures.[11] Some of these were later revised.[12]

Another reason why the jewels took so long to sell was because the market was flooded with Russian artefacts. When Xenia tried putting some of her mother's jewels on the market in France, she was unsuccessful.

'Thank you for the postcards that have been written by Mama,' Sandro wrote in November:

Now there is another business. Our dear F. [Felix, presumably] is getting closer to Mama's *bijou** and Irina told me that Cartier told him he could sell this *bijou* with great profit. He could get much more than their value because people will appreciate something that used to belong to Mama. This is the same as Gardner said but it was earnest and from the heart from his side. But from Cartier's side plus with the help of F. there is only greed. My advice to you and to anybody who will come to you with propositions will be to say that you do not think to sell. The less you are going to talk about them the better because the sharks do not sleep and are sharpening their teeth for these jewels.[13]

The Romanoffs and the aristocracy were selling the jewels they had saved from Russia, and after Lenin's death in 1924 the Bolshevik government began selling off confiscated jewellery and art treasures to prop up their tottering regime. An acquaintance showed Xenia her latest purchase, an exquisite rose jade box with an imperial crown surmounting a diamond and emerald monogram. 'I would be curious to know whose initials those are,' said the lady. 'They are mine,' Xenia replied, looking at the entwined 'KA'.[14] One of Xenia's Fabergé parasol handles, in gold, nephrite, diamonds, rubies and enamel, was acquired by Mrs Marjorie Merryweather Post. With it was a note from Xenia, stating it had been part of her Fabergé collection.[15]

Hvidøre was sold, and on 28 February 1929 Sir Frederick Ponsonby informed Hugh Cassells, the British Consul in Copenhagen holding power of attorney for Queen Alexandra's heirs, that Princess [sic] Brassova had every intention of claiming a share of the sale proceeds for her son George, the Empress's grandson. King George V and his sisters had agreed to give up their half share in favour of Olga and Xenia, and the estate would therefore be divided between Olga, Xenia and George Brassov. Most of the contents were sold at auction in April.

By a Deed of Conveyance dated 1 July 1929, the buildings and landward portion of the Hvidøre estate were sold to Mr Jacob Koefoed, a retired wine merchant, and the rest was purchased in

---

* In Russian in the original typewritten letter

November by Gentofte municipality. The buildings fetched Kr 320,000, and the contents Kr 119,494.94 at auction. Some items privately purchased by Xenia and Princess Victoria were shipped to England, ironically on the SS *Dagmar*, including the Delauney Belleville car which Xenia kept. On 22 November 1929 the executors paid the sum of £11,704 16*s* 3*d* to Peter Bark to be invested on behalf of the Grand Duchesses.

The contents of the Kejservilla fetched Kr 15,000 at an auction held at Hvidøre on 28 May 1929. The villa itself was inherited by Olga but had been used as security for a loan of Kr 10,000 from the Østifternes Kreditforening. The house was sold on 10 June 1929 for Kr 14,000, considerably less than the Kr 25,000 paid by Alexander III, and that same day Olga discharged Kr 8,000 of the debt, the rest being cleared in 1930. The documents make no mention of Xenia having jointly inherited the Kejservilla, so perhaps the Empress had intended it as a home for Olga and her family.[16]

After settling her mother's estate, Xenia closed her account with Coutts. In 1930 she and Olga both opened accounts with the Bank of England; in Xenia's case this reflected Peter Bark's involvement in her affairs and was done at the British royal family's suggestion.[17]

At the end of 1928 Sandro left on the *Leviathan* to take up a long-standing offer of a lecture tour of the United States. 'Again in America, for the third time – 1893, 1913 and 1928.' The Anastasia controversy continued to bother him. After describing his heavy schedule and writing about Dmitri, now working successfully in New York, he continued: 'Nina met me on the pier, Xenia did not want to come [his nieces, daughters of his brother George and Greek Minny] but said through Nina that she will be happy to see me at her [place]. Children are very strange these days and I think that something is not right in her soul and she really does not want to see me. I met many reporters. I had to receive them because of my special visit [the lecture tour], but everyone was asking about [Frau] Tchaikovsky. I told everyone the same, that I know she is not Anastasia and do not wish to go into details.'[18]

Later that month he described his lectures, which took him to the Grand Rapids, Indianapolis, Philadelphia and Chicago, where he planned to meet Rostislav. 'Xenia does not make any effort to see me. I think she feels guilty and she wants to avoid unpleasant talks about Tchaikovsky. But I cannot forgive her behaviour towards me.'[19]

He was also worried about a letter that he needed Xenia to sign, concerning the three relics from the possessions of the Dowager Empress that had been given as a gift to Berlin Cathedral. Xenia, it appears, refused to sign. Sandro was displeased with her decision and worried about the future of the relics.[20]

Even as he sailed home he returned to the problem of Anastasia. 'Today is Tuesday and we are at sea for four full days. . . . I am worried about the story of Tchaikovsky and am afraid that Botkin and company will not let me alone, there will be some sort of *blackmail* because they chose this way and nothing could stop them. But as I told you before I have a lawyer and he will handle the case if they start an attack.'[21]

And in an undated letter, after describing more of his travels, his lectures on spiritualism and his campaign for peace, there is a final plea: 'I do not have anything from you. I do not know what to think.'[22]

Frogmore Cottage and its twenty-three rooms had fallen into some dis-repair, and after an inspection in February 1928 a Ministry of Works official reported on its 'deplorable condition'. Apart from redecoration in one small bedroom, it gave every impression of not having been touched for several years. In most rooms the paper was torn and hang-ing in strips, the ceilings were filthy, plaster was broken and paintwork was down to the bare wood.[23] Gas lighting and new staff bells were also required, and a requisition was put in for £130 for the work but the provision had been cut out. 'As I understand the King has expressed a wish that the Grand Duchess be made as comfortable as possible and there is no doubt that the work is necessary, the Board may perhaps reconsider the matter.' A note at the bottom read, 'there appears to be special circumstances in this case apparently'.[24] Because of the King's concern, the work had to be undertaken urgently, and the use of oil lamps and candles for lighting was regarded as an unacceptable fire risk.

A convenient date was fixed with Xenia and that was the end of the matter. However, a request eighteen months later for a ground-floor lavatory basin to provide suitable washing facilities for guests led to further activity. It had come to the notice of someone in the Office of Works that 'Princess Xenia' [sic] was a grace and favour resident. 'If this is so,' the unknown correspondent continued, 'she should pay for this improvement. It is not quite clear, as she is a relative of the King, that she is an ordinary G & F resident.'[25] Sir Frederick Ponsonby was asked to clarify the situation, and reported that 'the King quite understands that as this is a G & F residence any work should be paid for by the occupants. In this case, however, H.M. does not wish the Grand Duchess troubled in the matter and is willing to pay for the basin from the Privy Purse.'[26] The new sink in the butler's pantry was likewise paid for by the King.

More quibbling followed over payment for improvements to the hot water service and cooking apparatus in September 1932; 'as the Grand Duchess is very poor, the King has been in the habit of paying for alterations and improvements', Ponsonby explained, wondering if the expense might be included in the programme for the Grant in Aid the following year.[27] The Treasury was unwilling and the bill was once again sent to the palace. Even then a second-hand gas cooker was supplied from stock at Windsor Castle. On every future occasion when work was required at Frogmore Cottage, the cost was borne by the King.

By the early 1930s all Xenia's sons were married. Rostislav had married Princess Alexandra Galitzine in America shortly before the death of the Dowager Empress. Vassili also married in America, his wife being Princess Natalia Galitzine, a distant cousin of Rostislav's wife, whose family also had a hair-raising escape from Russia during the revolution. Last to marry was Dmitri, whose wedding to Countess Marina Koutouzov took place in Paris on 25 November 1931, with a reception held at the Youssoupovs' house in Boulogne-sur-Seine. 'Dmitri and his wife have come here having been on their honeymoon,' Xenia told Nastya from Paris, 'and very soon they will be going to England.'[28] Felix had sold his main house, and the Theatre Pavilion in the grounds was to be the Youssoupovs' new home. While alterations were being carried out, Irina and Bébé, who was living with her parents again, stayed with Xenia at Frogmore. Xenia also attended the marriage of

Sergei Dolgoruky's niece Sofka to Lev Zinoviev in London that year, where Sergei gave the bride away. Afterwards Xenia and her daughter-in-law Elsa attended the reception at the London home of the Duchess of Hamilton.

Xenia still divided her time between London and Paris, although she rarely visited Denmark. On one trip to France, the French Embassy in London requested the Customs authorities to allow her luggage to pass through as 'Her Highness is the daughter of Emperor Alexander III of Russia and resides at Windsor Castle with H.M. King George V'.[29] Paris had a strong Russian community. Many of the emigrés were from the old Tsarist capital and they founded The St Petersburg Club. There were also Russian restaurants, bookshops, churches, newspapers, clubs, libraries – everything the emigrés needed. Xenia had many friends to visit, among them Count Fersen, Mme Verola, Greek Minny (who now lived mainly in Rome) and, of course, Sergei Dolgoruky. She was often seen in a chic Russian teashop, Le Tierem Boyard, on the rue de Berri just off the Champs Elysees, run by Princess Vera Orbeliani. The paintings, the decoration, even the smell made the emigrés feel they had returned to Russia.[30]

Sandro had continued his nomadic existence. In the late 1920s he was living in Princess Paley's large house 'Balindus', in Biarritz, and between 1927 and 1929 he spent the winters with Feodor and Irene in their Paris flat on the rue Liautey. In the autumn of 1931 Sandro returned to Europe after a lecture tour of New York. Shortly afterwards he fell seriously ill with a lung malady. Tuberculosis of the spine was also suspected, though it may have been cancer. In the autumn of 1932 he moved to the south of France. His first volume of memoirs, *Once a Grand Duke*, was published in 1931. During several months' illness he wrote *Twilight of Royalty*, and the posthumously published *Always a Grand Duke*.[31]

In November 1932, as his condition worsened, Xenia left for France with her maid Sasha. By the New Year he was clearly dying. Xenia hurried to the home of his friends Captain Nicholas and Mme Tchirikoff, the Villa St Therese at Carnolés, a seaside resort near Menton, where she found Irina. Mme Tchirikoff, formerly Olga Vassilievna, born the same year as Irina, had been with the imperial family during the last months in the Crimea and left Russia with the family, but was stranded in Malta. In May 1919 her name had appeared on a list of people whom the Dowager Empress and Xenia were endeavouring to have admitted to England.[32]

The Tchirikoffs had previously lived in Menton. 'Completely unexpectedly I found myself in Olga Tchirikoff's house, the most wonderful ancient house with twisted stone stairs,' Irina wrote to her mother in the summer of 1929. 'It is Château St Bernard. Here they used to breed dogs for rescue and founded the Order with the same name. . . .'[33] Now, three years later, Olga Tchirikoff devoted much of her time to nursing Sandro during these last few sad weeks, and giving the family moral support.

Unfortunately there were other complications. Xenia was torn between Sandro in the south of France and Sergei Dolgoruky, who was ill in Paris. 'I got yr sad letter this morning and it filled me with despair,' Toria wrote from Coppins on 27 February. 'All those long weeks out at Carnolés when you might have been with your dear friend* who also needed you. . . . It is *all too dreadful* for you and only two hours together through Paris with people interrupting! Please God you will go to Paris now *soon* and perhaps be able to make him understand things but certainly the news you give me does sound very bad.'[34]

On the evening of 25 February Xenia was to be guest of honour at a ball for graduates of the St Petersburg Corps des Pages. She left Sandro's bedside at 11pm and Irina kept him company. At 3am on 26 February he complained of terrible pains. Irina immediately sent for her mother and the doctor, but Xenia arrived too late. However, Sandro would probably not have wished it otherwise. He hated melodrama and the idea of 'last words', and passed away peacefully at 3.45am.** 'Oh! *Why? You* of all people so good should have *so* much sorrow to go through,' Toria wrote, referring perhaps both to Sandro and to Sergei Dolgoruky, and the fact that their aunt Thyra, Duchess of Cumberland, Xenia's godmother, had died on the same day. 'I hope Sandro did not suffer much – your heart is indeed broken. My only consolation is

---

* Prince Dolgoruky died in Paris in November 1933.
** The certificate, at Menton, does not state the cause of death.

to think you will be able to leave that sad place which appears to be so cold.'[35]

Sandro was buried with military honours[36] on 1 March with Xenia, four of her sons and Irina attending his funeral in the cemetery at Roquebrune-Cap-Martin. Rostislav sent a telegram from Chicago. Also present were Felix, King Christian X and Queen Alexandrine of Denmark, the Tchirikoff family and Sandro's major-domo, Korobasov. Despite his wishes, Sandro was given a religious funeral at the small Orthodox Church of Vierge, 'Joie des Tous les Affligés et St Nicolas le Thaumaturge' nearby. Adini's brother Fritz, the former Grand Duke of Mecklenburg-Schwerin, apologized for not attending,

but my actualy [sic] financial means do not allow me to do so.

I sincerely feel very sad and depressed, poor Uncle Sandro was Ma's last brother and was always so very nice and kind to me. . . .

I would also so much like to have the 'Icon' of Christ which used to be in Ma's room and which Uncle Sandro had taken after Ma's death . . . if you do not want to keep it yourself.[37]

Messages of condolence poured in from every royal house in Europe, and a memorial service was held in the Russian church, London, on 5 March. Among the letters from old friends in the south of France was one from one of Xenia's closest friends Mme Leglise (La Mouche) and her husband Jean at the villa Marthe-Marie in Biarritz, recalling former happy times at the Villa les Vagues.[38]

By the beginning of March Xenia was suffering from influenza. Immediately after Sandro's death she had moved from the villa to the Hotel Banastron round the corner, where she received a letter signed 'your old Grasshopper', from Greek Minny:

Xenia darling, it is quite *useless* for me to try and express all I *feel* for you. . . . Your one comfort, though, must be that he is at peace now and suffers no more. You must not grieve, it is bad for his soul, because as I gathered from your letters, he did not seem to wish to go on living. The shock must have been terrific for you, poor dear. . . . I am so dreadfully upset not to be with you at such a moment. I do not suppose anyone expected the end would come so suddenly and quickly. In your last letter dated 20 February you said he was no worse, though felt again depressed. I wonder what he really had and what those strange dark swellings could have been. . . . All too sad and tragic. Life is an agony now-a-days.[39]

Toria immediately told King George V that Xenia had further financial difficulties. Once again, Peter Bark was sent to help her sort things out. For some time Sandro had been living off the proceeds of his coin collection, and he had left his affairs in considerable disarray. After the publication of *Once a Grand Duke*, he had asked his niece Lady Zia Wernher for a loan of £500 as he was ill in bed, promising to repay her on publication on his second book and mentioning that he was working on some articles for the *Red Book Magazine*. Zia's husband, the extremely wealthy Sir Harold Wernher, was 'touchy' when she received what he termed as 'begging letters from impoverished Russian relatives'.[40] There was also no love lost, at least after the revolution, between Zia's father Miche-Miche, who died in 1929, and Sandro.[41] On instructions from Sir Harold, Zia replied that she could only lend £250, to be repaid within a year. Whether the offer was taken up is not known, but Sandro was 'not complimentary' about Zia and her sister Nada when *Always a Grand Duke* was published in 1933.[42]

Thankfully Zia had borne her widowed relation no rancour, and added her words of condolence to the rest:

I received your letter this morning, and on finishing it opened the papers and saw the death of dear Uncle Sandro. It was a great shock, although I knew how weak he was. Adini [her cousin, Queen Alexandrine of Denmark] wrote me how changed she had found him. For him, it is a blessing . . . as it must have been awful for him not to be able to move, but it is very hard to bear for those left behind. I *do* feel for you so deeply, dearest Auntie Xenia, as you have had such a difficult time through his illness. . . . It is so very sad to think he is the last of Papa's brothers to go. Please let me know when you return, as I should so love to see you again if you have a minute to spare.[43]

Meanwhile the Anastasia controversy continued. In 1929 Xenia received a letter from A.J. Wright, an American who described a test carried out to see whether the woman recognized her former home in Russia. Wright had seen photographs, published in the *New York Times* in 1927, of the Tsar's private apartments at Tsarskoe Selo, and forwarded these to Faith Lavington, governess to the Duke of Leuchtenberg, at a Bavarian castle where 'Anastasia' was staying. All clues showing where the photographs had been taken were blacked out, and Lavington let the pictures fall, as if by chance, into 'Anastasia's' sight. She placed one of them, showing a rather obscure picture of the Tsar's bathroom, in front of her and asked what this could be. She 'took it up quite indifferently', but after a few moments, she exclaimed with some surprise that it was her father's bathroom. When Miss Lavington showed her pictures of the study, bedroom, boudoir, music room and the children's playroom, she declared: 'But these are our rooms', and 'walked quickly away to her own room, with her head down, evidently labouring under strong emotion'. Wright said the Duke believed that 95 per cent of the evidence was proven, and while he realized Xenia would be distressed by the findings, he thought it better that 'Anastasia's' claim should be proven one way or another.[44]

The family were still divided on the issue. At some time during the 1930s Xenia received a visit from her niece Princess Xenia (Mrs William Leeds), with whom Anna Anderson had stayed in America. During a three-hour talk Princess Xenia confided her impressions of Mrs Anderson and her feeling that she *was* Anastasia. Among other evidence was the fact that Mrs Anderson had recognized the voice of Prince Dmitri, Xenia's son, without seeing him, when he was playing tennis outside the house. The Grand Duchess remained unconvinced, as did her children, but she heard Princess Xenia out, blessed her and remained as friendly and loving towards her as ever.[45]

In 1933 the Central District Court in Berlin finally ruled that Nicholas II and all his children were dead. This was at the insistence of Natasha Brassova, who wanted to claim a share of the Tsar's money in the Mendelssohn Bank as heir of her son George, killed in a car crash in France two years earlier. The other heirs were Xenia, Olga and the brother and sisters of Empress

Alexandra – Ernest Ludwig of Hesse; Victoria, Marchioness of Milford Haven; and Princess Irene of Prussia.

On 9 January 1934 they were granted the Tsar's assets in Germany, said to be worth 'between 7 & 14 million roubles (£700,000 and £1,400,000)' but wartime inflation and German hyper-inflation had significantly reduced the value of the deposit. The 1930s value, put at between £20,000 and £25,000, was finally paid to the Tsar's heirs in a Certificate of Inheritance dated 1938. By 1957 there was only £1,000 left in the account. Xenia had left her share of the money 'almost untouched'.[46] It was this action that spurred Anna Anderson's lawyers to lodge a petition for the revocation of the Certificate and to challenge, in court, the assumption that all the Tsar's children had died at Ekaterinburg. The Anastasia trial in Berlin was delayed while English translations of the documents were prepared for Sir Edward Peacock (who had retained a lawyer for Xenia and Olga) and Peter Bark.[47]

In February 1934 Xenia finally received a cheque in respect of compensation for her father's property at Halila in Finland. Her financial situation was still difficult but, though she had been quietly selling her things, her 54-piece solid gold set of plate 'was still in her possession in the mid-40s'.[48] She was also involved in litigation again. In 1931 she and Olga brought a lawsuit* in America 'to restrain the sale of art objects that had belonged to Tsar Nicholas'.[49]

Rumours were still circulating that a fortune in banks in London, New York and elsewhere awaited the Tsar's rightful heirs. Anna Anderson's lawyer, Edward Fallows, was approached by Rasputin's former secretary Aaron Simanovich, who offered 'to reveal the source of $17 million of tsarist money in a New York bank if Fallows would do a deal with him'.[50] Fallows' efforts to persuade Xenia's lawyers to 'make a joint deal' foundered, because Peter Bark insisted 'on his personal knowledge' that no tsarist deposits existed in London or New York. Xenia and Olga were contacted by a Russian lawyer, who said he knew of tsarist money in England, Germany, Switzerland and America. He offered to provide them with 'authentic documents stolen from Russia'

---

* The outcome of this case is unknown.

giving the details, in exchange for half of the money.[51] In the late 1920s a 'Baron von Cuyck' in Belgium claimed to know the location of a sizeable deposit which he would reveal in exchange for a suitable 'retainer'. He promised Sandro £1,000 a year 'for at least five years' in exchange for Xenia's signature.[52]

In the wake of all these rumours and counter-rumours Xenia was introduced to the formidable American lawyer Fanny Holtzmann. During Christmas 1932, the MGM film *Rasputin and the Empress* opened to a mixed reception in New York. The following year, it opened at the Empire, Leicester Square, as *Rasputin, the Mad Monk*. Purporting to tell the story of the murder of Rasputin, it starred Ethel, John and Lionel Barrymore. In a key scene Rasputin hypnotized and then violated the Tsar's beautiful niece Natasha, whose fiancé Prince Paul Chegodieff murdered Rasputin in his cellar in revenge. Although the picture bore little resemblance to the facts, a preface was shown on screen at the beginning, saying: 'This concerns the destruction of an empire, brought about by the mad ambition of one man. A few of the characters are still alive. The rest met death by violence.'[53]

MGM were soon to learn that their preface, doubtless intended to enhance the drama of the film, was a costly mistake. One reviewer 'had been immediately satisfied' that the Prince Paul in the film was Felix Youssoupov – and everyone knew that he was married to Tsar Nicholas's niece. Felix and Irina had not seen the film, but they were soon alerted by friends. They had enjoyed mixed fortunes since the revolution, living off the proceeds of her jewels and two Rembrandts he had managed to bring out of Russia. In 1926 he opened Irfé, a *maison de couture*, and Irina was photographed in some of the clothes. Business prospered, and they began to sell soap and perfume, some of which was supplied to the Dowager Empress's lady-in-waiting Zina Mengden, who had opened a small shop in a private house in Copenhagen. Branches of Irfé in London and Berlin followed, but by 1931 the business was failing. Most of Irina's jewels had been sold and Felix, always more than generous to Russian refugees, found himself living an almost hand to mouth existence by his standards. In the summer of 1933, when Irina was staying at Roquebrune with the Tchirikoffs, they introduced her to Fanny Holtzmann who was staying nearby.

Brooklyn-born Fanny was a diminutive brunette of about thirty with a very acute mind. After passing her exams at night school she became a specialist in film and copyright law, her clients including Noel Coward and Fred Astaire. The one surprising thing about Fanny's involvement in the Youssoupov case, given the imperial family's well-known anti-Semitism, was that Fanny was Jewish. Irina told Fanny that the Natasha of the film was, according to friends, clearly recognizable as herself. Felix was anxious to discuss the matter and Fanny arranged to meet him at the Ritz in Paris. Despite Felix's Oxford education, his command of English was poor. He once sent a telegram to order a bull and three cows from England, which said, 'Please send me one man cow and three Jersey women.'[54] After paying for the dinner, Fanny understood only that Felix wanted to start legal proceedings against MGM. He suggested that she meet his mother-in-law, whose English was excellent.

One autumn day in 1933 Prince Andrei met the Green Line bus at Windsor and conducted Fanny to Frogmore Cottage. Also on the agenda was a meeting with King George and Queen Mary. If Fanny passed this inspection she would be allowed to act for the Romanoffs in the lawsuit against MGM. There was uncertainty on both sides. Xenia was unsure how to address her guest ('After all, you are a distinguished barrister') and Fanny supposed that 'Mrs Romanoff' would not be the correct form of address for her hostess. They settled on 'Fanny' and 'Xenia'. As an American Fanny was less dazzled than her European contemporaries might have been, but she was gratified to learn later that this privilege of first-name terms was only shared by King George and a few others. After a family lunch of *borscht* and *kasha*, followed by a tour of the house, they sat in the large drawing room 'huddled in shawls around the fireplace, as far as possible from the magnificent but draughty bay windows'.[55] Fanny noted the Grand Duchess's very erect posture, as she told her about the film and her daughter's grievance against MGM.

The King and Queen arrived punctually at 4pm, intrigued at the prospect of meeting a Hollywood lawyer. They questioned her intensely about America, her career and the people she knew. The Queen was surprisingly interested in John Gilbert, the great screen lover of the 1920s. At this point Xenia's butler brought in the tea, served Russian-style with lemon slices, and accompanied by 'yeast cake, cold cherries, jam and Russian coffee cake with raisins and spices'.[56] Fanny declined Xenia's invitation to stay the night, preferring the comfort of her suite in the Savoy.

The ice having been broken, on Fanny's second visit Xenia confided some of her innermost feelings over a lunch of pot roast and *kasha*. Her main invective was reserved for Alix, who 'really made a rag out of Nicky. She was never really one of us. She wouldn't speak a word of Russian unless she absolutely had to.'[57] While Xenia had been one of those most eager to welcome her sister-in-law into the family when she arrived in Russia as a painfully shy bride, she had steadily lost all patience with her in the last few months of the dynasty; even the memory of the slaughter at Ekaterinburg did not stop her speaking her mind on the woman who had done so much to lead them to the abyss. They then got on to the subject of Rasputin, and Xenia shook her head. 'We all warned Nicky, again and again.'[58] Fanny was concerned about the imperial family's anti-Semitism and the pogroms. Xenia assured her that this was something she knew nothing about, maintaining that all the very talented people in St Petersburg were Jewish. 'That's why, when we heard you were Jewish, we wanted to consult you.'[59]

There would be many more meetings, both in London and Frogmore, and telephone calls. To avoid the problem of curious telephone operators, before the days of direct dialling, Xenia needed a code name. She 'had heard Fanny Brice's radio portrayal of the willful Baby Snooks', and with deadpan humour suggested 'Mrs Snooks'. Even the republican Fanny thought that too much of a demotion for a Grand Duchess, and they decided on 'Lady Snooks'.[60]

With Fanny fully briefed about the matter with MGM, Xenia now confided that she and her family had other legal matters to attend to. There was the delicate aftermath of one of Sandro's affairs. He had sat to a sculptor named Sergei Yourievich 'and later adopted a less formal posture with his wife Helene', who had collected and carefully preserved his love letters. Yourievich, a Russian born in Paris in 1876, had been a chamberlain at the Russian Embassy and was decorated with the Legion d'Honneur. He became attracted to sculpture and studied under Rodin, giving up his formal position to become a sculptor in 1909. During the war he served in the Russian army and, after losing everything in the revolution, returned to Paris. Among his works was a bust of Queen Marie of Roumania, Xenia's cousin.

His wife, Helene Ivanovna Yourievich, 'an opulent blonde with a Wagnerian figure',[61] was now living in London. Xenia was furious to learn that Helene planned to publish Sandro's letters, but Fanny Holtzmann persuaded her to abandon the idea. Madame Yourievich pleaded that she only wanted to show the world how the Grand Duke 'hated being tied down to that dreadful Xenia',[62] but Fanny pointed out that the widowed Grand Duchess would surely emerge as the heroine of the story, the ill-treated wife.

Next there was the search for the Tsar's enormous wealth believed to be held overseas. Apart from the litigation over the money in the Mendelssohn Bank in Berlin, and the dispute over the property in Finland, Xenia placed everything in Fanny's capable hands. On Xenia's behalf, Fanny visited various emigrés in Paris, often accompanied by Irina, Dmitri and Feodor. In 1935 she even tried to enter the Soviet Union, intrigued by Xenia's claim, as Sandro's widow, 'to a vast stretch of woodland between Minsk and Pinsk'. Fanny was turned away at the Russian border as 'she was too closely associated with the decadent Czarist aristocracy'.[63] As she continued to investigate rumours of deposits in San Francisco and New York, gold bullion secretly sent to London and heavy investments in America, as well as banks in London, each lead 'slipped away into insubstantiality'.[64]

They had more success in 1934. When the case of Youssoupov vs. MGM came to court, Irina won damages of £25,000, with an immediate payment of £5,000. After Sir Harold and Lady Zia Wernher had 'turned down the suggestion' of helping Irina fund her lawsuit,[65] Nikita introduced Felix to Baron Erlanger, who either gave or lent him the money. Payment of the initial fees had come 'discreetly from Buckingham Palace'.[66] However, a suspicion remains that Fanny advanced the costs 'in return for a share of the proceeds of the judgment or any compromised settlements'.[67] An appeal failed, and MGM were forced to pay Irina undisclosed damages and a sum of £10,000 in return for an undertaking that all actions elsewhere in the world would be dropped.[68] After telling the press that she was putting the money in trust for Bébé and her future children, 'so that she and they shall never know the poverty I have endured',[69] Irina spent two weeks with Xenia at Frogmore.

Fanny continued to visit. Once, as she was signing Xenia's guest book, Nikita asked her to sign an autograph for seven-year-old Princess Elizabeth, daughter of the Duke of York. Xenia, who was a frequent guest at Buckingham Palace, issued a standing invitation to Fanny to drop by any time she was in London.

By the spring of 1934 Frogmore Cottage was evidently too small for Xenia and her family. After a case of scarlet fever, it was established that twenty-one people were living in the house. Xenia also entertained many guests. Galitzines, Zinovievs, and other emigrés came to Frogmore, where they were just as likely to bump into Xenia's royal relatives, such as her cousin Princess Anne of Bourbon-Parma (now HM Queen Anne of Roumania).

A frequent visitor was Andrew Briger, who spent the school holidays with his close friend, Xenia's grandson Prince Michael Andreievich. Andrew remembered Xenia as 'an extremely gracious lady'. One day, when he was about twelve years old, he recalled:

I invited one of her female guests to accompany me on a bicycle tour of 'MY' grounds of Windsor. The gracious lady accepted and we set off on the tour without ever mentioning who she was. After the lunch (and my bike tour) a photo was taken of us all. It was only years later, when looking at the photo with my mother, I discovered that I had shown with great pride, Princess Victoria . . . the estate she had grown up in [70]

It was originally thought that the most cost-effective solution would be to move Xenia to Frogmore House, but the greater part of this property already contained a family museum. Also, as Ponsonby explained to the Office of Works, 'once the Russian Royal Family were allowed to spread into Frogmore House there would be no limit to the numbers that came. The Grand Duchess has to pay for feeding all these people and already she finds it as much as she can manage.'[71]

The King and Queen therefore approved designs for a new wing, comprising three bedrooms and a bathroom on the ground floor adjacent to the old coal store, with a further three bedrooms and bathroom above. Xenia was shown the plans on 19 April. 'She appeared quite well pleased with the lay-out of the rooms,' wrote Mr Lamb afterwards, 'but remarked in a casual way to her lady-in-waiting, the rooms looked small! I remarked that the two rooms were larger than the smallest of the existing rooms . . . then measured out roughly on the floor the size the rooms would be, and said they would be quite big enough for a single bed, small wardrobe and dressing table. The Grand Duchess passed no further remark. . . .'[72] According to Ponsonby, the King and Queen 'did not want large rooms, as in this event, two beds would probably be put into the rooms and this was not advisable'.[73] After the usual haggling (it was 'quite out of the question to expect the Treasury to defray the cost',[74] Duff told Ponsonby), the King agreed to pay for the alterations, though he made one stipulation about the gas fires. 'H.M. hopes you will put up a notice in each room, asking that fires may not be lit until the heating is actually required,' Ponsonby wrote.[75]

By June the King was complaining about delays. 'H.M. is personally interested in requests made by the Grand Duchess,' minuted an official. 'It must be understood that any work for her, or in any connection with the Royal Family generally, is to be given priority treatment as a matter of course.'[76] After the King had paid £882 10s 4d for the alterations, it was found that the gas meter was too small to cope with the increased demand. The Privy Purse was required to pay £13 for a larger meter.

In 1934 Princess Marina of Greece married the King's youngest surviving son George, Duke of Kent. Marina was the youngest daughter of Xenia's cousin Grand Duchess Elena Vladimirovna, who had married Prince Nicholas of Greece in 1902. The new Duchess would always regard Xenia as one of her closest friends in England. After the wedding in Westminster Abbey on 30 November, at which Xenia wore a draped dress in oyster grey, an Orthodox ceremony was performed in the private chapel at Buckingham Palace. The Great Archimandrite officiated at the service which, apart from the bridal blessing, was conducted in Greek. During the ceremony, in the course of which the Prince of Wales 'absentmindedly' lit a cigarette from a candle held by one of the priests, Marina's wedding ring was transferred to her right hand, where it remained for life. Xenia and her sister-in-law Greek Minny were among the foreign members of royalty in the chapel who listened to a mixed choir from the Greek Cathedral. It may have been the last time the two old friends met.

One of the Duchess's first public duties in England, not long after her wedding, was to open an exhibition of Russian art held in a house in Belgrave Square, London. Although she was required to do little more than say a few formal words, she was extremely nervous beforehand, and grateful for the moral support given by members of the family sitting prominently in the audience. Among them were her parents, Princess Victoria, and appropriately enough Xenia, all leading 'such noisy and prolonged applause that it was as if she had made a brilliant and masterly oration'.[77] Xenia was also one of the large number of royal ladies who lent exhibits.

In May 1935 came the triumphant swansong of King George V's reign, the celebrations for his silver jubilee. A couple of days after the main procession in London and service of thanksgiving in St Paul's, Xenia wrote to Queen Mary:

Let me tell you how *touched* I was by all your kindness & sweetness to me & *how* I loved being with you & Georgie on such a memorable occasion. Thank you both from all my heart for letting me be near you & be able to *share* everything with you. It was like a lovely dream & a glimpse into *the past* – a ray of sunshine amidst one's sadness. . . .[78]

That same year there was a small fire at Frogmore Cottage and the King again paid for the redecoration of two rooms. The King, Ponsonby wrote, 'said he hoped everything would be done to study the convenience of the Grand Duchess in carrying out the decorations'.[79] After both rooms were finished, Xenia asked for her own suite to be decorated when she was away after Ascot. The Office of Works confirmed this would be done and hoped that the other bedrooms could be redecorated before then but, with the court coming for the race meeting, the men could not be spared to move the furniture. 'H.M. has always expressed a wish that everything should be done to make the Grand Duchess comfortable at Frogmore Cottage,' Ponsonby told Duff, 'and I cannot imagine that the decoration of a few rooms will be a very expensive matter.'[80]

By the time the invoice for £151 2s 2d was submitted in April 1936, Xenia's position had changed once more. The unhappy spinster Princess Victoria, who had always been one of her most supportive friends, was ailing and died on 3 December 1935. Affection between the cousins had deepened with the years, as a short letter from Queen Maud of Norway (undated but from Christmas five or six years earlier) to Xenia made clear: 'Glad we met, but sorry *only* once. Toria *misses you frightfully*. We had a quiet little Xmas together, just "we four" and the grandchild [Princess Ragnhild]. It was sad leaving home. I had a delightful stay there [England].'[81]

Six days after Toria's death, Princess Henry of Battenberg wrote to Xenia:

I feel I must send you a little line, for I know how sad you must be feeling at the loss of dear Victoria, whom you saw so much, and you were so attached to one another. You have gone through so much sorrow that I grieve for you that you should now have this added to it all, and I fear dear Victoria will leave a great blank in your life. . . . For her, I think we must all thank God to have taken her to Himself and to have spared her further suffering and ill health. . . .[82]

Xenia was among the mourners at her old friend's funeral. At Christmas she wrote to her cousin:

I must send these lines to tell you that my thoughts are with you today – & tho' these last years Toria dear was away for Xmas, I know you must miss her. . . .

I heard you speak on the wireless, it reminded me so of darling Toria.

We used to sit together in Coppins & listen to yr voice & we both had a lump in the throat.

I just can't tell you (tho' you know) *all* she meant to me & how terribly I miss her & *how* terribly I will as long as I live &

how lonely I feel . . . no use trying to explain – the feelings I bore her & all I have lost in her – you know it. Two days ago several boxes were sent here with a lot of her clothes & small belongings. May kindly wrote that you wished me to have them. Let me tell you how touched & grateful I am & thank you from the bottom of my heart. The small things which she always used are very dear to me & I will always treasure them. . . .[83]

In January 1936 Xenia wrote to Princess Olga Alexandrovna Wiassemskaya thanking her for sympathy on the loss of her lady-in-waiting and friend Sophie Evreinoff, who had been with Xenia for forty years and died in the autumn of 1935, aged sixty-four. It had been a sad Christmas and New Year, but yet another blow was to come. King George V was now losing his own fight for life, and he passed away on 20 January. 'No words of mine will ever be able to express all I feel & how my heart aches for you darling May in your terrible sorrow,' she wrote to the widowed Queen. 'You know how I loved him – he was just like a brother to me but it is you I am thinking about & yr sorrow is incomparable to my own.'[84]

In the space of just a few months Xenia had lost her three closest friends and supporters.

12 (1936–45)

'The Grand Old Lady of the North'

The death of King George brought his eldest son, the Prince of Wales, to the throne as King Edward VIII. Early in the new reign Xenia was advised that the new monarch intended to retain Frogmore Cottage as a private sanctuary for the immediate royal family, and to offer her and the family another grace and favour residence, Wilderness House at Hampton Court. 'Glad David [Edward VIII] has offered Xenia a house at H. Court as it will be further away for *all* her tiresome family,' Queen Maud of Norway, King George V's last surviving sibling, wrote to Queen Mary. 'But fear *she* will be unhappy to leave Frogmore as *she* loved it. Hope only she won't be hurt, poor dear she has *so* much sorrow & so many worries with that large useless family.'[1]

Originally called the Master Gardener's House, Wilderness House was built around 1698/9 as an official residence for the royal gardener. Among the earlier occupants, during his brief sojourns at Hampton Court, was 'Capability' Brown, who had complained of the small, uncomfortable rooms, an offensive kitchen and bad offices. A new dining room, complete with cellar underneath, was built at his request.[2] On the retirement of the last royal gardener to occupy the house, it was given over to grace and favour in 1881. When Xenia inspected the property on 26 June 1936 various proposed alterations were explained and she suggested others, including installation of a bathroom in the flat above the Coach House and the construction of an Orthodox chapel in the main house. On 2 July the Privy Purse Office formally notified the Office of Works that the King intended to offer her use of the house, and that the alterations were under consideration.

By July the usual haggling over who should pay for the alterations – including those to the Coach House, which it was understood was to be used by one of Xenia's sons – was under way. King Edward undertook to bear the extra expenses over and above those falling on the Office of Works, but wanted Xenia to move in as soon as possible. Around this time the last reunion of all Xenia's children at Frogmore Cottage took place, with Vassili and Rostislav coming from America, Irina and Felix from France. In the autumn Xenia was at St Genevieve-des-Bois with Irina and Vassili, and the Office of Works complained that it was 'not possible to ascertain her wishes about the property'.[3]

As well as visiting the old people's home at St Genevieve-des-Bois, Xenia inspected the Russian children's camp at Capreton, Landes. She was one of the patrons of the Russian Ball held at the Ritz Hotel in aid of these camps in 1939. Once again her family was involved as her daughter-in-law Marie (Princess Nikita) was chairman of the committee, and her granddaughter Xenia sold programmes. In the meantime Xenia suffered another personal blow with the death of Sir Peter Bark. He had become a British subject in 1935 and was knighted by King George V, with whom he had frequently discussed Xenia's financial affairs at the palace. Count Vladimir Kleinmichel succeeded him as the Grand Duchess's adviser and trustee. Not admired by everyone with whom he came into contact, Bark was unlamented by Edward Fallows, Anna Anderson's lawyer, who advised Sir Harold Brooks, an attorney involved in the Rasputin film libel case, that he had 'kept both Xenia and Olga under his thumb, and how bitter he was against Anastasia'.[4]

The abdication of King Edward VIII in December 1936 over his determination to marry the twice-divorced Wallis Simpson brought his brother 'Bertie', Duke of York, to the throne as King George VI. In the following month the Office of Works concluded that Xenia was 'reluctant to leave Frogmore Cottage and move into Wilderness House', as she had failed to keep an appointment with the architect. In fact she was unwell, but her son visited the house on 22 January and said his mother would move in towards the end of February.[5] After a further delay, on 18 March the Lord Chamberlain confirmed that the Grand Duchess would accept the property, emphasizing that she would 'be required to defray the rates, insurance and other incidental expenses in connection with the house'.[6] Xenia hoped to be settled in before the end of March. She was allowed to take with her 'furniture from Frogmore which belonged to the Crown' and the Office of Works was asked to undertake any repairs that should become necessary and charge the cost to the Privy Purse.[7]

Various alterations were carried out at Wilderness House for Xenia's benefit. The 22-roomed house had a basement with kitchens and servants' quarters, and two sitting rooms, a large drawing room, a dining room and a bedroom on the ground floor. On the first floor were four bedrooms and a bathroom, with further servants' bedrooms and bathroom in the second floor attic. An Orthodox chapel was constructed in the drawing room, and Father George Cheremetev of the Greek Orthodox Church came to conduct the services. Xenia's children and grandchildren were quick to visit, and it became a tradition for members of the family to scratch their names on a window pane. As the house was near the Lion Gate of Hampton Court Palace, to the children's delight they could look out of the windows and watch visitors getting lost in the maze.

From time to time Xenia was to be seen shopping in Kingston. For many years she was a customer at Benson's Nurseries in St James's Road, which supplied and arranged the floral decorations inside Wilderness House. It may have been about this time, when she was feeling the loss of Sophie Evreinoff, that Mara Sanders, sister of the actor George Sanders, became her aide and companion.

Having settled into her own new home, the next year Xenia visited Olga in Denmark. After the death of the Dowager Empress, Olga and Nicholas lived at Rygaard, near Holte, before buying Knudsminde, a farm at Ballerup, 15 miles north-west of Copenhagen, in 1932. It stood in 185 acres of farmland, where they kept horses, pigs, chickens and geese and grew vegetables. Among the heirlooms scattered around the house was the dining-room furniture from Hvidøre. Olga had her two elderly Russian maids Emilie Tenso ('Mimka') and Tatiana Gromova, but like any other Danish housewife she went shopping, did the washing and mending and tended the garden, while Nicholas took care of the farm. Their sons Tihon and Guri had both entered the Royal Danish Guards. Xenia frequently received news of her sister from other relatives. 'I have just seen Olga,' Prince George of Greece wrote in March. 'She and her husband are well and both sons delighted to be soldiers.'[8]

Xenia and one of her sons, probably Feodor, spent two months at Knudsminde. When they visited Alfred Jacobsen at Malov, Xenia admired the flowers in his garden but her son was more interested in the Danish beer.

On 19 June 1938 Xenia's eldest granddaughter Bébé married Count Nicholas Cheremetev, a first cousin of Nikita's wife Marie Vorontzov-Dashkov, in the Russian Church in Rome. The marriage had been delayed while the bridegroom spent two years in a Swiss sanatorium seeking a cure for his tuberculosis.*

That same month King George VI asked the Home Office in London to expedite naturalization papers for Xenia's grandchildren who lived with her at Hampton Court, namely Xenia and Michael Andreievich (their brother Andrew, godson of the Duke of Windsor, was born in London); Elizabeth Frederiki, Elsa's daughter by her first marriage; and Alexander Nikititch (his brother Nikita was also born in London). Those who had been born in England were automatically British subjects and no such formality was required in their case. Lord Wigram explained to Lord Boyd that by royal standards Grand Duchess Xenia was 'very badly off'. Her sons were not employed and not making their own living, and she had to support them all: 'funds are very short as unfortunately many of the investments in the trust Fund are in these international securities like Austrian Loan, etc., which are not paying dividends. It is very pathetic to see these exiled members of the Royal Family of Russia in such a parlous state.'[9]

When the Home Office demanded the customary £10 fee for each, Lord Wigram replied that although they lived at Hampton Court the Romanoffs' finances were in a very precarious condition and requested that the sum should be waived, adding in a jocular fashion, 'I must arrange a flag day at Hampton Court for them.'[10] A further exchange of correspondence between Sir Alexander Maxwell and Sir James Rae emphasized that the family were 'in an

---

* His sister Prascovia was married to Prince Roman, son of Grand Duke Peter and Grand Duchess Militza.

impecunious position' and 'largely dependent on the bounty of the King'[11] and the £40 fees were indeed waived.

Around this time a new figure entered Xenia's life. Vera Maslenikoff, nine years younger than her, came from a family whose 'well-connected' relatives included the Stroganovs. Her mother, the illegitimate daughter of 'someone well-known', was married off to the land agent or the bailiff. Vera's training as a nurse and her personal skills led to her being deputed by Prince Alexander of Oldenburg, head of the Russian Red Cross during the First World War, to travel to the front, where she put her considerable energies to good use by reorganizing hospitals and Red Cross arrangements. She was also sent on special missions to POW camps in Austria and Germany. Later she became a nun, taking the name Mother Martha.[12] After the death of Sophie Evreinoff, she moved into Wilderness House to look after the Grand Duchess. Princess Alice of Greece visited in 1938, sat talking to Xenia at some length and helped in the kitchen. Anxious to emulate the example of her aunt, Grand Duchess Ella, Alice consulted Mother Martha, who told her about Read House, a rest home for Orthodox clergy in Kent. Alice went to work there in June.[13]

Xenia maintained contact with Russian emigrés both in England and France, never failing to send Easter and New Year greetings to Eugene Sabline, former Russian Chargé d'Affaires in London, and his wife. She also continued to keep in regular touch with members of the family around Europe, all too often as a result of deaths and subsequent letters of condolence. In July 1938 the irrepressible widowed Marie, Queen of Roumania, passed away, and a letter to her younger sister Sandra of Hohenlohe-Langenburg brought forth a heartfelt answer:

Yes, it is almost impossible to realize that Missy, with all her great and wonderful personality, has really left us for ever. What it means to me to have lost my two most beloved sisters so soon one after the other I shall never be able to say. . . . I had been so much with her [Missy] during this whole last year and know perhaps better than anyone how she bore her trial, which was so doubly hard just for her, so full of life and energy, forced to complete inactivity. . . .

Yes, it is ages and ages since we met last, but also my

thoughts have so often wandered to *you* in deep sympathy for all the tragic suffering you have gone through. Oh, yes, life has become one huge tragedy, which one often hardly knows how to bear and with every day one becomes more lonely.[14]

Four months later Queen Maud of Norway, the last survivor among aunt Alix's children, came to London for an operation, had a sudden relapse, and died unexpectedly. Maud had written from Claridges six days before her death, saying she was about to undergo surgery and was sending Xenia a velvet coat which she hoped might be useful.[15] When King Haakon opened Maud's safe afterwards, he divided the money found inside between Xenia and Olga, as he was aware that his late wife had often helped them in various ways.[16]

It may have been the shock of these deaths, or the liver trouble that Xenia complained of when writing to her Uncle Waldemar to congratulate him on his eightieth birthday in October, that had prompted Xenia to make her will. 'I am sending you the copy of the letter . . . from Baring Bros. in which they confirm that they are holding your Will,' Count Kleinmichel wrote earlier that year, on 12 January 1938. 'Please keep this letter in case something happens to me otherwise it's possible to forget where the Will is kept.'[17]

Waldemar sent condolences to his niece:

I am very sorry to hear, that you are suffering from your liver, I do hope you have got a good doctor, who can examine you thoroughly from head to bottom and find out, what it is, please do that for us all. . . .

Now I just return from the unveiling of a monument for Uncle Fredy [Frederik VIII] and Aunt Louise, an Obelisk with their portraits in relief. It stands at Charlottenlund in front of the house in the garden and was unveiled today, A. Louise's birthday. Dear Olga is well, also her Kukuschkins. I see them often here at Ballerup. . . .[18]

Having reached the same age as his mother and two of his sisters, Waldemar passed away in January 1939.

Xenia continued to receive many invitations to family events which she was unfortunately unable to accept. One of these was the marriage of Ducky's daughter Kira to Prince Louis Ferdinand of Prussia, second son of the ex-Crown Prince of Germany, a family alliance of which his mother Cecilie wrote to Xenia in glowing terms:

> We are *so* happy about Lulu's engagement! Kira is a dear, and so clever, and *kind*, the right girl to be a good companion to him, in all the different difficult situations. . . .
>
> The Orthodox wedding will be here on May 2nd. We would have been delighted to have had you here with us, dear Xenia, but I'm afraid the long journey would be too complicated for you? We thought of asking your son Dmitri with his wife, if they care to come. They would be 'quartered' in a hotel in Potsdam. I would be grateful to hear if they can come over.[19]

On the outbreak of war in September 1939, Xenia's family were scattered. Irina and Felix were in France. Bébé and her husband were in Rome, where they were later joined by Nikita, Marie and their sons who had left England in the spring of 1939. Feodor had left France in 1937 after his divorce and was now living with Xenia. His young son Michael, who had visited Wilderness House in 1937, remained with his mother in France. Dmitri was a Lieutenant-Commander in the Royal Navy and served as Naval Attaché to the Royal Hellenic and Royal Yugoslav navies stationed in British waters, also accompanying the armament convoys from England to Murmansk. Rostislav and Vassili had settled in America.

Andrusha and his family were also at Wilderness House. His sons Michael and Andrew were serving in the Royal Navy, while his daughter Xenia ('Mysh') trained as a nurse at Great Ormond Street Children's Hospital, also doing voluntary work for the Russian Benevolent Society. The war and the separation from her family left Xenia low-spirited, especially at Christmas. Writing to an old friend who had sent a photograph of the Dowager Empress's Cossack bodyguard Koudinoff, who died in 1915, she commented with sadness: 'We were happy in those days and *so* much has happened since as you say. It was a *cleaner* and better world altogether.'[20]

By the New Year Xenia was laid low with influenza, and the Duchess of Kent wrote in January:

Georgie and I are back in London since a few days, and I have thought of you so much all this time. I have the most awful 'remorse' that I haven't seen you for so long! May I come with Zoia? She and A [Aunt] Agnes* long to see you too.

I am so sorry your beastly flu won't leave you in peace! Do you look after yourself properly and stay in bed?[21]

Prince George of Greece wrote in the spring of 1940 with further dispiriting news of the family:

May God help us all against these swines and anti-Christ who are behaving worse than Barbarians. The great English successes in Norway give me hope and courage and my sailor heart rejoiced with what the navy of navies has done and is doing. And poor Carl!** He is also going through terrible moments and they are after him trying to shoot him like a rabbit or a hare. Fancy if dear Maud was there!

I got news from Christian [X] yesterday . . . they are all well [living under the German occupation]. . . . Only Harald's Helena,*** that fat German swinish being, is satisfied! Christian ought to kick her out of the country.[22]

'It is terrible to have one's country occupied,' the Dowager Marchioness of Milford Haven wrote, sympathizing with the family in Denmark, 'and with the ghastly fear when it can be free

---

* Agnes de Stoeckl and her daughter Zoia. Agnes and her husband had been part of Greek Minny's household and knew Xenia well. The Duke and Duchess of Kent had given her a house on the Coppins estate.
** King Haakon VII of Norway, who strove to maintain his kingdom's neutrality, until events later that spring brought the country into the war on the side of Great Britain and her allies.
*** Princess Helena of Glucksburg, the German-born wife of Prince Harald of Denmark, younger brother of Kings Christian X and Haakon VII. Much to the family's embarrassment and fury, she remained unashamedly committed to the Nazi cause, even entertaining some of Hitler's officers at their home during the occupation of Denmark. After the war she was banished to the land of her birth.

again. Now perhaps people will realise, what you and your Russian friends have gone through and how hard exile is.'[23]

The war also brought forth a declaration of loyalty from Eugene Tseshkovsky in Belgrade, a member of Xenia's old regiment:

On behalf of the Ukrainian Hussars, I would like to send your Imperial Highness our most heartfelt . . . wishes for prosperity, happiness, health and joy.

During this time of terrible historical events, we want you to know that, with a calm and clear awareness of our duty, we are prepared to face any new ordeals and sacrifices for Russia, for the glory of our Throne, for Russian personal interests and in these turbulent times our eyes and hearts are turned to you . . . and the whole meaning of our services is concentrated in Your Person as a living symbol of past greatness and future glory. . . . our only joy is your prosperity and longevity and the restoration of Your Throne, the Motherland and our regiment is our only happiness. . . .[24]

As in 1914, many of her relatives experienced the heartbreak of having relatives so widely dispersed, and often on opposite sides in the conflict. From Adsdean, Chichester, the Dowager Marchioness of Milford Haven wrote to Xenia:

I am thinking so much and lovingly of you, to whom this war under such altered circumstances will bring back so many recollections. One is grateful for all our dear ones, now we trust and pray for ever at peace in God's merciful keeping, that none of our sorrows and anxieties can trouble them any more. May He grant you and all of us patience and strength. . . .

Alice and Philip are together in Athens, it will be a comfort to her to have him there. Louise, thank goodness is in a completely neutral country and may be able perhaps to hear from time to time how Alice's daughters and Irene are keeping. In the great war Daisy was able to do that too. If I can be of any help to you and your family please always count on me.[25]

On 29 October 1940 Wilderness House was bombed and the windows were shattered. Elisabeta, who had been suffering from cancer for some time, died that day. Queen Mary immediately sent 'loving sympathy' to Xenia and Andrusha,[26] and in a letter of condolence Victoria Milford Haven wrote of Elsa being 'released from her long and cruel sufferings'. After a funeral service at Wilderness House, at which Father Michael Malchanoff, a family friend, officiated, she was buried at Old Windsor.

'I hope all this bombing, which, not as terrible as in London, is frequent round here and at Hampton Court I am sure too, is not too trying on your nerves,'[27] wrote the Dowager Marchioness of Milford Haven from Maidenhead a few days later. Soon afterwards another blow fell, with the death of Greek Minny on 14 December: 'I can't get over dear Minnie's *sudden* death, it gave me such a shock,' Xenia told Queen Mary a week later. 'I feel terribly sad – we were such friends all our life ever since we were *small* children. She sent me a few lines last August . . . saying that she was going to Dresden for a cure . . . because she felt rotten and everything seemed to have gone wrong. She came back – to pack and close the house all by herself, because her husband was stopped at the frontier and was obliged to stay in Germany – Naturally all this and the beastly war must have affected her health.'[28]

The King now decided that Xenia should be moved somewhere safer, where they 'could keep an eye on her'.[29] By Christmas she was safely and happily installed at Craig Gowan, about a mile from Balmoral Castle. Described as a 'very pleasant, medium-sized country house'[30] with five bedrooms, it was built on the east end of Craig Gowan Hill around 1870. Various alterations have been made over the years but it is still used by the royal family today, notably by Queen Elizabeth II and the Prince of Wales. From here Xenia wrote to Queen Mary with her hopes and 'loving good wishes' for the festive season and 1941: 'may the New Year bring us both better times & all the evil & wickedness vanish with the old one!' After several years of living close to London, the Scottish Highlands were an unexpected delight. 'Here in this lovely country (& remote spot) we have found real peace & I can't say what it means & feels like. I am ever so grateful to Bertie for letting me come here. The house is ever so cosy & comfortable, no wonder the Wigrams are so fond of it.'[31]

There she stayed for the rest of the Second World War. Though bitterly cold, it was the lesser of two evils. 'There have been 7°

below Fara at Balmoral,' Queen Mary wrote to her brother Alexander, 'Alge', Earl of Athlone, 'which is unfortunate for poor Xenia & co, who have gone to live at Craig Gowan, as their house at H. Ct, had had all the windows shattered, & Xenia could not stand the bombs & no wonder – so Bertie let her go there, tho' there is no central heating. However, she loves it & is quite happy.'[32]

Safe from the bombing which ravaged London and several other cities in England, Xenia's main concern was the health of her son Feodor, suffering from tuberculosis. 'I have been so worried all these months about my poor Feodor,' she wrote to Queen Mary in December 1941, 'who . . . after being laid up for weeks at home – had to go to the sanatorium at Torna-dee for a treatment. He feels much better and the doctors are more satisfied with his general condition. It is his left lung that is affected. . . . He feels very lonely and dull over there cut off as he is from us all. . . .'[33] The following year Feodor spent Easter at Craig Gowan, but after a few days he was back at the sanatorium, though feeling stronger and looking much better, cut off from his young son Michael. Through the kindness of a mutual friend in Madrid, Xenia and Feodor were able to send letters via the South Express, which Michael and his mother then collected from the station. This correspondence was always wrapped between two bars of chocolate, and the young prince always associated news from Balmoral with the taste of dessert.[34]

Occasionally Xenia received a letter from Bébé in Rome, sent via Lisbon. On 1 March 1942 she became a great-grandmother when Bébé gave birth to a daughter, also called Xenia ('Punka') in Italy. Like Nikita, who received regular amounts from his mother's bank account (despite selling his wife's fur coat and other possessions) and had to ask her to increase the payment in 1942, Bébé had money worries. As Irina, living in occupied France, could not receive money from her mother, she wanted it to be used by Bébé. In December Bébé sent her grandmother some photographs of baby Xenia and asked again if she could receive the money usually paid to her mother, giving the address of a man in Sweden who would be able to forward a letter.[35] Xenia had little news of Irina and Felix but Dmitri, who had helped with the evacuation of Dunkirk, was able to visit them later in the war.

Xenia was also cut off from direct contact with Olga, living in German-occupied Denmark. '. . . Ingeborg [Xenia's cousin,

Princess Charles of Sweden] has just returned from a visit to Denmark,' the Dowager Marchioness of Milford Haven wrote in October 1940, 'where she saw Olga, who was quite well and delighted with her daughter-in-law [Ruth, Guri's new wife].'[36]

Sometimes messages were passed on via Switzerland:

'I have news of Olga – through our old Swiss tutor [Thormeyer] in Geneva,' Xenia told Queen Mary in May 1941. 'Her youngest son [Guri] married last year and his wife is expecting a baby.'[37] 'I got a letter from Olga two months ago,' Xenia reported in December. 'She is delighted with her little granddaughter [Xenia Kulikovsky] who was born last June. . . .'[38]

The correspondence sometimes came via Crown Princess Louise of Sweden, who copied out Olga's letters in her own hand and forwarded them by courier to Xenia. One example of this tactic came in a letter from Louise in June 1941, though by the time the letters arrived, the information was often out of date.

> I know that any news of one's dear ones is welcome. She writes: 'I have such a dear sweet young daughter-in-law and am looking forward to become [sic] a grandmother . . . in June. It will be a blessing when it will all be over and the little one has arrived safely. Our boys and Ruth live with us still, but for how long is impossible to say as they finish the officers school this autumn and may be moved. My garden is so lovely . . . so full of flowers, there is lots to paint. . . .
>
> 'I have no news from my sister but I know where she is, and her family. Her last letters are from October.'[39]

The Duchess of Kent was another recipient of Louise's letters from neutral Sweden, and was able to forward any copied letters from Olga. Marina told Xenia to send letters for Olga to Coppins and she would forward them to Louise, who would send them to Denmark. By this convoluted route the sisters managed to keep in touch throughout the war.

Xenia received regular letters from the Duchess of Kent and other royal relatives, and even Easter greetings from the family's old nanny. She saw the King and Queen when they could come to Balmoral, and also the Duke and Duchess of Gloucester. Queen Elizabeth remembered Xenia as 'dear, small and kind', quite thin and often dressed in black (perhaps in mourning for her daughter-in-law Elsa). Although the Grand Duchess never visited Balmoral Castle, the King and Queen occasionally went to Craig Gowan. The Queen admired Xenia's 'charming, delicate nature' and the fact that, despite everything, she never complained. On their rare wartime visits to Scotland the King, Queen and their young daughters Princesses Elizabeth and Margaret Rose always sang the 'Volga Boat Song' as they drove past Craig Gowan, in salute to the Russians.

One of Xenia's favourite occupations, in true Russian tradition, was gathering mushrooms in the woods. She knew all the various types, and taught the local people which ones could be eaten and which were poisonous. Sometimes one or more of the Grand Duchess's 'tall and handsome' sons, or her grandsons were there. One day 'one of the sons got very merry in the village'.[40] The New Zealand and Canadian troops whom Xenia entertained to tea when they were stationed nearby always called her 'The Grand Old Lady of the North'.[41]

She still needed to watch her finances carefully, and was particularly grateful for Queen Mary's Christmas gift, a dressing gown, for Christmas 1941: 'it is just the right material, soft and not too thick, will keep me nice & warm & also save me the expense of buying a new one, which I was on the verge of doing!'[42] Queen Elizabeth allegedly sent her food hampers.[43] Like many other households, they were also busy sawing and chopping wood.

In August 1942 the Duke of Kent was killed when his plane crashed on a flight over Scotland. The King and Queen and the Duke and Duchess of Gloucester were staying at Balmoral when the tragic news arrived. Shattered by her sudden bereavement, with their younger son Michael a newly christened baby of three weeks at the time of his father's death, the widowed Duchess clung ever more resolutely to Xenia's friendship. 'Poor Marina, one's heart aches for her,'[44] she wrote to Queen Mary. Feodor's health continued to worry her. 'He is with me again,' she told Queen Mary in April 1943, '& was kept in the sanatorium for 10 days only. Dr Anderson is coming over to see him one of these days. It is very hard for him to be laid up again (7 weeks already) after having been so much better and able to go about.'[45]

A few years previously Andrei had made friends with Nadine McDougall, who lived in Kent. A friend of Field-Marshal

Mannerheim, a one-time aide-de-camp to Tsar Nicholas II, she already had a passing acquaintance with the imperial family. Soon after moving to Scotland during the war she re-established contact with the young widower. He proposed to her at a picnic in the Balmoral woods, and in September 1942 they were married. Xenia was also cheered by visits from Andrusha's sons Michael and Andrew, who enjoyed skiing in the snow-capped hills. 'I have got a dear friend staying here besides – who came over with us,' she told Queen Mary on 17 December 1942, 'she is a *nun*, Mother Martha. Bertie and Elizabeth know her.'[46] Because Mother Martha had rather large feet, Princesses Elizabeth and Margaret Rose thought she must be a man. Although the princesses made fun of her feet, Mother Martha, Queen Elizabeth recalled, was devoted to Xenia.[47]

Family concerns continued to trouble her. Earlier in the war Nikita and Marie had been able to send letters to Xenia via Queen Ena of Spain, with whom he played bridge, but now there had been no news of Nikita or Bébé, both in German-occupied Italy, for over a year. The Duchess of Kent, who was cut off from members of her own family, understood Xenia's worries and was full of sympathy.

'I am so sorry to hear about Feodor's illness, and I do hope he is much better,' she wrote in July 1943. 'What a worry for you – also Nikita and Marie and all the others in Rome, do you ever have news? Not easy, I know, from enemy territory.'[48]

'Yes, isn't it beastly being separated for so long from one's loved ones,' the Duchess reiterated in spring the following year, 'and when will this bloody war ever end! Sometimes one feels it is going on for ever.'[49]

News of Olga, who now had two grandchildren, came mainly via Geneva. Among friends Xenia made locally were the Abercrombies, the Mosses and Nadine's mother Sylvia McDougall, whom she sometimes met in Aboyne. She was an indefatigable walker, visiting many of the tenants on the Balmoral estate, including a former housemaid from Balmoral Castle, Charlotte Gordon, who remembered the visit of Nicky and Alix in 1896. Seton Gordon, who had travelled to Russia with Felix in 1913, was a frequent visitor, and Xenia loved reminiscing with him about the 'Old Russia' and her brother the Tsar. A photograph of

Nicholas in the uniform of a private soldier stood on her writing desk.[50] When she watched the summer sunset over Deeside, she said her thoughts always turned to Russia; she never lost her love for the country.

She was distressed on hearing that the retreating Germans had destroyed the Russian palaces of her childhood, including Tsarskoe Selo, Peterhof and Pavlovsk. 'It hurts to think that nothing has been spared by the enemy (*beasts*) & all those beautiful Palaces & lovely parks exist no longer – & everything is now a mass of ruins! Gatchina Palace has also been burnt down & as to Peterhof – nothing is left of it by the continual bombardment by both sides. Pavlovsk, which belonged to the Constantine family, was a real gem. . . .'[51]

She continued to paint, among other things a Christmas card for the Duchess of Kent. Many of her miniature watercolours were sold for charity or given to friends. There were gifts each Christmas from Queen Mary, all received gratefully. 'I was so touched with yr kind thought,' she wrote after her fifth season at Balmoral, 'the shawl & book of Raphael's beautiful paintings. It is so refreshing looking at them . . . it is so sweet of you to remember me every Christmas. . . .'[52]

In May 1944 Sylvia McDougall booked the annexe of the Dinnet Profeits Hotel for Andrusha's family, Mother Martha and Xenia, who had been feeling 'rather seedy'.[53] The change did her good, though she was still worried about Feodor, who suffered a relapse the previous September. She had been to visit him in the sanatorium near Aberdeen and he received regular presents from Mother Martha. Feodor asked Xenia to subscribe to two English papers for him, *Tablet* and *Nineteenth Century and After*. He complained of hunger – he had only eaten bread and a piece of cheese that day, he wrote in April 1944 – and found the ration book a bore.[54]

Early in 1945 Xenia received a letter from Bébé, the first for some time. She had spent the last four years in Italy, living in the countryside with Tatiana and Jacques de Rham. Eventually, after a terrible journey through bombing and machine-gun fire, Bébé and her two-year-old daughter 'Punka' reached Switzerland. They spent three weeks in a camp and Bébé had to spend her days peeling potatoes. At night they slept on the floor without sheets. By January 1945 they were at the Hotel Beau-Rivage in Lausanne and Bébé had been having treatment for a slight fever, but she needed money. She again asked if her grandmother could help, or whether she should try to obtain money from the Trust fund set up by her mother after the Youssoupov court case.

Xenia had been staying in Banchory and returned to Balmoral in April, mainly on account of Feodor, but was delighted to be able to give Queen Mary some family news. Her granddaughter Xenia, Andrei's eldest child, announced her engagement to 2nd Lieutenant Calhoun Ancrum from South Carolina, 'a huge surprise as we never suspected anything'.[55] 'Cal' Ancrum, serving abroad with the US Army, was relieved to know that after their wedding they would be living near the Grand Duchess and that 'Mysh' would see her grandmother every day.[56]

There were also worries about Nikita. He and Marie had left Italy, against Tatiana de Rham's advice, and were refugees in Germany. Bébé was hoping they would join her in Lausanne. The Queen of Spain was in Switzerland, but Bébé did not know her. 'Do you think [she] could do something for them?', Bébé asked Xenia, '. . . perhaps you could write and ask her.'[57]

Xenia was back at the Tor-na-coille Hotel at Banchory, and had asked Princess Marina to forward a letter to another regular correspondent, her old friend Countess Fersen [Sophie Fersen, sister of Sergei Dolgoruky]. The Duchess of Kent had been worried about her mother, Xenia's cousin Princess Nicholas of Greece [Grand Duchess Elena Vladimirovna], who was living in Athens. The electricity and hot water had been cut off and food was in short supply. 'I can't think what is going to happen after the war,' Marina continued. 'I fear there will be many difficulties ahead . . . and that "your" people are going to be the great trouble! I am so sorry you don't get any news of Nikita it must be dreadfully worrying for you. . . .

'I laughed over your description of the inhabitants of your hotel! So typical!!'[58]

May 1945 saw the end of the war in Europe and in July Xenia received news of Nikita, now in a camp near Munich, from her distant cousin Princess Tatiana Constantinovna. 'They are not alone, there are 200 Russian people with them, they all arrived together,' Tatiana wrote. 'They can get out of there because they've got visas but for some reason they didn't do it. . . .' There was another problem; Bébé still needed money. Could Xenia send 300 Swiss Francs?[59] In August Xenia's grandson Nikita arrived at Newhaven from France. Some of his documents were impounded by the Immigration Officer and the Home Office Aliens Department was anxious to inspect them. His application for a commission in the British Army was eventually declined, though he was a British subject.[60]

By September Xenia's son Nikita and his wife Marie were staying with the Duchess of Kent's sister Elizabeth (called 'Woolley' 'because of her masses of dark curly hair'[61]) and her husband Count Toerring at Schloss Winhöring, Germany. Cal Ancrum had managed to take them tea, coffee and other necessities and bring back news to Xenia. She, meanwhile, had written to 'Paulik' [Prince Chouvalov], who eventually managed to bring them out. They had been unable to understand why it was so difficult for them to obtain British visas, and while they waited the Red Army was coming dangerously close. Finally they were able to reach Felix and Irina in Paris. It appears that of all Xenia's sons Nikita was closest to the Nazis. He lived in Italy under Mussolini and when Italy left the Axis he moved to Berlin, from where he was rescued by Prince Chouvalov in 1945 because he was in danger of being arrested.[62]

To Xenia's letter of thanks, Woolley replied that she was happy to help and that Marie, whose health had suffered during the war, was looking much better.[63] A curious document from Paris, which Xenia preserved for the rest of her days, welcomed her home. 'Discovering that you are in good health having safely returned to your former residence, the Order of Preobrajensky, under your esteemed patronage, warmly welcome Your Imperial Highness,' it began, before listing members of the Order who had been killed during the war. 'The fund in the name of the Emperor the Great Nikolai II, created in 1935, graciously helped by Your Imperial Highness, was of great use to the seriously wounded and their families. The remaining uninjured, having endured such an ordeal . . . convey to Your Imperial Highness the heartfelt feelings of your devoted followers and the deepest respect.'[64]

For the festive season friends managed to procure a goose, while others made Christmas pudding, mince pies and even a cake.[65] At Wilderness House Christmas 1945 was celebrated in style.

13 (1945–60)

'Always a Grand Duchess'

At the end of the war Xenia had moved back with a maid and a cook to Wilderness House. The postwar years brought inevitable changes to her world. Rostislav and Vassili both had families in the United States, though Xenia's grandson Alexander recalled that she had no desire to go to America and could not understand her sons and grandsons making a life there. Dmitri and Marina were divorced in 1947; Rostislav and Alexandra had divorced in 1944, and his subsequent marriage to Alice Baker ended likewise in 1952. By the time of her death Xenia had thirteen grandchildren and four great-grandchildren.

Now in her seventies, her health was beginning to give cause for concern. Queen Mary went to see her in March 1946, the first time they had met since before the war, and reported sadly to the Earl of Athlone afterwards that she had been suffering from a duodenal ulcer and still looked very ill. Feodor, who was living with her at the time, seemed even worse: 'he is eaten up with lung trouble & looks awful, he is so ill that Xenia's doctor will not allow her young grandson* to live in the house in case of infection . . . but F refuses to move!'[1]

Felix and Irina came to stay in April, the first time Xenia had seen them since 1939. Xenia was grateful to Felix for managing to 'liberate' her from Lala, a troublesome member of staff.[2] Feodor was now little more than skin and bone, and Irina and Felix took him back to France in the hope that a better climate would help. The British doctor accompanying Feodor gave him six months to live.[3] A Parisian doctor sent him to a sanatorium near Pau, and after several operations his ex-wife Irene, Felix and Irina paid for

---

* Prince Alexander had returned to England in the autumn of 1945.

him to live in Ascain, near Biarritz, for the rest of his life. Xenia was also able to see Vassili again after a 'long separation'.[4]

Increasing heart trouble led to various cancelled invitations and inevitable regrets. She found the severe winter of 1947 particularly hard. Accepting an invitation to lunch with Queen Mary in February, Xenia wrote, 'I am afraid you will find me very dull and "ramoline" as the arctic weather has run havoc with my head and added to the state of stupor I have been long drifting to! . . .'[5]

'I just can't tell you how wretched I felt about yesterday – what a *bitter* disappointment it was & oh! How ashamed & disgusted I am with myself,' she wrote to Queen Mary later that week. 'That heart of mine (the cause of all this upheaval) is allright [sic] again. I slept & *cried* alternatively – sleep did me good, but tears brought nothing! . . . It's so kind of you saying I may come another day, I would love to come & see you more than anything!'[6]

Occasionally she also had to apologize for muddling dates of appointments. 'I am so ashamed of myself – having produced such a blunder,' Xenia told Queen Mary in May 1947. '. . . I can't imagine how and why I got so muddled with the date.'[7] She was invited to the wedding of Princess Elizabeth to Prince Philip of Greece & Denmark, another of Xenia's cousins, in 1947 but did not attend, though she sent a present of 'an agate snuff box set with a ruby'.[8] Her grandson Prince Michael Feodorovich, who visited that week, recalled her suffering from a cold or influenza. There were also the usual domestic crises. In August 1947 the cook was replaced, and Mara Sanders left Wilderness House in the interests of 'peace and harmony'. A couple was engaged so there would be a man in the house if anything went wrong.[9]

As ever, Xenia worked hard to ameliorate the plight of refugees. She continued as patron of various social events, notably in New York, such as the annual dinner dance of the Association of Former Imperial Russian Naval Officers, and was also committee chairman of New York's Annual Russian Easter Ball. Sometimes she was unsuccessful in obtaining help, such as a request to the Duchess of Kent in February 1946 to give her patronage to a charity ball which was refused. As Marina explained to Xenia, unless she was personally connected with the charity, 'if one says yes to one it makes it difficult to refuse others. I am sure you will understand the complication.'[10]

Xenia was patron of the Legat School of Russian Ballet, founded in 1923 by Nicholas Legat, a former principal dancer at the Maryinsky Theatre. In the 1920s she had attended 'elegant little soirées' in Legat's Baron's Court studio where prominent Russian emigrés watched the pupils perform. Some of the costumes had belonged to Anna Pavlova. Andrusha's daughter Xenia was having ballet lessons at the Legat School in 1938. The school logo was based on the crest of the Maryinsky Theatre. A letter from Grand Duchess Xenia, giving them permission to use this crest, was framed and kept at the school.

Xenia and Andrusha were also patrons of the Association of Russian Ballet, founded by Legat's widow Nadine Nicolaeva Legat. Xenia had a personal connection with Mme Legat's family. Nadine's sister Olga Briger had been married to Leontieff, one of the Court Chamberlains who was close to the imperial family; her brother Vladimir married Zenaide Soumarokoff-Elston, a cousin of Prince Felix Youssoupov. It was Zenaide Briger who invited Xenia, whom she had known in St Petersburg, to become patron of the ballet school. In 1945 the school and association moved to Warberry House, near Tunbridge Wells, where the Grand Duchess attended the annual garden party and performance by the pupils.

Other Russian affairs called for her involvement. In July 1947 she received a letter from the Royal Netherlands Embassy in London, officially conveying the Dutch government's thanks 'for your willingness to transfer to the Netherlands State your rights to the House of Czar Peter [the Great] at Zaandam'.[11] The Sisterhood of St Xenia, of which the Grand Duchess was also patron, collected money for the education of children. They also organized Christmas parties, for which the Russian Benevolent Society contributed funds. In 1950 Xenia agreed to go to the Society headquarters and accept funds collected by the Sisterhood of St Xenia.

In 1948 Xenia saw her sister again for the first time in ten years. During the war Olga, in occupied Denmark, had been helping Russian emigrés who were also defectors from the German army. Warned in 1948 that her safety in Denmark could no longer be guaranteed, she and the family sold the farm, and decided to make a new life in Canada. Before emigrating, they paid what would be their final visit to England.

The news worried one of Xenia's correspondents, the Revd

Bousfield S. Lombard, chaplain of the English church in Petrograd at the time of the revolution. 'I am puzzled by this alarming news that dear Olga Alexandrovna and family are coming to England,' he wrote from Rhodesia on 6 April. 'Is there any truth in these accusations? . . . I should be grateful for a few lines from you to say when they are arriving and where they are going to live? The Rhodesia Herald states that they are leaving for England in a few days' time – so they should be on their way now.' He signed himself 'your affectionate old Padre'.[12]

Olga, Nicholas and their maid 'Mimka' stayed with Xenia at Wilderness House for about a month, while their two sons, daughters-in-law and grandchildren Xenia and Leonid stayed in 'a hotel which used to be a palace', possibly the London Savoy. Many years later Ruth Kulikovsky, Olga's daughter-in-law, recalled that they visited Xenia once for afternoon tea. Some of her children were also there. Ruth remembered Xenia as 'a very snobbish old lady' whom she could not really take to, so she went out into the garden and began talking to Mother Martha, 'who was very sweet and kind'. They even corresponded for a while after Ruth left for Canada but eventually it lapsed.

At about this time Xenia closed her account at the Bank of England, and both sisters opened accounts with Baring Brothers. These few weeks in England were the last time the sisters, the last survivors of Alexander III's family, saw each other. On 2 June Olga and her family boarded the *Empress of Canada* at Liverpool bound for Halifax, Nova Scotia.

In 1949 Nikita and Marie came to stay. It was the first time Xenia had seen Marie since the war. She was looking thin and tired, the Grand Duchess told Queen Mary. By the early 1950s they had joined Rostislav and Vassili in America. Other Russians, particularly the Kleinmichels and Zinovievs, also visited and Irina came regularly from France. Callers first had to get round Mother Martha, who was a fierce protector of the Grand Duchess.

Between 1953 and 1957 a fairly regular visitor was Princess Margarita of Baden, who used to travel by bus from London to Hampton Court for tea. Everything was 'very Russian', she said. She remembered Xenia as 'a charming person', very religious, 'gentle and shy'. 'There is not a nasty thing to be said about her,' the princess added. At that time Xenia's son Rostislav and grandson Alexander were living there, and Princess Margarita recalled how, before visitors arrived, Rostislav 'helped himself to the goodies' on the tea table and then climbed out of the ground floor window. 'But once he knew me and realised that I would not bite – he stayed.' She recalled that Mother Martha was 'very protective', always hovering. The princess was never really alone with Xenia, only for as long as it took Mother Martha to put the kettle on. Mother Martha 'cooked and did everything' and Princess Margarita never saw any other staff in the house. They had a Russian-style tea but the conversation was in English. Xenia called the princess '*Malenkiya Margarita*', 'Little Margarita'. Princess Margarita, who was a nurse, wanted to take Xenia for drives in the car but the Grand Duchess always protested that she would feel giddy, or was too frail, or some such excuse. The princess thought she was afraid of the formidable Mother Martha.

Xenia's grandson Prince Alexander recalled that Mother Martha, who waited on Xenia hand and foot, was 'extremely jealous of visitors', even members of the family. She was an 'extremely controversial figure in the family' and he was one of the few who really got on with her.

King Haakon of Norway always took care to make a good impression on Mother Martha. The Duchess of Kent and her sister Olga, Princess Paul of Yugoslavia, also came to Wilderness House. Princess Olga persuaded Sandro's niece Lady Zia Wernher to call on Xenia, 'now that the ice is broken'.[13] Apparently there had been a rift between the two ladies for many years, although neither of Lady Zia's daughters can recall this.[14] Lady Zia resumed her visits to Wilderness House, often bringing 'a gift of a brace of pheasants or asparagus'.[15] The widowed Queen Alexandrine of Denmark, another of Sandro's nieces, hoped to see her aunt while she was in England. 'Of course, I was coming to see you,' she wrote from Marlborough House in early 1948, 'but unfortunately, I was laid up and the doctor has forbidden me to move. I was *furious* and so disappointed not to see you. I am sending you some cheese which Margaretha* asked me to give to you.'[16] A more poignant caller was

---

* The wife of Prince Axel of Denmark.

Captain Robert Ingham who, as a young ADC to the Governor, had looked after the Romanovs in Malta so many years before.

In April 1950 Nadine gave birth to a daughter and Xenia stayed with them in Kent. Their house 'Provender' dated partly from the thirteenth century and the Black Prince had slept there on his way to France. Unfortunately, Xenia suffered a heart attack and spent much of her time in bed. Nevertheless, 'it was lovely being in the country,' she told Queen Mary. 'The old Tudor house [sic] and grounds are charming. My little granddaughter Olga is very sweet and a wonderfully good natured baby.'[17]

The heart attack took its toll on her remaining strength. She recovered slowly, and seven months later she wrote to Queen Mary apologizing for her continued poor health: 'Am feeling better on the whole, but rather weak still & am never up till 3.0, ashamed to say so. I do envy yr energy.'[18] Two months later she reported being 'laid up with horrid lumbago & pains in [the?] neck & shoulders'.[19] The Duchess of Kent sympathized with her trials: 'I am *so* sorry you have had a liver upset! really how maddening on top of your rheumatism! & I don't suppose this damp weather helps!'[20]

By the end of 1951 she obviously had difficulty in writing letters. 'Haven't written to Olga for ages – she's furious,' she told Queen Mary, 'but Mother Martha wrote and explained all! They are selling the farm, which is a pity, but are unable to cope with it any longer. . . . They have found a smaller house near Toronto. . . . Mother Martha is wonderfully good – a real angel but a very tired one!'[21] In 1954, on an official visit to Canada, the Duchess of Kent was able to visit her Aunt Olga and bring back first-hand news to Xenia, as well as some photographs.

Nevertheless she battled against pain in keeping up her correspondence with relatives. She was reluctant to throw anything away, and after her death a few unfinished letters to friends were found. Written in the last five years or so of her life, they are in very shaky handwriting, full of mistakes and crossings out. Yet, from a careful study of the originals it is clear that she continued to write herself, rather than dictate. Her grandsons would recall that she spent hours writing at her desk every day. She always enjoyed receiving regular replies, though frequent letters of thanks from friends and family for 'a short note' suggest that lengthy messages were beyond her. One grateful item of correspondence from Sandro's niece, the former Crown Princess Cecilie, acknowledged her sympathy on the death of her son Hubertus:

It was such a joy to see your handwriting again after such a long time and hear all the news, and then so full of deep sympathy in our great loss! . . . Your granddaughter Xenia met him in the Burg Hohenzollern for Cecilie's wedding [Crown Princess Cecilie's daughter], and they all got on so well together. . . .

Lulu and Kira [her son and Ducky's daughter] named their 7th child after you, she seems to be [a] sweet little creature. Their children are charming and I find the 5th, Louis Ferdinand, reminds me of your father! He has the broad and sturdy figure of U. Sasha! I was delighted to see your charming granddaughter [Xenia] last June, she reminds me of Mamma and Irina. I thought her husband very nice too.[22]

One of Xenia's most regular correspondents was Grand Duchess Elena Vladimirovna, Princess Nicholas of Greece, the mother of the Duchess of Kent. In 1950 Xenia received a letter from Elena's daughter Olga:

Mummy has asked me to . . . thank you for your Easter letter as she is still too weak to write herself. She has been in bed since May 27th having overtired herself rather and had rather bad pains round the heart. . . . Thank God she at last took herself in hand and did what her doctor told her and has completely given up smoking and any form of wine – all this as well as the rest and quiet have helped and it is now just over a week that she is without pain, thank God. . . .

She kisses you very much and was happy to get your letter and hear about my visit to you. In the great heat here I can hardly believe it was over cold and snowed the day I saw you!! I have seen Baby [Irina Cheremetev] once or twice but not long enough, but I hope she will come to tea one of these days.[23]

The family of Xenia's aunt and godmother, Thyra Duchess of Cumberland, also kept in touch. Her cousin Alexandra had married Frederick Franz IV of Mecklenburg-Schwerin, a nephew

of Sandro. Barely escaping from falling into the hands of the
Russian army in 1945, Alix then learnt that her second son,
Christian Ludwig, had been caught behind Soviet lines. After
being held in a Berlin prison he was taken across the Soviet
border. Not until 1954 was he freed:

> I must tell you that my dear son Christian Ludwig has come
> back in the evening of Sylvister and the next evening he arrived
> here, that is not to describe what a joy it was. We screamed
> loud of happiness. We are all so thankful that God helped him
> during all these 8 and a ½ years and has sent him back to us.
> Thank God he is healthy and has not changed a bit.[24]

In August 1952 Xenia went to stay at Abinger Manor in the
Surrey countryside, to try to recover her strength.

For several years Queen Mary had sent regular hampers of food,
and Lady Astor* gave her a dressing gown for Christmas 1948.
Sometimes Olga sent her paintings to try to sell, and an apologetic
Xenia would ask her friends to help. Her sons Andrusha, Feodor and
Nikita had become keen philatelists, and with Xenia's
correspondents in so many different countries it was not difficult for
them to add to their collection. 'Margaretha told me you hoped I
could send you some stamps,' Crown Prince Olav of Norway wrote
in 1953. 'Here are some of those which have been sent out after the
War and I hope some of them may be of interest.'[25] Usually a
delivery of mail at Wilderness House would elicit the question
'What's the stamp?' rather than 'Who's the letter from?'

Queen Mary was nearly eight years older than Xenia, yet in her
eighty-fifth year she suffered a major blow that, though not
unexpected, was the final family tragedy from which she never really
recovered. After several years of poor health, culminating in a major
operation for lung cancer, King George VI died in his sleep at
Sandringham early on 6 February 1952. Xenia knew instinctively
what a devastating shock the news would be to her beloved cousin. 'I

---

* Nancy, Lady Astor, Member of Parliament (Conservative) for Plymouth
sutton, 1919–45, who numbered several members of British and
European royalty among her friends.

long to be near you, to hold you in my arms, kneel by your side & kiss yr hands & say *how* I suffer & share yr terrible grief.'[26] The Queen only survived her second son, the third to predecease her, by just over a year, and died in March 1953. Although Xenia was sent an invitation to the coronation of Queen Elizabeth II in June that year, again she did not attend. Coronations brought back too many memories of her father and brother.

Writing letters of condolence unfortunately became ever more frequent. A further sadness was the death from cancer in 1955 of the Duchess of Kent's sister Woolley, who had done so much to help Nikita and Marie after the war. 'I still feel stunned,'[27] Woolley's mother, Grand Duchess Elena, understandably wrote from Greece.

In 1955 Xenia celebrated her eightieth birthday, but for the last years of her life poor health prevented her from leaving Wilderness House. There was a steady flow of visitors to her door, and none more regular than the Duchess of Kent, who continued to call and write, once even asking if Mother Martha would make her a *Paskha* (Russian Easter cake).[28] Sometimes Marina brought her youngest son, Prince Michael of Kent.* Flowers and plants always arrived on her birthday, or during her increasingly frequent illnesses. Christmas cards, letters and photographs came from her grandsons and royal relatives all over Europe. She even continued to receive greetings from members of her old regiment. The Grand Duchess possessed a good vocabulary in her native Russian and gave the impression of being extremely well educated. From 1953 her grandson Alexander, whose parents Nikita and Marie were in America, lived with her.

The Anastasia case still dragged on, and in 1958 it reached the German courts when a judge at the Berlin Court of Appeals advised Anna Anderson's lawyers that she had enough evidence

---

* Prince Michael of Kent doubtless owed part of his later fascination with his Romanov ancestry and heritage to these visits. In middle age, with his beard and moustache, he bore a striking facial resemblance to Tsar Nicholas II; he presented a major BBC television documentary on the last Tsar and Tsarina, and he represented the British royal family at the reburial of the Romanovs in St Petersburg in July 1998.

to sue for recognition as the Grand Duchess Anastasia. The family was still divided; Xenia's goddaughter Princess Xenia, Mrs William Leeds, was convinced 'Anastasia' was genuine. '[Princess] Xenia's irresponsible statement should be somehow refuted,' Prince Dmitri wrote to Prince Louis of Hesse, the only surviving child of Empress Alexandra's brother, in Darmstadt. 'We know that she left Russia in 1914 aged 10 years old. I also know that Nina [her sister] and Xenia never saw Uncle Nicky's family very often, and when they did see them that was when they were very young.'[29]

Dmitri enclosed a short, typed statement from his mother, hoping it would be enough: 'This is to state that I am convinced that Mrs Anderson or Tchaikovsky is an imposter. I believe in the statement my sister the Grand Duchess Olga, made in 1925 that this woman was not Anastasia. I also believe in the statements made by my son-in-law Prince Felix Youssoupoff, the Baroness Buxhoeveden and M. and Mme Gilliard.

(Signed) Xenia. March 16th 1958.'[30]

Other 'Anastasia' claimants also continued to appear. While living at Wilderness House, Xenia received an undated report from Baroness Buxhoeveden about two meetings with a Mrs Eugenia Smith from New York. In a six-page report, which included a description of Mrs Smith, the Baroness reported that neither she nor the former imperial dentist Sergei Kostritsky could recognize her as Anastasia. 'I found no likeness whatsoever to the Grand Duchess physically . . .', wrote the Baroness. 'Although a total stranger, she is sympathetic on the whole, but seemed to be labouring under a mental delusion.'[31]

When the Baroness died on 26 November 1956 she bequeathed to Xenia several items which had belonged to the imperial family at Tobolsk, including 'a green enamel Fabergé pencil given to me by Empress Alexandra . . . a white china cup with a pattern of cornflowers and the mark NII used by the Emperor at Tobolsk . . . a small wooden Ikon . . . with a few words of prayer written by the Empress at Tobolsk. . . .'[32]

Prince David Chavchavadze, an officer in the United States Army, had been an occasional caller over the years when he was able to visit London. The last time he saw his aunt Xenia was in early 1956 when he was on leave from his unit, stationed in Berlin. He was warned by Nikita and Alexander that he would first have to get by Mother Martha, but they did not think he would be prevented from seeing his aunt, as Mother Martha was so fond of him.

'So I met Mother Martha,' he recalled. 'A tall, healthy looking woman in white robes and a very red face (or was she blushing?). She was obviously the guardian of the gate. "Yes," she said, "you may see the Grand Duchess but only for ten minutes! Not one minute more!"' Xenia said he was to call her 'Aunt Amama'. He had wanted to ask about her life before the revolution but 'all she was interested in was the Soviets in Berlin, how they talked, how they treated me, the political situation etc. She was very interested in my answers and laughed when I said anything funny.' During the conversation, he noticed, Xenia chain-smoked the whole time, flicking cigarette butts into what she called 'a small spitoon' about four feet away. 'She never missed once.' After an hour and a half Prince David left. Mother Martha did not interfere, nor did she reprimand him or throw him out for staying too long. He noticed that Xenia did not seem afraid of Mother Martha.

Indeed, Xenia had only praise for her. 'Poor Verucha's [Mother Martha] life is that of a real martyr, never having any rest,' she wrote to Olga in February 1957. '. . . To have me on her hands is a *task* of its own – but what with all the domestic troubles, demands . . . unwillingness to pull together, *show* some Christian feeling. One can only *marvel* at her unlimited . . . patience & endurance – strength of character. . . . – she is a striking personality. . . . capable of taking up some big works and *instead* here she sits – and all thanks to me! You can imagine my feelings – . . . to know that she has given up everything for my sake – independent life and be reduced to this kind of existence, her health ruined, nerves all shattered, and I sit and look on, sick at heart, and *worried* beyond words and unwell myself.'

These domestic troubles were the result of differences between the cook and Narnya, one of the staff, with the result that the cook had suddenly given notice. 'But we like Narnya and are keeping her,' Xenia continued, 'regardless of the fact that we have no-one to replace the cook. The latter thinks herself very superior – a "lady", no help at all, uses up any amount of pans & retires to her room leaving everything in a mess! But she is honest – . . . very discreet . . . a church goer, but. . . . No "humilité chrétianne", which doesn't correspond with all she says! She came with the intention to stay for good, came out with wonderful phrases – *how* happy she was to be here & silly things like "such an honour" etc. Well such is life. Luckily we have a kind soul who comes in 3–4 times a week to tidy the rooms & help Verucha.'[33]

In March 1957 Xenia learnt of her cousin Elena's death from the latter's eldest daughter, Princess Olga of Yugoslavia. 'I know how your own heart aches as you loved her and knew her all your life and shared so many memories of a bygone happy period when all was peace and security,' Olga wrote. 'What a blessing it is not to know what the future holds, else one could not go on. Darling Aunt Xenia, I have given you all these details [of Elena's last moments] because they will comfort you. We were so afraid that the shock of this news might injure your health.'[34]

In May 1957 the author James Pope-Hennessy, engaged at the time on writing an official biography of Queen Mary, was granted an appointment to speak to Xenia at Wilderness House by writing to Mary, Princess Royal, who arranged an invitation from Xenia's grandson Prince Alexander Romanoff. On arrival he was shown into her main room which faced on to the front garden and main road, and immediately struck him as 'small, pretty and light,' very white, full of photographs and one or two portraits. A long desk, covered with every sort of souvenir, including a cheap china bust of King George V, jutted out from one window into the middle of the room; and in the corner opposite the windows was a divan draped with shawls. Xenia sat on a hard armchair at the end of this desk, in the centre of her small cluttered room. The mantelpiece and every available wall-space were crammed with photographs, with a large tinted group of the Tsar, Tsarina and their children prominent on a small table by itself facing her chair.

He took in every detail of her dress and mannerisms: the dark dress, ropes of big pearls, curled grey hair with centre parting, and the 'old-fashioned gesture' of constantly placing her hand at her breast and fingering the pearls. He thought her face 'a synthesis, so to speak, of all the Danish Family's faces, with large slightly protuberant eyes, and the narrow heart-shape of Queen Alexandra.' She reminded him of 'an exceedingly nervous wild bird, which felt trapped. Her voice and hands fluttered; and her remarks trailed nervously away. It was as if she had been too stringently protected from strangers for too long, as it were the member of an enclosed order suddenly brought face to face with a strange man.' She spoke in 'a *floating* voice, vague and, in some curious way, outside herself. It is as if she is trying to catch it and bring it back again to say something else. You could almost see the sentence trailing like thin smoke around the room.'

Keen to gather her impressions about Danish court life, Pope-Hennessy asked her about life at Fredensborg and Bernstorff. Though her memory was failing by this time, she could still recall life at the court of her maternal grandparents, who 'had grand dinners, of course; but they were happiest leading a simple life'. He was particularly struck by her 'innocent girlish charm which was very fetching'. When he enquired politely after her health, she told him resignedly that she suffered from fibrositis in the neck and had a headache all the time, aggravated if not caused by living so close to the River Thames. She would not see an osteopath: 'the whole thing is such a bore; I just don't think about it.'[35]

For the last few years Xenia did not go into the garden or even into the dining room on the ground floor, but was confined to her room. Prince Michael Feodorovich recalled the atmosphere as 'out of time' – it could be Paris, or St Petersburg or anywhere. He remembered his grandmother as 'an old lady, looking very fragile most of the time sitting at her desk, or with several pillows in her bed', surrounded by several small icons and photographs of children and grandchildren. On the mantelpiece above the small gas fire were photographs of Alexander III and Dagmar, Nicky and some of her sons. In a corner of the room was a bust of Alexander III and a photograph of Empress Alexandra, with a portrait of Irina hanging on the wall nearby. Souvenirs of Russia were everywhere.

'Whenever we used to visit grandmother,' Prince Michael recalled, 'we were announced and we were told to keep our voices low. She would arrive and we would bow in front of her. Then she would kiss us in the front and in the cheeks.'[36] The house was a peaceful place and Xenia loved welcoming her children and grandchildren. Prince Michael paid his last visit in the spring of 1957, ironically, when he was assisting Anatole Litvak, Ingrid Bergman and Yul Brynner on a film based on the Anastasia and

Anna Anderson saga. Litvak, the director, wanted to recreate the Dowager Empress's room at Hvidøre, and Prince Michael was asked by the art director to take photographs of his grandmother's surroundings as a guide to recreating the atmosphere of the Dowager Tsarina's sitting room. The interiors of the imperial palaces were also reconstructed from photographs in Xenia's possession.

Religion continued to play an important part in Xenia's life, and she maintained a regular correspondence with the deeply respected Metropolitan Vladimir. When the Russian Orthodox Church of St Philip in Buckingham Palace Road was demolished, she became patron of the 1957 effort to raise funds for another building. Her grandson Alexander was among those who ran a stall at the 'bring and buy' sale.[37]

In March 1958 her mother's coffin was moved from King Frederik V's chapel in Roskilde Cathedral to the private royal crypt. Neither Xenia nor Olga was able to attend, and 'Rico', King Frederik IX of Denmark, sent her an account of the transfer:

I have just returned from Roskilde from the consecration of the vault underneath the Chapel of Christian IX. Your dear mother's coffin was placed there yesterday. The bishop of Roskilde consecrated the chapel by saying the Lord's Prayer and pronounced the blessing making the sign of the Holy Cross towards the coffin. It was short and solemn; I thought so much of you and Olga. When the Orthodox arms have been put up I shall send a photo of the place to you.[38]

Other relations continued to keep in touch, and in 1957 Xenia received news of Aunt Thyra's family from her cousin Princess Olga of Cumberland:

I am staying here [in Glucksburg] with Alix [Grand Duchess of Mecklenburg] and her daughter Thyra. Her second daughter lives quite close by the castle with her sweet family of four daughters, of which the eldest is 11 and the youngest 2, a very sweet baby, big and fat, who loves her Amama. Some time ago I had a letter from Olga [Kulikovsky], we don't often write but it does happen sometimes. She is pleased to have her granddaughter staying with her, what a shame Guri left her. . . .[39]

On 11 January 1959 Princess Ileana, youngest daughter of Queen Marie of Roumania, heard the tragic news that her eldest daughter 'Minola', Archduchess Maria Ileana, had been killed in a plane crash with her husband in Rio de Janeiro. 'I am sending this card about the Memorial Service for Minola and Rus, and let you know that there will be another Service in our Church on the 24th of February,' Ileana's sister 'Mignon', Queen Marie of Yugoslavia, wrote to Xenia. 'We are all shattered by the death of two young and happy children.'[40] Aged only twenty-six, Minola left a daughter of five months and had also been expecting a second child.

Her mobility now severely restricted by age, Xenia remained a voracious reader. One of her most treasured books was a limited edition volume about the English royal silver belonging to the Tsars, which had been published at the request of Edward VII. Her grandson Prince Alexander recalled that, although the Grand Duchess lived very much in the present, she would discuss the past if it came up in conversation. She liked recalling the grand receptions, fancy dress balls and her brief time living in the Winter Palace.[41] Always happy to help others, in 1956 she wrote the Foreword to *Close of a Dynasty*, Sir Francis Pridham's account of the voyage of the *Marlborough*. Pridham, who had visited several times over the years, had been the young Lieutenant whom Xenia had helped to allocate the cabins. The British Ambassador's daughter, Meriel Buchanan, published *Victorian Gallery* the same year. Xenia read and corrected the chapter about the Dowager Empress and the book was, with permission, respectfully dedicated to 'H.I.H. The Grand Duchess Xenia of Russia, in gratitude for her many kindnesses to me and in memory of other days.'[42]

In her last years she suffered increasingly from fibrositis, which stopped her from moving around easily. On her eighty-third birthday in April 1958 Seton Gordon recalled that she looked 'frail and sad'.[43] 'It has been to [sic] nice for words to see you again after all these years,' wrote Alix, Grand Duchess of Mecklenburg, after visiting her in the autumn of 1959. 'I enjoyed it ever so much and it was the best of my stay in England. It was very sad that you could not have us again but I do hope you feel better now. . . .'[44]

In June 1959, on a state visit to Canada, Queen Elizabeth and Prince Philip invited Grand Duchess Olga to lunch on board the royal yacht *Britannia*. 'I saw Lilibet to say goodbye last week,' the Duchess of Kent reported to Xenia in August, 'and she told me all about seeing dear Aunt Olga. She loved her and said she was too sweet! She also said she was going to write and tell you. I wonder if she did?'[45]

By November 1959 Xenia's health was giving cause for concern. The family tried to persuade her to go to Rome, and Prince Roman had also offered the use of his place at Antibes-Bergerie, but neither offer was taken up.[46] Shortly afterwards Xenia's grandson Nikita spent a month at Wilderness House, where he was thrilled to spend time looking at his grandmother's family photographs dating from the reign of Alexander II. Early in the new year she was evidently failing. Her back was causing her considerable pain and Irina arrived to keep a close eye on her. On 1 April a bulletin stated that she had suffered a relapse, but was improving slightly. By 4 April she was out of bed for a short time and no further bulletins were envisaged.[47]

Two weeks later the end was evidently near. On 20 April, as her condition worsened, Father George gave her the last rites. Later that day she passed away, with Irina and Andrusha at her bedside, and her icon lamp burning nearby. The official cause of death was given as heart trouble and bronchial pneumonia. Shortly afterwards Mother Martha appeared carrying a box marked 'black mourning veils', kept in readiness for such eventualities.

On Sunday 24 April members of the Russian community in London attended a memorial service at the Russian Orthodox church in Knightsbridge. The following evening the coffin was taken to the Church of the Holy Assumption (Russian Orthodox Church in Exile), Kensington, for a memorial service at noon on 26 April. Mourners included Xenia's children Prince and Princess Andrei; Prince and Princess Dmitri; Princess Irina Youssoupov; Princess Rostislav; her grandchildren Princess Xenia and Prince Alexander, as well as representatives of the Queen and of foreign royal families. Among those attending in person were the Duchess of Kent and her sister Olga, Princess Paul of Yugoslavia; Princess Margarita of Baden and her husband Prince Tomislav of Yugoslavia; Earl Mountbatten of Burma; and Sir Harold and Lady Zia Wernher. Archbishop John, head of the Russian Orthodox

Church of Exiles in Western Europe, came from Paris to conduct the service and Father George was among the clergy who officiated. Candles burned at each corner of the catafalque, beside which six members of the Old Guard stood rigidly to attention. All the women, dressed in black and heavily veiled, carried a lighted candle. As the service ended, the Duchess of Kent approached the open coffin where Xenia lay with a Russian cross clasped in her hands, and gently kissed the prayer silk which swathed the Grand Duchess's head.[48] Mother Martha stood to one side, away from the family. When they came out of the church she had disappeared.

The funeral service took place at the Russian Church, Kensington, after Mass at 10am on Wednesday 27 April, one week after Xenia's death. Her coffin was then taken to the south of France, along a narrow, winding, corniche-style road to the cemetery at Roquebrune in a wonderful position overlooking the sea. Here, on Friday 29 April, as a *Panikhida* took place at the Russian church in Paris, Xenia was finally laid to rest next to the wayward Sandro.

Count Vladimir Kleinmichel and Baring Bros were appointed executors of Xenia's estate. She left £117,272 16s 2d net. Most of her money and property went to a Trust fund 'from which her children would benefit in equal proportions'. This included 'a property agreed between herself and the three Trustees in 1929', shortly after the death of the Dowager Empress.[49] A legacy of £1,000 to each of her grandchildren later had to be reduced to £250, a measure taken with great regret on her part, she wrote in a codicil made in 1953, 'necessitated on account of the great increase in Estate Duty since I made my original Will'. But £500 was left to Vera Maslenikoff, 'as a token of my gratitude to her for her devoted care given to me over very many years past'.[50]

As tributes poured in, on 29 May there was the usual service at the Russian church to mark the fortieth day since her death. She had 'charm and distinction, great sympathy and simplicity, and great honesty,' wrote Seton Gordon; '. . . in every sense of the term she was a great lady, humble and upright, an inspiring example to all who knew her.'[51] As her daughter-in-law Nadine said: 'She was one of the angels of the world. She would do anything for anybody.'[52]

Xenia's St Petersburg palace at 106 Moika is now the Lesgaft Sports Institute. The interior was virtually destroyed by Nazi bombs and the rebuilding was haphazard. Only the hall and the grand staircase, now with Soviet murals covering the walls, are original. Until at least the 1960s they had kept Xenia's tradition of placing an aspidistra on every other step. The palace chapel in the second courtyard, now the gym, retains what was probably its original dark red colour.

Ai-Todor fared less well; the Crimea was under Nazi occupation for three years and no trace of the main building apparently remains. One of the children's houses is believed to be still standing, but tourists are not allowed to approach the estate. When Xenia's grandson Prince Alexander visited Ai-Todor it had become 'a sanatorium or something' with people walking around in prison-style striped uniforms. It was so depressing that he did not even get out of the car.

Ropsha, where Xenia and Sandro spent the first two nights of their honeymoon, is now only a shell. Scaffolding surrounds what remains of the palace. The lawn has become a local picnic area, but it is still possible to stroll along the red and white tiled terrace.

At least one of Xenia's court dresses is preserved at Tsarskoe Selo, and icons belonging to her are in St Job's, the Russian Orthodox church in Brussels.

Frogmore Cottage has been divided into five flats, now occupied by staff from Windsor Castle. Wilderness House is still a grace and favour residence, although all trace of the Orthodox chapel has been removed from the drawing room. After Xenia's death it was thought that Princess Alice of Greece, the mother of Prince Philip, might move in, but nothing came of this idea.

Grand Duchess Olga survived Xenia by a mere seven months. Though she was seven years younger, she had likewise been in frail health for some time. A telegram of condolence was sent by Queen Elizabeth II and the Duke of Edinburgh, but in order to spare her distress well-meaning friends thought it prudent not to pass it to her.[53] Aged seventy-eight, she died in Toronto on 24 November 1960.

When people expressed astonishment at Xenia's simple ways, dislike of pomp and ceremony, and retiring nature, she told them: 'The

Russian Revolution took almost everything from me, but the Bolsheviks left me with one privilege – to be a private person.' During her forty years of exile, it was a privilege of which she made full use.[54] Yet her dignity and bearing left nobody in any doubt that once a Grand Duchess, she was always a Grand Duchess.

Notes

Abbreviations: AE – Argyll Etkin Archive; Alexander, *AGD* – Alexander, *Always a Grand Duke*; FO – Foreign Office; GD – Grand Duke or Grand Duchess, as appropriate; HO – Home Office; MA – Mainau Archives; M & M – Maylunas & Mironenko, *A Lifelong Passion*; NAM – National Archives of Malta; nd – undated (no day, month or year)*; *OGD* – Alexander, *Once a Grand Duke*; PRO – Public Record Office; RA – Royal Archives; tr – translated; Tsch – Tsarevich

Unless otherwise stated, documents cited were written in English. Grand Duchess Xenia's diary for 1916–19, in the Hoover Institution, has been translated from Russian.

* certain documents cited below are dated only by month and/or year.

Chapter 1

1. Massie, 247, quoting Gautier.
2. Madol, 100.
3. Lowe, 17.
4. Vorres, 58.
5. Addendum to *Pravitelstvennyj Vestnik*, 67, 26.3.1875, tr. from Russian.
6. *The Times*, 15.4.1875. (NS).
7. *Pravitelskvennyj Vestnik*, No. 82, 13.4.1875, tr. from Russian.
8. Rigsarkiv, Danicasamling, Danica arkiv 455, Fond 642, Pakke 1–3, Princess of Wales to GD Marie Feodorovna, 9.4.1875 (NS), tr. from Danish.
9. *ibid*, Princess of Wales to GD Marie Feodorovna, 26.10.1875, (NS), tr. from Danish.
10. *ibid*, Princess of Wales to GD Marie Feodorovna, 7.7.1876, (NS), tr. from Danish.
11. Klausen, 136, 9/21.1.1877.
12. Bing, 28, 7.10.1879.
13. Rigsarkiv, Danicasamling, Danica arkiv 455, Fond 642, Pakke 1–3, Princess of Wales to GD Marie Feodorovna, 10.3.1879 (NS), tr. from Danish.
14. Klausen, 138, nd.
15. Pope-Hennessy, Una, 126.
16. Klausen, 156.
17. Ryzhnenko & Barkovets, 11.
18. Pope-Hennessy, Una, 127.
19. Conway, 133.
20. Klausen, 156.
21. Ryzhnenko & Barkovets, 31.
22. Klausen, 161.
23. *ibid*, 167, nd.
24. Waddington, 51.
25. *ibid*, 66.
26. Vorres, 54.
27. Kongehusets Arkiv, Christian IX's Arkiv. PK40. GD Xenia to Queen Louise, 8.12.1885.
28. Det Kongelige Bibliotek, Music Dept.
29. Ryzhnenko & Barkovets, 42.
30. *ibid*, 31.
31. *ibid*, 41, GD Xenia's diary, March 1892.

32. *ibid*, 22, GD Xenia's diary, 14.12.1884.
33. *ibid*, 21.
34. *ibid*, 42.
35. *ibid*, 20–1, GD Xenia's diary, 24.3.1887.
36. Obolensky, 54–5.
37. M & M, 11, Nicholas's diary, 8.6.1884.
38. George, 26.
39. Marie, Queen of Roumania, I, 90.
40. *ibid*, I, 216.
41. Obolensky, 62.
42. Ryzhnenko & Barkovets, 23, 45.
43. *ibid*, 45–6.
44. Sikorsky, 42–3.

Chapter 2

1. Poliakoff, 179.
2. GARF, Fond 662, Section 1, File 3622, GD Xenia to Queen Louise, 9.12.1889.
3. *ibid*, GD Xenia to Queen Louise, 27.12.1891.
4. Alexander, *OGD*, 116.
5. AE, GD Alexander to GD Xenia, 4.8.1889, tr. from Russian.
6. Alexander, *OGD*, 11.
7. GARF, Fond 662, Section 1, File 3622, GD Xenia to Queen Louise, 12.3.1891.
8. Naryshkin-Kurakin, 97.
9. *The Times*, 21.7.1891. (NS).
10. Perry & Pleshakov, 58–9.
11. M & M, 32, Princess Alix to GD Xenia, 8.11.1893.
12. Alexander, *OGD*, 128.
13. *ibid*, 129.
14. *ibid*, 44.
15. Vorres, 59.
16. AE, Sandra Vorontzov to GD Xenia, 13.1.1894, tr. from Russian.

17. Klausen, 213, Empress Marie to GD Alexandra Josifovna, 12.1 1894.
18. M & M, 50, GD Xenia to Tsch Nicholas, 10.4.1894.
19. *ibid*, 54, GD Xenia to Tsch Nicholas, 14.4.1894.
20. Klausen, 214.
21. Bing, 87.
22. M & M, 66, Tsch Nicholas to GD George, 9.5.1894.
23. Alexander, *OGD*, 131.
24. M & M, 73, GD George to Tsch Nicholas, 9.6.1894.
25. *ibid*, 80, GD Constantine's diary, 10.7.1894.
26. Alexander, *OGD*, 132.
27. Bing, 88, 27.6.1894.
28. M & M, 87, GD Constantine's diary 25.7.1894
29. *The Times*, 7.8.1894 (NS).
30. RA, GV/CC45/145, Princess Maud of Wales to Duchess of York, 14.8.1894 (NS).
31. Alexander, *OGD*, 134.
32. *ibid*, 135.

Chapter 3

1. M & M, 97, Tsch Nicholas to Alix, 27.9.1894.
2. GARF, Fond 662, Section 1, File 3622, GD Xenia to Queen Louise, 4.11.1894.
3–6. *ibid*.
7. *ibid*, GD Xenia to Queen Louise, 29.12.1894.
8. as 3–6.
9. as 7.
10. Alexander, *OGD*, 203–4.
11. M & M, 133, Nicholas II to GD George, 18.12.1895.
12. *ibid*, 127, GD Xenia to Nicholas II, 23.8.1895.
13. Vorres, 73.

14. Youssoupov, *Lost Splendour*, 107–8.
15. Alexander, *OGD*, 172.
16. M & M, 147, GD Xenia's diary, 19.5.1896.
17. *ibid*, 149, GD Xenia's diary, 26.5.1896.
18. GARF, Fond 662, Section 1, File 3622, GD Xenia to Queen Louise, 8.12.1896.
19. M & M, 154, GD Xenia to Nicholas II, 4.11.1896.
20. *ibid*, 160, Nicholas II to Empress Marie Feodorovna, 9.1.1897.
21. *ibid*, 162, Nicholas II to GD George, 3.4.1897.
22. *ibid*, 172, GD Xenia to Nicholas II, 26.4.1898.
23. Rørdam, 184.
24. M & M, 190, GD Xenia to Nicholas II, 11.10.1899.
25. AE, GD Olga to GD Xenia, 4.1.1900, in English and Russian.
26. *ibid*, Queen Olga of Greece to GD Xenia, 19.2.1910, tr. from Russian.

Chapter 4

1. M & M, 206, GD Xenia's diary, 5.6.1901.
2. *ibid*, 204, 9.1.1901.
3. *ibid*, 210, Empress Alexandra to GD Xenia, 7.11.1901.
4. *ibid*, 228, GD Xenia's diary, 10.7.1903.
5. *ibid*, 218, GD Xenia to Countess Apraxine, 20.8.1902.
6. Alexander, *OGD*, 210–11.
7. M & M, 232, GD Xenia's diary, 21.12.1903.
8. *ibid*, 239, GD Xenia's diary, 25.1.1904.
9. Salisbury, 95.
10. M & M, 241, GD Xenia's diary, 31.3.04.
11. Vorres, 118.
12. Kongehusets Arkiv, Christian IX's Arkiv, PK 13, GD Xenia to Christian IX, 29.12.1904.
13. M & M, 277, GD Xenia's diary, 18.6.1905.
14. *ibid*, 280, GD Xenia's diary, 17.8.1905.
15. Ai-Todor wine list, courtesy of Prince Michael Feodorovich Romanoff, tr. from Russian.
16. M & M, 209, GD Xenia to Nicholas II, 31.10.1901.
17. *ibid*, 282, GD Xenia's diary, 14.10.1905.
18. George, 121.
19. M & M, 291, GD Xenia's diary, 30.1.1906.
20. *ibid*, 293, GD Xenia's diary, 27.4.1906.
21. *ibid*, 293, GD Xenia's diary, 30.4.1906.

Chapter 5

1. M & M, 306, GD Xenia's diary, 30.7.1907.
2. Leon, 162, Empress Marie Feodorovna to Nicholas II, 5.8.1906.
3. Alexander, *OGD*, 228.
4. *ibid*, 230–1.
5. Cerda, 78.
6. Alexander, *OGD*, 231.
7. *ibid*, 232.
8. Fabergé, Prolet & Skurlov, 251–2.
9. Alexander, *OGD*, 234.
10. Alexander, *AGD*, 94.
11. M & M, 313, GD Xenia's diary, 24.6.1908.
12. Alexander, *OGD*, 236.
13. M & M, 312, GD Xenia's diary, 15.6.1908.

NOTES

14. Ulstrup, in *Ruslands Skatte*, 166–8.
15. M & M, 313 & footnote, 24.6.1913.
16. Alexander, *OGD*, 240.
17. Private information – Arthur Addington.
18. Romanov, Pr. Roman, 44–5.
19. MA, GD Marie to Prince William of Sweden, 22.8.1907.
20. *ibid*, GD Marie to Prince William of Sweden, 9.9.1907.
21. AE, Queen Olga to GD Xenia, 19.2.1910, tr. from Russian.
22. *Daily Telegraph*, 22.4.1960.
23. RA, GV/AA55/43, GD Xenia to George V, 2.5.1910.
24. AE, George V to GD Xenia, 29.12.1910.
25. M & M, 345, GD Xenia's diary 13.11.1911.
26. Perry & Pleshakov, 106.
27. Vorres, 118.
28. M & M, 331, GD Xenia's diary, 15.3.1910.
29. AE, GD Elisabeth Feodorovna to GD Xenia, 27.2.1912.
30. M & M, 377, GD Xenia's diary, 24.5.1913.
31. Anon, *Russian Court Memoirs*, 113
32. Neerbek, 88.
33. M & M, 375, GD Xenia's diary, 19.3.1913.
34. *ibid*, 376, GD Xenia's diary, 22.3.1913.
35. *ibid*, 379, GD Xenia's diary, 4.6.1913.
36. *ibid*, 379, GD Xenia's diary, 23.6.1913.
37. *ibid*, 381, GD Xenia's diary, 19.8.1913.
38. Youssoupov, *Lost Splendour*, 168.
39. Softky, 'Growing up Royal in Imperial Russia'.

Chapter 6

1. Alexander, *OGD*, 259.
2. *ibid*, 258.
3. Trevelyan, 264.
4. Alexander, *OGD*, 265.
5. Fuhrmann, 97, Empress Alexandra to Nicholas II, 8.3.1915.
6. AE, unfinished draft of letter from Wilderness House, nd, in Russian and English.
7. *Poslednie Novosti*, July 1933, Empress Marie Feodorovna's diary, 18.8.1915, tr. from Russian.
8. Fuhrmann, 254, Empress Alexandra to Nicholas II, 20.9.1915.
9. *ibid*, 405, Empress Alexandra to Nicholas II, 9.3.1916.
10. Hoover, Box 6, Folder 7, GD Olga to GD Xenia, 5/6.5.1916, in English and Russian.
11. Fuhrmann, 628, Empress Alexandra to Nicholas II, 27.10.1916.
12. Hoover, Box 1, Folder 16, GD Xenia to Empress Marie Feodorovna 28.10.1916, quoted in Belyakova, 113.
13. Fuhrmann, 640, Empress Alexandra to Nicholas II, 4.11.1916.
14. Hoover, Box 6, Folder 13, GD Xenia's diary, 18.12.1916.
15. *ibid*, GD Xenia's diary, 19.12.1916.
16. Alexander, *OGD*, 278.
17. M & M, 515, quoting Anna Vyrubova in *Memoirs*.

Chapter 7

1 Radzinsky, 487.
2. Hoover, Box 2, Folder 2, GD

Xenia to Empress Marie
Feodorovna, 21.1.1917, quoted
in Belyakova, 115.

3. M & M, 536, Empress Alexandra
to Nicholas II, 22.2.1917.

4. Hoover, Box 2, Folder 2, GD
Xenia to Empress Marie
Feodorovna, 26.1.1917, quoted
in Belyakova, 115.

5. *ibid*, GD Xenia to Empress Marie
Feodorovna, 21.2.1917.

6. Hoover, Box 6, Folder 13, GD
Xenia's diary, 24.2.1917.

7. *ibid*, GD Xenia's diary,
25.2.1917.

8. *ibid*, GD Xenia's diary,
26.2.1917.

9. Bashkiroff, 27.

10. Hoover, Box 6, Folder 13, GD
Xenia's diary, 27.2.1917.

11. *ibid*, GD Xenia's diary,
28.2.1917.

12. *ibid*, GD Xenia's diary, 1.3.1917.

13. *ibid*, GD Xenia's diary, 2.3.1917.

14. *ibid*, GD Xenia's diary, 3.3.1917.

15. *ibid*.

16. Poutiatine, 141.

17. Buchanan, Sir George, II, 101;
Stopford, 123.

18. Hoover, Box 6, Folder 13, GD
Xenia's diary, 4.3.1917.

19. Hoover, Box 2, Folder 2,
Empress Marie Feodorovna to
GD Xenia, 22.3.1917, quoted in
Belyakova, 116.

20. Hoover, Box 6, Folder 13, GD
Xenia's diary, 5.3.1917.

21. Phoenix, 110, GD Olga to GD
Xenia, 28.2.1917.

22. Hoover, Box 6, Folder 13, GD
Xenia's diary, 5.3.1917.

23. *ibid*, GD Xenia's diary, 6.3.1917.

24. *ibid*, GD Xenia's diary, 7.3.1917.

25. *ibid*, GD Xenia's diary, 8.3.1917.

26. *ibid*, GD Xenia's diary, 9.3.1917.

27. Hoover, Box 6, Folder 12, GD

Xenia's diary, 12.3.1917,
quoted in Belyakova, 117.

28. Klausen 311, Empress Marie
Feodorovna to GD Xenia,
13.3.1917.

29. M & M, 567, GD Xenia to
Nicholas II, 23.3.1917.

30. Hoover, Box 6, Folder 2, GD
Xenia to Empress Marie
Feodorovna, 14.3.1917, quoted
in Belyakova, 117.

31. PRO, FO 800/205, Sir George
Buchanan to FO, 12.4.1917 (NS).

32. Youssoupov, *Lost Splendour*, 255.

33. Hoover, Box 7, Folder 1, GD
Xenia's diary, 28.3.1917.

34. Perry & Pleshakov, 176.

35. Hoover, Box 7, Folder 1, GD
Xenia's diary, 30.3.1917.

36. PRO, FO800/205, Sir George
Buchanan to FO, 25.4.1917 (NS).

37. Hoover, Box 7, Folder 1, GD
Xenia's diary, 16.4.1917,
quoted in Belyakova, 124.

38. Alexander, *OGD*, 89.

39. Anon, *Fall of the Romanovs*, 181.

40. Klausen, 316, GD Xenia's diary,
2.5.1917.

41. Belyakova, 119.

42. Romanov, Pr. Roman, 465.

43. Hoover, Box 7, Folder 1, GD
Xenia's diary, 1.4.1917.

44. *ibid*, GD Xenia's diary, 2.4.1917.
Quoted in Belyakova, 120.

45. Hoover, Box 7, Folder 1, GD
Xenia's diary, 26.4.1917,
quoted in Belyakova, 126.

46. George, 221.

47. *ibid*.

48. *ibid*, 222.

49. Klausen 319, Empress Marie
Feodorovna to Queen Olga, June
1917.

50. Mengden, 115.

51. Anon, *Imperial House of Russia*,
194, 1917, (ND).

52. Hoover, Box 7, Folder 1, GD Xenia's diary, 25.5.1917.
53. *ibid*, GD Xenia's diary, 26.5.1917.
54. *ibid*, GD Xenia's diary, 27.5.1917.
55. Skipwith, 37.
56. Stopford, 165.
57. *ibid*, 164.
58. Anon, *Imperial House of Russia*, 194–6, GD Xenia to GD Nicholas Michaelovich, 21.6.1917.
59. *ibid*.
60. AE, Queen Olga of Greece to GD Xenia, 31.7.1917, tr. from Russian.
61. Hoover, Box 7, Folder 1, GD Xenia's diary, 12.8.1917.
62. Hall, 296.
63. Hoover, Box 7, Folder 1, GD Xenia's diary, both quotations from 12.8.1917.
64. *ibid*, GD Xenia's diary, 13.8.1917.
65. AE, GD Cyril to GD Xenia, 6.8.1917.
66. M & M, 587, GD Xenia to Nicholas II, 15.10.1917.
67. PRO, 371/3015; RA, GV/M1067/75.
68. Hoover, Box 1, Folder 6, Alexandra Feodorovna to GD Xenia, 23.9.1917. Tr. from Russian.
69. Klausen, 323.
70. Hoover, Box 7, Folder 2, GD Xenia's diary, 16.10.1917.

Chapter 8

1. Hoover, Box 7, Folder 2, GD Xenia's diary, 30.10.1917.
2. M & M, 592, GD Xenia's diary, 30.11.1917.
3. AE, Paul Cheremetev, 30.11.1917; Sergei Cheremetev, 20.11.1917; both to GD Xenia, tr. from Russian.
4. M & M, 592, GD Xenia to Nicholas II, 6.12.1917.
5. *ibid*, 592, GD Xenia to Nicholas II, 30.11.1917.
6. *ibid*, 603–4, GD Xenia to Nicholas II, 31.1.1918.
7. Hoover, Box 7, Folder 2, GD Xenia's diary, 31.12.1917.
8. *ibid*, GD Xenia's diary, 19.2/4.3.1918.
9. *Ibid*, GD Xenia's diary, 26.2/11.3.1918.
10. *ibid*, GD Xenia's diary, 7/20.3.1918.
11. *ibid*, GD Xenia's diary, 8/21.3.1918.
12. *ibid*, Box 6, Folder 6, GD Xenia to Nicholas II, 5.4.1918, quoted in Belyakova, 150.
13. Perry & Pleshakov, 117.
14. AE, nd, in Russian.
15. Hoover, Box 7, Folder 1, GD Xenia's diary, 17/30.4.1918.
16. *ibid*, GD Xenia's diary, 18.4/1.5.1918.
17. *ibid*.
18. *ibid*.
19. *Ibid*, GD Xenia's diary, 26.5/8.6.1918.
20. *ibid*.
21. *ibid*.
22. *ibid*, GD Xenia's diary, 29.5/11.6.1918.
23. Belyakova, 111.
24. AE, Ferdinand Thormeyer to GD Xenia, 23.7.1918, tr. from French; Clarke, 282.
25. Hoover, Box 7, Folder 1, GD Xenia's diary, 31.5/13.6.1918.
26. *ibid*, GD Xenia's diary, 1/14.6.1918.

27. *ibid*, GD Xenia's diary, 2/15.6.1918.
28. *ibid*, GD Xenia's diary, 3/16.6.1918.
29. AE, GD Marie Pavlovna to GD Xenia, 28–9.8.1918, tr. from Russian.
30. Hoover, Box 7, Folder 1, GD Xenia's diary, 7/20.7.1918.
31. AE, GD Cyril to GD Xenia, 26.7.1918.
32. Hoover, Box 7, Folder 1, GD Xenia's diary, 7/20.7.1918.
33. AE, Queen Marie of Roumania to GD Xenia, 19.9.1918.
34. *ibid*, GD Cyril to GD Xenia, 22.10.1918.
35. Hoover, Box 7, Folder 4, GD Xenia's diary, 26.10/8.11.1918.
36. *ibid*, GD Xenia's diary, 27.10/9.11.1918.
37. AE, Queen Marie of Roumania to GD Xenia, 19.11.1918.
38. *ibid*, Queen Marie of Roumania to GD Xenia, 1918 (ND).
39. Hoover, Box 7, Folder 5, GD Xenia's diary, 28.10/10.11.1918.
40. *ibid*, 29.10/11.11.1918.
41. AE, GD Cyril to GD Xenia, 1918 (ND).
42. Hoover, Box 7, Folder 5, GD Xenia's diary, 31.10/13.11.1918.
43. *ibid*.
44. Youssoupov, *Lost Splendour*, 277.
45. PRO ADM 1/8938. 5.11.1918
46. Hoover Box 7, Folder 5, GD Xenia's diary, 9/22.12.1918.
47. *ibid*, GD Xenia's diary, 11/24.12.1918.
48. *ibid*, GD Xenia's diary, 12/25.12.1918.
49. *ibid*.
50. *ibid*, GD Xenia's diary, 13/26.12.1918.

51. Klausen, 337, GD Alexander to GD Xenia, 17.1.1919.
52. AE, Ferdinand Thormeyer to GD Xenia, 28.1.1919, tr. from French.
53. *ibid*, GD Marie Pavlovna to GD Xenia, 19.2.1919, tr. from Russian.
54. *ibid*, GD George to GD Xenia, 9.3.1919.
55. Hoover, Box 1, Folder 1, GD Alexander's staff to GD Xenia, 24.3.1919, tr. from French.
56. *ibid*, Box 7, Folder 5, GD Xenia's diary, 25.3/7.4.1919.
57. Youssoupov, *En Exile*, 101.
58. Berkman, 140.
59. AE, Admiral Auret to GD Xenia, 25.3.1919, tr. from French.
60. *San José Mercury News*, 17.4.1989.
61. Pridham, 62.
62. *ibid*, 67–8.
63. Hoover, Box 7, Folder 5, GD Xenia's diary, 25.3/7.4.1919.
64. AE, Dmitri Cheremetev to GD Xenia, 11.4.1919, tr. from Russian.
65. Softky, 'Growing Up Royal in Imperial Russia'.
66. Southworth, 'The Last Man with the Right to Rule Russia', *Daily Mail*, 31.3.1979.
67. Alexander, *OGD*, 133.

Chapter 9

1. AE, 11.4.1919.
2. Pridham, 90.
3. Hall, 323.
4. Pridham interview, transcript kindly provided by Anthony Summers.
5. NAM, to Coryne Hall, 18.10.1995.

6. *ibid*, FO telegram to Governor of Malta, 12.4.1919.
7. Ingham, 26.
8. *ibid*, 36.
9. *ibid*, 28.
10. *ibid*, 49.
11. Poutiatine, 237.
12. Ingham, 65.
13. Alexander, *AGD*, 92.
14. RA, GV/M1344A/115, GD Alexander to Lord Hardinge, 23.4.1919.
15. Perry & Pleshakov, 252.
16. AE, GD Alexander to GD Xenia, 28.4.1919.
17. PRO, HO 45/11549, FO to Under-Secretary of State, HO, 3.5.1919.
18. Ingham, 79.
19. Skipwith, 55.
20. PRO, ADM1/8938, 6.5.1919.
21. *The Times*, 9.5.1919.
22. Trevelyan, 283.
23. PRO, HO45/11549, 12.6.1919, FO Minute.
24. *ibid*, Sir Arthur Davidson to Sir Ronald Graham, FO, 19.5.1919.
25. *ibid*, 28.5.1919.
26. *ibid*, Sir Stuart Coates, 16.3.21.
27. RA, GV/CC45/532, GD Xenia to Queen Mary, 14.6.1919.
28. Marie, GD, 102.
29. Information from Suzy Payne, Penhaligon's, 4.4.2001.
30. AE, GD Cyril to GD Xenia, 28.8.1919.
31. PRO, FO371/4026, Sir G. Grahame to FO, 7.8.1919.
32. *ibid*, Lord Cromer to A. Hay, FO, 13.8.1919.
33. PRO, FO371/4026, Sir Arthur Davidson to Under-Secretary of State, FO, 13.8.1919.
34. GD Xenia to Prince Feodor, 29.1.1920, by kind permission of Prince Michael Feodorovich Romanov.
35. Vorres, 163–8.
36. AE, GD Cyril to GD Xenia, 13.11.1920.
37. *ibid*, Prince George of Greece to GD Xenia, 2.11.1920.
38. Clarke, 142.
39. RA, PS/GV/J1601/19, Sir Charles Russell to GD Xenia, 15.6.1920.
40. Clarke, 193.
41. Summers & Mangold, 380.
42. AE, GD Nicholas to GD Xenia, 23.7.1920.
43. *ibid*, GD Cyril to GD Xenia, 13.11.1920.
44. Hoover, Box 1, Folder 3, GD Alexander to GD Xenia, 11.1.1922, tr. from Russian.
45. *ibid*, Box 1, Folder 12, Irina Youssoupov to GD Xenia, 12.10.1922, tr. from Russian.
46. George, Foreword.
47. Hall, 328.
48. AE, menu, 20.4.1923.
49. Nadelhoffer, Ch. 7, note 3.
50. *The Times*, 18.4.1923.
51. Wig, 58.
52. Ponsonby, 336.
53. Ferrand, *Album de Famille*, 204.
54. AE, 'Anna' to GD Xenia, nd.
55. Hoover, Box 1, Folder 12, Irina Youssoupov to GD Xenia, 12.10.1922, tr. from Russian.
56. *ibid*, Irina Youssoupov to GD Xenia, 1.9.1922 or 1929 [date unclear], tr. from Russian.
57. AE, Queen Olga to GD Xenia, 29.1.1923, tr. from Russian.
58. Alexander, *AGD*, 210.
59. AE, GD Xenia to Nastya, 1924 (ND), tr. from Russian.
60. *ibid*, Olga to Nastya, 1924 (ND), tr. from Russian.

61. *ibid*, GD Xenia to Nastya, 12.1.1925, tr. from Russian.
62. PRO, FO242/4, Sir Charles Marling to Henry Toms, 18.10.1924.
63. Crawford, 381.
64. AE, Queen Olga to GD Xenia, 21.2.1925, tr. from Russian.

Chapter 10

1. RA, GV/AA43/234, GD Xenia to George V, 18.2.1925.
2. AE, Prince Nicholas to GD Xenia, 23.7.1926.
3. Berkman, 10.
4. PRO, WORK19/755, Sir Frederick Ponsonby's memo, 9.2.1928.
5. Ponsonby, 337.
6. RA, GV/AA43/238, GD Xenia to George V, 15.5.1926.
7. Vorres, 53.
8. Private information – Prince Andrew.
9. Private information – Prince David Chavchavadze.
10. *Hello*, Prince Andrew interview, 2.8.1997.
11. RA, Queen Mary's diary, 21.6.1925.
12. *ibid*, 11/12.8.1925; *The Times*, 13.8.1925.
13. Kurth, 110, 408.
14. Vorres, 174.
15. Kurth, 112.
16. *ibid*, 114.
17. *ibid*, 151.
18. *ibid*, 222.
19. RA, GV/AA56/86, GD Xenia to George V, 22.11.1925.
20. AE, Prince Christopher to GD Xenia, 18.7.1926.
21. *ibid*, Prince Nicholas to GD Xenia, 23.7.1926.

22. *ibid*, Queen Marie of Roumania to GD Xenia, 27.7.1927.
23. *ibid*, GD Xenia to Nastya, 1924 (ND), tr. from Russian.
24. Ballerup Egnsmuseum, Russian Red Cross to various recipients, 31.1.1926, tr. from Danish.
25. Vorres, 180.
26. AE, Empress Marie Feodorovna to GD Xenia, 23.8.1928.
27. *Berlingske Politiske og Avertissements Tidende*, 14.10.1928.
28. Alexander, *AGD*, 215.
29. RA, GV/CC45/729, GD Xenia to Queen Mary, 1.11.1928.

Chapter 11

1. AE, Deeds, 9.11.1928, 29.4.1932, tr. from Russian.
2. *ibid*, Belgian Legation, 28.11.1928, tr. from French.
3. *ibid*, GD Xenia to Nastya, 9.3.1929, tr. from Russian.
4. Kurth, 229; Summers & Mangold, 209–10.
5. AE, Botkin to GD Xenia, 18.10.1928.
6. Kurth, 162, GD Andrei to Serge Botkin, 4.8.1927.
7. *ibid*, 231, GD Andrei to Tatiana Botkin, 29.10.1928.
8. Hoover, Box 1, Folder 4, GD Alexander to GD Xenia, 20.11.1928, tr. from Russian.
9. Godl [web pages] – Prince Michael Andreievich interview.
10. as 8.
11. AE, Provisional Valuation, 22.5.1953.
12. Exhibition catalogue, Maria Feodorovna, 344–51, jewel list

of the Empress Marie Feodorovna.
13. as 8, 10.
14. Youssoupov, *En Exile*, 102.
15. Odum, 16–17.
16. Hall, 'Our Dear Miniature Gatchina'.
17. Clarke, 315.
18. Hoover, Box 1, Folder 4, GD Alexander to GD Xenia, 4.12.1928, tr. from Russian.
19. *ibid*, GD Alexander to GD Xenia, December 1928, tr. from Russian.
20. *ibid*, GD Alexander to GD Xenia, 23.12.1928, tr. from Russian.
21. *ibid*, Box 1, Folder 5, GD Alexander to GD Xenia, undated, probably 1929, tr. from Russian.
22. *ibid*, GD Alexander to GD Xenia, undated, probably 1929, tr. from Russian.
23. PRO, WORK19/755, WHB to CA, 7.2.1928.
24. *ibid*, memo, 7.2.1928.
25. *ibid*, 13.1.1931.
26. *ibid*, Sir Frederick Ponsonby to Sir Lionel Earle, 20.1.1931.
27. *ibid*, Sir Frederick Ponsonby to Sir Lionel Earle, 20.9.1932.
28. AE, GD Xenia to Nastya, 4.1.1932, tr. from Russian.
29. *ibid*, French Embassy travel document, 15.7.1935, tr. from French.
30. Russie, 121.
31. Alexander, *AGD*, viii.
32. PRO, HO45/11549, 1923.
33. Hoover, Box 1, Folder 12, Irina Youssoupov to GD Xenia, 8.8.1929, tr. from Russian.
34. AE, Princess Victoria of Wales to GD Xenia, 27.2.33.
35. *ibid*.

36. *New York Times*, 27.2.1933.
37. AE, Frederick Franz IV of Mecklenburg-Schwerin to GD Xenia, 8.3.1933.
38. *ibid*, Mme Leglise to GD Xenia, 28.2.1933, tr. from French.
39. *ibid*, GD George to GD Xenia, 2.3.1933.
40. Trevelyan, 337.
41. *ibid*, 286.
42. *ibid*, 338.
43. AE Lady Zia Wernher to GD Xenia, 27.2.1933.
44. AE, A.J. Wright to GD Xenia, 29.5.1929, and Lavington's report of 5.11.1927.
45. Prince Paul Chavchavadze to Greg Rittenhouse, 18.9.1965; Greg Rittenhouse to Coryne Hall, 7.5.2001.
46. Kurth, 389; Clarke, 165.
47. *ibid*, 239.
48. Clarke, 143.
49. *New York Times*, April 1960.
50. Clarke, 249.
51. *ibid*, 250.
52. *ibid*, 251.
53. Napley, 62.
54. Youssoupov, *Lost Splendour*, 139.
55. Berkman, 5.
56. *ibid*, 9.
57. *ibid*, 139.
58. *ibid*, 140.
59. *ibid*, 139.
60. *ibid*, 140.
61. *ibid*, 141.
62. *ibid*, 142.
63. *ibid*, 170–1.
64. *ibid*, 149.
65. Trevelyan, 338.
66. King, Greg, 246; Berkman, 151.
67. Napley, 202.
68. Berkman, 160.
69. Napley, 197.
70. Private information – Andrew Briger.

71. PRO, WORK19/755, Sir Frederick Ponsonby to Sir Patrick Duff, 7.3.1934.

72. *ibid*, Lamb to Heasman, 19.4.1934.

73. *ibid*, Lamb to Heasman, 30.4.1934.

74. *ibid*, Duff to Sir Frederick Ponsonby, 14.4.1934.

75. *ibid*, Sir Frederick Ponsonby to Duff, 1.3.34.

76. *ibid*, ?16.6.34.

77. King, Stella, 136.

78. RA, GV/CC45/960, GD Xenia to Queen Mary, 8.5.1935.

79. PRO, WORK19/755, Ponsonby to Duff, 17.5.1935.

80. *ibid*, Ponsonby to Duff, 7.6.1935.

81. AE, Queen Maud of Norway to GD Xenia, nd, but Xmas 1930 or 1931.

82. *ibid*, Princess Henry of Battenberg to GD Xenia, 9.12.1935.

83. RA GV/AA57/132, GD Xenia to George V, 25.12.1935.

84. *ibid*, GV/CC45/990, GD Xenia to Queen Mary, 21.1.1936.

Chapter 12

1. RA, GV/CC45/1048, Queen Maud to Queen Mary, 19.7.1936.

2. Heath, 86.

3. PRO, WORK19/830, 9.10.1936.

4. Kurth, 239, Fallows to Brooks, 9.11.1937.

5. PRO, WORK19/830, 25.1.1937, 6.2.1937.

6. *ibid*, 18.3.1937.

7. *ibid*, 5.5.1937, 11.5.1937.

8. AE, George of Greece to Xenia, 1.3.1938.

9. PRO, HO382/5, 877097, Wigram to Boyd, 21.6.1938.

10. *ibid*, Wigram to Boyd, 27.6.1938.

11. *ibid*, Maxwell to Rae, 28.6.1938.

12. Private information – Prince Alexander; Pridham, 172.

13. Vickers, 280.

14. AE, Princess Alexandra of Hohenlohe-Langenburg to GD Xenia, 4.8.1938.

15. *ibid*, Queen Maud to GD Xenia, November 1938.

16. *ibid*, King Haakon VII of Norway to GD Xenia, 13.1.1939.

17. *ibid*, Count Kleinmichel to GD Xenia, 12.1.1938, tr. from Russian.

18. *ibid*, Prince Waldemar to GD Xenia, 31.10.1938.

19. *ibid*, Crown Princess Cecilie to GD Xenia, 25.3(?).1938, date unclear.

20. *ibid*, GD Xenia to Mrs Sinclair, 29.12.1939.

21. *ibid*, Duchess of Kent to GD Xenia, 24.1.1940.

22. *ibid*, Prince George of Greece to GD Xenia, 15.4.1940.

23. *ibid*, Dowager Marchioness of Milford Haven to GD Xenia, 31.10.1940.

24. *ibid*, Eugene Tseshkovsky to GD Xenia, 26.4.1940.

25. *ibid*, Dowager Marchioness of Milford Haven to GD Xenia, 8.9.1939.

26. *ibid*, Queen Mary to GD Xenia, and Andrusha telegram, 31.10.1940.

27. *ibid*, Dowager Marchioness of Milford Haven to GD Xenia, 31.10.1940

28. RA, GV/CC45/1248, GD Xenia to Queen Mary, 21.12.1940.

29. Interview with HM Queen

Elizabeth The Queen Mother, 4.12.2001.

30. Hoey, 57.

31. RA, GV/CC45/1248, GD Xenia to Queen Mary, 21.12.1940.

32. *ibid*, GV/CC53/826, Queen Mary to Earl of Athlone, 7.2.1941.

33. *ibid*, GV/CC45/1306, GD Xenia to Queen Mary, December 1941.

34. Ferrand, *Complement*, 18.

35. AE, Irina Cheremetev to GD Xenia, December 1942 (ND).

36. *ibid*, Dowager Marchioness of Milford Haven to GD Xenia, 31.10.1940.

37. RA, GV/CC45/1287, GD Xenia to Queen Mary, 23.5.1941.

38. *ibid* GV/CC45/1306, GD Xenia to Queen Mary, December 1941 (ND).

39. AE, Crown Princess Louise of Sweden to GD Xenia, 2.6.1941.

40. as 29.

41. *Daily Telegraph*, 22.4.1960.

42. RA, GV/CC45/1306, GD Xenia to Queen Mary, December 1941.

43. Klier & Mingay, 116.

44. RA, GV/CC45/1342, GD Xenia to Queen Mary, 17.12.1942.

45. *ibid*, GV/CC45/1322, GD Xenia to Queen Mary, 26.4.1943, wrongly dated 1942.

46. *ibid*, GV/CC45/1342, GD Xenia to Queen Mary, 17.12.1942.

47. as 29, 40.

48. AE, Duchess of Kent to GD Xenia, 23.7.1943.

49. *ibid*, 11.4.1944

50. *The Times*, 21.4.1960.

51. RA, GV/CC45/1734, GD Xenia to Queen Mary, 29.2.1944.

52. *ibid*, GV/CC45/1405, GD Xenia to Queen Mary, 12.1.1945.

53. *ibid*, GV/CC45/1383, GD Xenia to Queen Mary, 26.5.1944.

54. AE, Prince Feodor to GD Xenia,

24.4.1944, 27.4.1944, tr. from Russian.

55. RA, GV/CC45/1414, GD Xenia to Queen Mary, 25.4.1945.

56. AE, Lt Calhoun Ancrum to GD Xenia, 5.10.1945.

57. *ibid*, Irina Cheremetev to GD Xenia, postmarked 5.1.1945.

58. *ibid*, Duchess of Kent to GD Xenia, 28.4.1945.

59. *ibid*, Princess Tatiana Constantinovna to GD Xenia, 17/30.7.1945, tr. from Russian.

60. PRO, HO382/5, naturalization files, 29.7.1945.

61. Buchanan, *Victorian Gallery*, 55–6.

62. AE, Princess Marie to GD Xenia, 16.9.1945; Private information – Prince Michael Feodorovich Romanoff.

63. AE, Countess Toerring to GD Xenia, 29.10.1945.

64. *ibid*, Order of Preobrajensky to GD Xenia, 14.11.1945.

65. *ibid*, Evelyn Pearson to Prince Alexander, 4.1.1946.

Chapter 13

1. RA, GV/CC53/1462, Queen Mary to Earl of Athlone, 2.3.1946.

2. AE, Prince Nikita to GD Xenia, 4.8.1946.

3. Ferrand, *Grand-duc Paul*, 268.

4. AE, Alexandra Leuchtenberg de Beauharnais to GD Xenia, 29.7.1947.

5. RA, GV/CC45/1493, GD Xenia to Queen Mary, 19.2.1947.

6. *ibid*, GD Xenia to Queen Mary, 24.2.1947.

7. *ibid*, GV/CC45/1508, GD Xenia to Queen Mary, 12.5.1947.

8. Menkes, 144.
9. AE, Prince Alexander to GD Xenia, 25.8.1947, in Russian and English.
10. *ibid*, Marina, Duchess of Kent to GD Xenia, 18.2.1946.
11. *ibid*, Royal Netherlands Embassy in London to GD Xenia, 3.7.1947.
12. *ibid*, Revd B.S. Lombard to GD Xenia, 6.4.1948.
13. Trevelyan, 416.
14. Private information – Lady Myra Butter.
15. As 13.
16. AE, Queen Alexandrine to GD Xenia, 27.2.1948.
17. RA, GV/CC45/1702, GD Xenia to Queen Mary, 21.12.1950.
18. *ibid*, GV/CC45/1728, GD Xenia to Queen Mary, 1.7.1951.
19. *ibid*, GV/CC45/1742, GD Xenia to Queen Mary, 25.9.1951.
20. AE, Duchess of Kent to GD Xenia, 10.11.1951.
21. RA, GV/CC45/1742, GD Xenia to Queen Mary, 19.11.1951.
22. AE, Crown Princess Cecilie to GD Xenia, 19.6.1950.
23. *ibid*, Olga, Princess Paul of Yugoslavia, to GD Xenia, 3.6.1950.
24. *ibid*, Alix, GD of Mecklenburg to GD Xenia, 16.1.1954.
25. *ibid*, Crown Prince Olav to GD Xenia, 6.1.1953.
26. RA, GV/CC45/1777, GD Xenia to Queen Mary, 7.2.1952.
27. AE, Princess Nicholas of Greece to GD Xenia, 6.1.1955, in Russian and English.
28. *ibid*, Duchess of Kent to GD Xenia, 8.5.1953.
29. Hessisches Staatsarchiv, Darmstadt, Prince Dmitri to Prince Louis of Hesse, 11.3.1958.
30. *ibid*, GD Xenia's statement, 16.3.1958.
31. AE, report from Bss Buxhoeveden, nd.
32. Will of Sophie Buxhoeveden, 28.5.1954.
33. GD Xenia to GD Olga, 14.2.1957, by kind permission of Paul C. Byington, in English and Russian.
34. AE, Olga, Princess Paul of Yugoslavia, to GD Xenia, 29.3.1957.
35. Pope-Hennessy, James, 257–60.
36. Private information – Prince Michael Feodorovich.
37. *Daily Telegraph*, 8.4.1957.
38. AE, King Frederik IX of Denmark to GD Xenia, 4.3.1958.
39. *ibid*, Princess Olga of Cumberland to GD Xenia, 27.7.1957.
40. *ibid*, Queen Marie of Yugoslavia to GD Xenia, 21.1.1959.
41. Romanoff, Alexander, 'A Romanoff in Soviet Russia'.
42. Buchanan, *Victorian Gallery*, vi.
43. *The Times*, obituary, 21.4.1960.
44. AE, Alix, Grand Duchess of Mecklenburg to GD Xenia, 8.10.1959.
45. *ibid*, Duchess of Kent to GD Xenia, 10.8.1959.
46. *ibid*, Prince Nikita Nikititch to Prince Alexander Nikititch, 25.11.1959.
47. *The Times*, 1, 2 and 4.4.1960.
48. *Daily Express*, 27.4.1960.
49. Clarke, 270.
50. GD Xenia's will and codicil.
51. *The Times*, 21.4.1960.
52. Obituary, source unknown.
53. Vorres, 220.
54. *The Times*, 21.4.1960.

Bibliography

I Manuscript Sources

Argyll Etkin, London
Hessisches Staatsarchiv, Darmstadt
Kongehus Arkiv, Rigsarkiv, Copenhagen
Mainau Archives
National Archives of Malta
Public Record Office, London
Rigsarkiv, Copenhagen
Royal Archives, Windsor
State Archive of the Russian Federation (GARF), Moscow
Xenia Alexandrovna, Grand Duchess, papers – Hoover Institution on War,
    Revolution & Peace, California

II Books

The place of publication is London unless otherwise stated

Abela, Major A.E. *A Nation's Praise*, Progress Press, Valletta, 1994
Alexander, Grand Duke. *Once a Grand Duke*, Cassell, 1932
—— *Always a Grand Duke*, New York, Farrar & Rinehart, 1933
Anon. *The Fall of the Romanovs*, Ian Faulkner, 1992
—— *The Imperial House of Russia – Diaries, Letters, Photographs*,
    Perspektive, Moscow, 1992
—— *Russian Court Memoirs*, Ian Faulkner, 1992
Aronson, Theo. *A Family of Kings: The Descendants of Christian IX of
    Denmark*, Cassell, 1976
Baedeker's Russia 1914, David & Charles/George Allen & Unwin, 1971
Bashkiroff, Zenaide. *The Sickle and the Harvest*, Neville Spearman, 1960
Belyakova, Zoia. *The Romanovs: The Way it Was*, St Petersburg, Ego, 2000
Berkman, Ted. *The Lady and the Law: the Remarkable Life of Fanny
    Holtzmann*, Boston, Little, Brown, 1976
Bing, Edward J. (ed.). *The Letters of Tsar Nicholas & Empress Marie*, Ivor
    Nicholson & Watson, 1937
Buchanan, Sir George. *My Mission to Russia and Other Diplomatic
    Memories*, 2 vols, Cassell, 1923
Buchanan, Meriel. *Dissolution of an Empire*, John Murray, 1932
—— *Victorian Gallery*, Cassell, 1956
Cantacuzene, Princess Julia. *Revolutionary Days*, Chapman & Hall, 1920

Cerda, Alexandre de la. *La Tournée des Grands-Ducs*, Biarritz, Atlantica, 1999

Chavchavadze, Prince David. *The Grand Dukes*, New York, Atlantic International Publications, 1990

Clarke, William. *The Lost Fortune of the Tsars*, Weidenfeld & Nicolson, 1994

Conway, Sir Martin. *Art Treasures in Soviet Russia*, Edward Arnold, 1925

Crawford, Rosemary & Donald. *Michael and Natasha: the Life and Love of the last Tsar of Russia*, Weidenfeld & Nicolson, 1997

de Stoeckl, Baroness. *Not All Vanity*, John Murray, 1950

Dobson, Christopher. *Prince Felix Yusupov, The Man Who Murdered Rasputin*, Harrap, 1989

Eagar, Miss Margaretta. *Six Years at the Russian Court*, Hurst & Blackett, 1906

Enache, Nicolas. *La Descendance de Pierre le Grand, Tsar de Russie*, Paris, Sedopols, 1983

Eugenie, Princess of Greece. *Le Tsarevitch, Enfant Martyr*, Paris, Perrin, 1990

Exhibition catalogue. *Maria Feodorovna, Empress of Russia – An Exhibition about the Danish Princess who became Empress of Russia*, Copenhagen, Christiansborg Slot, 1997

Fabergé, Tatiana, Prolet, Lynette G. & Skurlov, Valentin V. *The Fabergé Imperial Easter Eggs*, Christie's, 1997

Ferrand, Jacques. *Romanoff – Un Album de Famille*, Paris, 1989
—— *Romanoff – Un Album de Famille, Complement*, Paris, 1990
—— *Les Princes Youssoupoff et les Comtes Soumarokoff-Elston*, Paris, 1991
—— *Le Grand-Duc Paul Alexandrovitch de Russie*, Paris, 1993
—— *Il est Toujours des Romanovs*, Paris, 1995
—— *Romanoffs, Fragments de Vie*, Paris, 1998

Field, Leslie. *The Queen's Jewels*, Weidenfeld & Nicolson, 1987

Fuhrmann, Joseph T. (ed.). *The Wartime Correspondence of Nicholas & Alexandra*, USA, Westport, Connecticut, 1999

Galitzine, Katya. *St Petersburg: The Hidden Interiors*, Hazar, 1999

George, H.I.H. Grand Duchess. *A Romanov Diary*, New York, Atlantic International, 1988

Glenny, Michael & Stone, Norman. *The Other Russia*, Faber & Faber, 1991

Hall, Coryne. *Little Mother of Russia: a Biography of the Empress Marie Feodorovna, 1847–1928*, Shepheard-Walwyn, 1999

Harcave, Sidney (ed. and tr.). *The Memoirs of Count Witte*, New York, M E Sharpe, 1990

Heath, Gerald. *Hampton Court*, Hampton Court Association, 2000

Hoey, Brian. *Monarchy*, BBC Enterprises, 1987

Ingham, Robert. *What Happened to the Empress*, Hamrun, Malta, St Joseph's Institute, 1949

Jaschik, Timofey. *En livkosacks Erindringer*, Denmark, Forlaget Zac, 1968

Jensen, Bent. *Zarmoder blandt Zarmordere*, Denmark, Gyldendal, 1997

BIBLIOGRAPHY

King, Greg. *The Murder of Rasputin*, Century, 1996

King, Stella. *Princess Marina, her Life and Times*, Cassell, 1969

Klausen, Inger-Lise. *Dagmar, Zarina fra Danmark*, Copenhagen, Lindhardt & Ringhof, 1997

Klier, John & Mingay, Helen. *The Quest for Anastasia*, Smith Gyphon, 1995

Kurth, Peter. *Anastasia: The Life of Anna Anderson*, Jonathan Cape, 1983

Lowe, Charles. *Alexander III of Russia*, Heinemann, 1895

Madol, Hans Roger. *Christian IX*, Collins, 1939

Marie, Grand Duchess of Russia. *A Princess in Exile*, Cassell, 1932

Marie, Queen of Roumania. *The Story of my Life*, 3 vols, Cassell, 1934–5

Massie, Suzanne. *Land of the Firebird*, Hamish Hamilton, 1980

Maylunas, Andrei, & Mironenko, Sergei. *A Lifelong Passion: Nicholas & Alexandra, Their Own Story*, Weidenfeld & Nicolson, 1996

Mengden, Countess Zenaide. *Grevinde Zinaide Mengdens Erindringer*, Copenhagen, H. Hagerup, 1943

Menkes, Suzy. *The Royal Jewels*, Grafton, 1985

Michael, Prince of Greece. *Imperial Palaces of Russia*, Tauris Park, 1992

Mossolov, Alexander A. *At the Court of the Last Tsar*, Methuen, 1935

Nadelhoffer, Hans. *Cartier, Jewellers Extraordinary*, Thames & Hudson, 1984.

Napley, Sir David. *Rasputin in Hollywood*, Weidenfeld & Nicolson, 1990

Naryshkin-Kurakin, Elizabeth. *Under Three Tsars*, New York, Dutton, 1931

Neerbek, Hans. *Søstrenes Slot*, Copenhagen, Hernovs Forlag, 1990

Nicholas II, Tsar of Russia. *Journal Intime de Nicolas II*, Paris, Payot, 1925

—— *Lettres de Nicolas II et de Sa Mere*, edited by Paul Leon, Paris, Simon Kra, 1928

Obolensky, Dimitri. *Bread of Exile*, Harvill, 1999

Odum, Anne. *Fabergé at Hillwood*, Washington DC, Hillwood Museum & Gardens, 1996

Perry, John Curtis, & Pleshakov, Constantine. *Flight of the Romanovs*, New York, Basic Books, 1999

Phenix, Patricia. *Olga Romanov, Russia's Last Grand Duchess*, Canada, Viking, 1999

Poliakoff, Vladimir. *The Empress Marie of Russia & Her Times*, Thornton Butterworth, 1926

Ponsonby, Sir Frederick. *Recollections of Three Reigns*, ed. Colin Welch, Eyre & Spottiswoode, 1951

Pope-Hennessy, James. *A Lonely Business: a Self-Portrait*, ed. Peter Quennell, Weidenfeld & Nicolson, 1981

Pope-Hennessy, Una. *Leningrad, the Closed and Forbidden City*, Hutchinson, 1938

Poutiatine, Princess Nathalie. *Princess Olga, My Mother*, Valletta, Gulf, 1982

Pridham, Vice-Admiral Sir Francis. *Close of a Dynasty*, Allan Wingate, 1956

Radzinsky, Edvard. *Rasputin*, Weidenfeld & Nicolson, 2000

Rørdam, C.H. *Hofdage Hos Christian IX*, Copenhagen, H Hagerups Forlag, 1929

Romanoff, Prince Roman. *Det var et rigt hus, et lykkeligt hus*, Copenhagen, Gyldendal, 1991

Russie, Leonida, Grande-duchesse de. *Chaque matin est une grace*, France, editions J.C. Lattes, 2000

Ryzhnenko, Irina & Barkovets, Olga. *Alexander III at Gatchina*, St Petersburg, Abris Art, 2001

Salisbury, Harrison E. *Black Night, White Snow*, New York, Da Capo, 1977

Scavenius, Anna Sofie. *Diplomatfrue ved Zarhoffat*, Copenhagen, Martins Forlag, 1960

Sikorsky, Hilary. *Boobi's Memoirs*, Book Guild, 1989

Skipwith, Sofka. *Sofka, the Autobiography of a Princess*, Rupert Hart-Davies, 1968

Solodkoff, Alexander von. *The Jewel Album of Nicholas II*, Ermitage, 1997

Spiridovich, A. *Les Derniers Années de la Cour de Tzarskoie Selo*, Paris, Payot, 1925

Stopford, Hon. Albert. *The Russian Diary of an Englishman*, New York, Robert M. McBride, 1919

Summers, Anthony, & Mangold, Tom. *The File on the Tsar*, Victor Gollancz, 1976

Trevelyan, Raleigh. *Grand Dukes and Diamonds*, Secker & Warburg, 1991

Tudor, Dawn & Armeanu, Hilary Hunt. *Recollections of Legat*, Privately printed, 1998

Ulstrup, Preben. *Danmarks kongefamilie og Ruslands kejserfamile*. In *Ruslands Skatte – Kejserlige Gave*, exhibition catalogue. Denmark, Christiansborg Slot 2002.

Van der Kiste, John. *Crowns in a Changing World: the British and European Monarchies 1901–36*, Stroud, Sutton, 1993

—— *Princess Victoria Melita, Grand Duchess Cyril of Russia, 1876–1936*, Stroud, Sutton, 1991

—— *The Romanovs 1818–1959: Alexander II of Russia and his Family*, Stroud, Sutton, 1998

Vickers, Hugo. *Alice, Princess Andrew of Greece*, Hamish Hamilton, 2000

Vorres, Ian. *The Last Grand-Duchess: Her Imperial Highness Grand-Duchess Olga Alexandrovna*, Hutchinson, 1964

Waddington, Mary King. *Letters of a Diplomat's Wife, 1883–1900*, Smith, Elder, 1903

Wainman, Paul (Mrs Sylvia MacDougall). *Let's Light the Candles*, Methuen, 1944

Wig, Kjell Arnljot. *Konges ser tilbake*, Norway, J.W. Cappenlens Forlag AS, 1977

Youssoupov, Prince Felix. *Lost Splendour*, Jonathan Cape, 1953

—— *En Exile*, Paris, Librairie Plon, 1954

Zeepvat, Charlotte. *Romanov Autumn*, Stroud, Sutton, 2000

BIBLIOGRAPHY

Zemlyanichenki, Marina & Kalinin, Nikolai. *The Romanovs and the Crimea*, Moscow, Russian Nobility Descendants Union, Kruk, 1993

III Journal Articles

Hall, Coryne, 'Our Dear Miniature Gatchina', *Royalty Digest*, Vol. X, No. 4
—— 'The Queen of Resorts, The Resort of Kings', *Royalty Digest*, Vol. IX, No. 12
Romanoff, Alexander, 'A Romanoff in Soviet Russia', *Sunday Telegraph*, 27.8.1961
Softky, Marion, 'Growing Up Royal in Imperial Russia', *The Imperial Russian Journal*, Vol. 2, No. 3
Southworth, June, 'The Last Man with the Right to Rule Russia', *Daily Mail*, 31.3.1979

IV Journals – General References

Berlingske politiske og Avertissements Tidende
Cercle d'Etudes des Dynastes Royales Européennes
Daily Mail
Daily Telegraph
Hello
Illusteret Tidende
Imperial Russian Journal
New York Times
Poslednie Novosti
Pravitelstvennyj Vestnik
Royalty Digest
Surrey Comet
The Times

V Web Pages

Godl, John. *Remembering Anna Anderson Part II*
www.intlromanovsociety.org/expressions/gold2.htm
A Romanoff Album. Hoover Digest 1999, No. 3
www-hoover.stanford.edu/publications/digest/993/toc993.html

Index

INDEX

INDEX